MARTHA'S VINEYARD & NANTUCKET

2ND EDITION

Where to Stay and Eat
for All Budgets

Must-See Sights
and Local Secrets

Ratings You Can Trust

Fodor's Travel Publications   New York, Toronto, London, Sydney, Auckland
www.fodors.com

FODOR'S MARTHA'S VINEYARD & NANTUCKET
EDITOR: William Travis

Editorial Production: Jacinta O'Halloran
Editorial Contributors: Andrew Collins, Sandy MacDonald, Phyllis Meras
Maps: David Lindroth Inc., *cartographer;* Rebecca Baer and Bob Blake, *map editors*
Design: Fabrizio La Rocca, *creative director;* Moon Sun Kim, *cover designer;* Guido Caroti, *art director;* Melanie Marin, *senior picture editor*
Cover Photo: (Edgartown Lighthouse, Martha's Vineyard): Jeane Vogel Photography
Production/Manufacturing: Colleen Ziemba

COPYRIGHT

Second Edition

ISBN 1–4000–1448–4

ISSN 1541–2911

SPECIAL SALES

This book is available for special discounts for bulk purchases for sales promotions or premiums. Special editions, including personalized covers, excerpts of existing books, and corporate imprints, can be created in large quantities for special needs. For more information, write to Special Markets/Premium Sales, 1745 Broadway, MD 6-2, New York, New York 10019 or e-mail specialmarkets@randomhouse.com.

AN IMPORTANT TIP & AN INVITATION

Although all prices, opening times, and other details in this book are based on information supplied to us at press time, changes occur all the time in the travel world, and Fodor's cannot accept responsibility for facts that become outdated or for inadvertent errors or omissions. So **always confirm information when it matters,** especially if you're making a detour to visit a specific place. Your experiences—positive and negative—matter to us. If we have missed or misstated something, **please write to us.** We follow up on all suggestions. Contact the Martha's Vineyard & Nantucket editor at editors@fodors.com or c/o Fodor's at 1745 Broadway, New York, New York 10019.

PRINTED IN THE UNITED STATES OF AMERICA

10 9 8 7 6 5 4 3 2 1

DESTINATION MARTHA'S VINEYARD & NANTUCKET

artha's Vineyard and Nantucket remain oases of simplicity. Even during the busy summer months, it is possible to get away from it all on these twin jewels of the Atlantic: strolling along the shore gathering shells and beach glass, watching birds dive into the surf and emerge with their struggling supper, tramping through the shady woods, or just being seduced by the setting sun and the rhythm of the waves—all this is somehow life-affirming and satisfyingly real. Come and see for yourself.

Tim Jarrell, Publisher

CONTENTS

Maps

CloseUps

ABOUT THIS BOOK

The best source for travel advice is a like-minded friend who's just been where you're headed. But with or without that friend, you'll be in great shape to find your way around your destination once you learn to find your way around your Fodor's guide.

SELECTION

Our goal is to cover the best properties, sights, and activities in their category, as well as the most interesting communities to visit. We make a point of including local food-lovers' hot spots as well as neighborhood options, and we avoid all that's touristy unless it's really worth your time. You can go on the assumption that everything in this book is recommended wholeheartedly by our writers and editors. Flip to **On the Road with Fodor's** to learn more about who they are. It goes without saying that no property pays to be included.

RATINGS

Orange stars ★ denote sights and properties that our editors and writers consider the very best in the area covered by the entire book. These, the best of the best, are listed in the **Fodor's Choice** section in the front of the book. Black stars ★ highlight the sights and properties we deem **Highly Recommended**, the don't-miss sights within any region. In cities, sights pinpointed with numbered map bullets ❶ in the margins tend to be more important than those without bullets.

SPECIAL SPOTS

Pleasures & Pastimes and text on chapter-title pages focus on experiences that reveal the spirit of the destination. Also watch for **Off the Beaten Path** sights. Some are out of the way, some are quirky, and all are worthwhile. When the munchies hit, look for **Need a Break?** suggestions.

TIME IT RIGHT

Check **On the Calendar** up front and chapters' **Timing** sections for weather and crowd overviews and best days and times to visit.

SEE IT ALL

Use Fodor's exclusive **Perfect Days** as a model for your time on the islands. **Good Walks** guide you to important sights; ▶ indicates the starting points of walks and itineraries in the text and on the map.

BUDGET WELL

In the hotel and restaurant price categories, from ¢ to $$$$, we provide a balanced selection for every budget. For attractions, we always give standard adult admission fees; reductions are usually available for children, students, and senior citizens. Look in **Discounts & Deals** in Smart Travel Tips for information on destination-wide ticket schemes. Want to pay with plastic? **AE, D, DC, MC, V** following restaurant and hotel listings indicate whether American Express, Discover, Diner's Club, MasterCard, or Visa are accepted.

BASIC INFO

Smart Travel Tips lists travel essentials for the entire area covered by the book. To find the best way to get around, see the transportation section; see individual modes of travel ("Car Travel," "Train Travel") for details.

ON THE MAPS	Maps throughout the book show you what's where and help you find your way around. Black and orange numbered bullets ❶ ❶ in the text correlate to bullets on maps.
BACKGROUND	We give background information within the chapters in the course of explaining sights as well as in CloseUp boxes and in Understanding Martha's Vineyard & Nantucket at the end of the book.
FIND IT FAST	Within the book, the Martha's Vineyard and Nantucket chapters are divided by towns, Where to Eat, Where to Stay, Nightlife, Shopping, and Sports & the Outdoors. Heads at the top of each page help you find what you need within a chapter.
DON'T FORGET	Restaurants are open for lunch and dinner daily unless we state otherwise; we mention dress only when there's a specific requirement and reservations only when they're essential or not accepted—it's always best to book ahead. Hotels have private baths, phone, TVs, and air-conditioning and operate on the European Plan (a.k.a. EP, meaning without meals). We always list facilities but not whether you'll be charged extra to use them, so when pricing accommodations, find out what's included.
SYMBOLS	

Many Listings

★ Fodor's Choice
★ Highly recommended
⊠ Physical address
✛ Directions
⌖ Mailing address
☎ Telephone
🖷 Fax
⊕ On the Web
✍ E-mail
🎫 Admission fee
🕐 Open/closed times
▶ Start of walk/itinerary
☐ Credit cards

Outdoors

⅃ Golf
⚠ Camping

Hotels & Restaurants

🏨 Hotel
🛏 Number of rooms
♨ Facilities
🍽 Meal plans
✕ Restaurant
🍸 Reservations
👔 Dress code
⚲ Smoking
🍷 BYOB
✕🏨 Hotel with restaurant that warrants a visit

Other

👪 Family-friendly
📞 Contact information
⇨ See also
⊠ Branch address
☞ Take note

ON THE ROAD WITH FODOR'S

A trip takes you out of yourself. Concerns of life at home completely disappear, driven away by more immediate thoughts—about, say, what marvels will beguile the next day or where you'll have dinner. That's where Fodor's comes in. We make sure that you know all your options, so that you don't miss something that's around the next bend just because you didn't know it was there. Mindful that the best memories of your trip might have nothing to do with what you came to Martha's Vineyard or Nantucket to see, we guide you to sights large and small all over town. On Martha's Vineyard, you might set out for dinner in Edgartown, but back at home you find yourself unable to forget watching the sun sink into the Aquinnah Cliffs. You might set out to wine and dine your way across Nantucket but back home you find yourself unable to forget the Emersonian feeling of an impromptu bike ride past cranberry bogs out to Siasconset Beach. With Fodor's at your side, serendipitous discoveries are never far away.

Our success in showing you every corner of Martha's Vineyard and Nantucket is a credit to our extraordinary writers. Although there's no substitute for travel advice from a good friend who knows your style, our contributors are the next best thing—the kind of people you would poll for travel advice if you knew them.

Former Fodor's editor and New England native **Andrew Collins,** who updated the Smart Travel Tips section, is the author of several books on travel in New England, including handbooks on Connecticut and Rhode Island.

Sandy MacDonald is a truly accomplished and prolific travel writer, having contributed to many Nantucket, Boston, and New England travel guides. She has also written about Nantucket for several newspapers and magazines, including *Boston Magazine, Boston Globe, Country Home, Country Inns,* and the *Nantucket Inquirer & Mirror.* For this book, she covered Nantucket's good life—including dining, lodging, nightlife, the arts, and shopping—and created the Perfect Days itineraries.

Phyllis Meras is a fourth-generation summer Vineyarder and has been a year-round Martha's Vineyard resident since the 1960s. She is a former managing editor of *The Vineyard Gazette* and is the author of 13 books, including a collection of essays about the island, "First Spring: A Martha's Vineyard Journal." She has previously contributed to Fodor's "Germany." She is also the former travel editor of the *Providence Journal* and has written for the *New York Times,* the *Boston Globe* and the *Washington Times,* among others.

Martha's Vineyard

The three towns that compose Down-Island (the east end of Martha's Vineyard)—Vineyard Haven, Oak Bluffs, and Edgartown—are the most popular and the most populated. Here you'll find the ferry docks, the shops, and a concentration of things to do and see, including the centuries-old houses and churches that document the island's history. A stroll through any one of these towns allows you to look into the past while enjoying the pleasures of the present.

However, much of what makes the Vineyard special is found in its rural reaches, in the agricultural heart of the island and the largely undeveloped lands south and west of the Vineyard Haven–to–Edgartown line known as Up-Island. Country roads meander through woods and tranquil farmland, and dirt side roads lead past crystalline ponds, abandoned cranberry bogs, and conservation lands. In Chilmark, West Tisbury, and Aquinnah, nature lovers, writers, artists, and others have established close, ongoing summer communities. In winter, the isolation sends even year-round Vineyarders from their Up-Island homes to places in the cozier Down-Island towns.

Nantucket

Tiny Nantucket is divided into town and country. Town, where the ferries dock, is the center of island activity, with historical homes and inns and boutiques, galleries, and restaurants leading up from the harbor and waterfront. The rest of the island is largely residential (trophy houses abound), and nearly all roads from town terminate at one of the island's teeny (and seasonal) beach communities. Surfside, 3 mi to the south of Nantucket Town, is the island's premier beach (although Jetties also draws a crowd). Well-loved bike paths crisscross the island, spoking from town to western Eel Point and Madaket, south to Surfside, and east to Siasconset, via straight Milestone Road or winding Polpis Road.

The Village of Siasconset (known locally as Sconset) lies 8 mi to the east of town, past Windswept Cranberry Bog, and has spectacular rose-covered cottages worth a peek. In spring, Milestone Road, the main route here, teems with millions of blooming daffodils, a project inspired by Jean MacAusland in the early '70s when she donated the bulbs. (An annual Daffodil Festival each April honors her contribution and the island's love of gardens.) The village is also near the majestic Sankaty Head Lighthouse and the turnoff for the remote spit of Coatue, Coskata, and Great Point. Biking is a popular way to see many of the tiny island's sights. Just be sure to bring a map, available at bike shops and at the Nantucket Visitor Services and Information Bureau, at 25 Federal Street in the center of town.

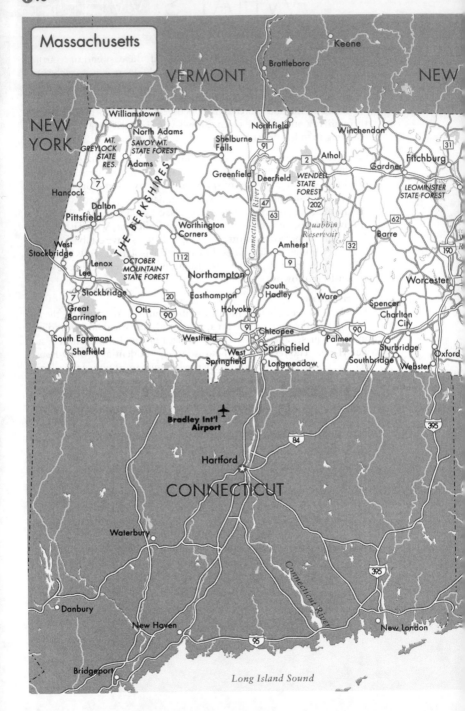

Massachusetts

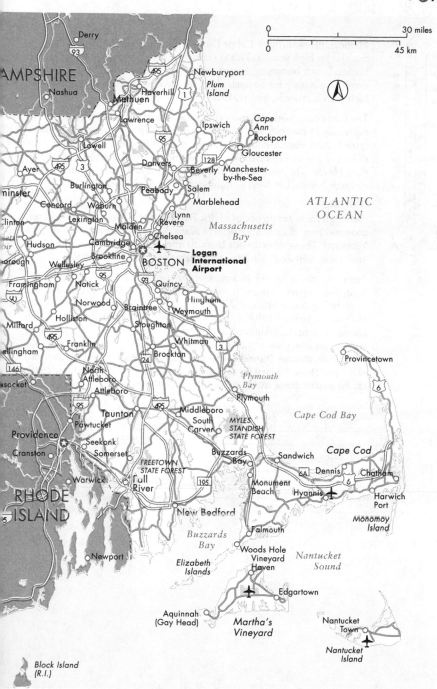

0 — 30 miles
0 — 45 km

NEW HAMPSHIRE

Derry

Nashua

Newburyport
Plum Island

Methuen
Haverhill

Lawrence

Ipswich

Cape Ann
Rockport

Lowell

Danvers
Gloucester

Ayer

Burlington
Peabody
Beverly Manchester-by-the-Sea

Leominster

Concord
Waburn
Salem

Clinton
Lexington
Marblehead

Malden
Lynn
Revere

Hudson
Cambridge
Chelsea
Massachusetts Bay

Marlborough
Brookline
BOSTON
Logan International Airport

Wellesley

Framingham
Natick
93
Quincy

Norwood
Braintree
Hingham

Holliston
Weymouth

Milford
Stoughton

Franklin
Whitman
ATLANTIC OCEAN

Bellingham
Brockton

146
North Attleboro
Plymouth Bay
Provincetown

Woonsocket
Attleboro
Plymouth

Taunton
Middleboro
Cape Cod Bay

Pawtucket
South Carver
MYLES STANDISH STATE FOREST

Providence
Seekonk
Somerset
FREETOWN STATE FOREST
Buzzards Bay
Sandwich
Cape Cod

Cranston
Dennis
Chatham

Warwick
Fall River
6A

RHODE ISLAND
New Bedford
Monument Beach
Hyannis
Harwich Port

Monomoy Island

Newport
Buzzards Bay
Falmouth

Elizabeth Islands
Woods Hole
Vineyard Haven
Nantucket Sound

Aquinnah (Gay Head)
Edgartown
Martha's Vineyard

Nantucket Town

Nantucket Island

Block Island (R.I.)

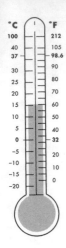

Memorial Day through Labor Day (and in some cases through Columbus Day) is high season. This is summer with a capital S, a time for barbecues, beach bumming, water sports, and swimming. During summer everything is open for business, but you can also expect high-season evils: high prices, crowds, and traffic.

The islands are, however, increasingly becoming year-round destinations, especially in the shoulder seasons of fall and spring, when the summer crowds have diminished. Martha's Vineyard puts bells on for all kinds of special events and celebrations, most notably in Edgartown and Vineyard Haven. On Nantucket, many shops and restaurants remain open through Nantucket Noel (Thanksgiving through December).

Climate

Although there are plenty of idyllic beach days, rain or fog is not an uncommon part of even an August vacation on Nantucket and Martha's Vineyard. Those who do not learn to appreciate the beauty of the land and sea in mist and rain may find themselves mighty cranky.

Temperatures in winter and summer are milder here than on the mainland, due in part to the warming influence of the Gulf Stream and the moderating ocean breezes. As a rule (and there have been dramatically anomalous years—1994 and 1999 in particular), the islands get much less snow than the mainland, and what falls generally does not last. Still, winter can bring bone-chilling dampness.

🗃 Forecasts **Weather Channel Connection** ☎ 900/932–8437, 95¢ per minute from a Touch-Tone phone. For local Cape weather, coastal marine forecasts, and today's tides, call the weather line of **WQRC** ☎ 508/771–5522 in Hyannis.

Jan.	40F	+4C	May	62F	17C	Sept.	70F	21C
	25	−4		48	+9		56	13
Feb.	41F	+5C	June	71F	22C	Oct.	59F	15C
	26	−3		56	13		47	8
Mar.	42F	+6C	July	78F	25C	Nov.	48F	9C
	28	−2		63	17		37	3
Apr.	53F	12C	Aug.	76F	24C	Dec.	40F	4C
	40	+4		61	16		26	−3

Both the *Martha's Vineyard Times* and the *Vineyard Gazette* publish weekly calendars of events on Martha's Vineyard. Also scan the *Best Read Guide* and *Vineyard Style Magazine*, found at many shops and hotels. The Nantucket events calendar published in the free handout *Yesterday's Island* (and also at ⊕ www.yesterdaysisland.com) lists every public happening, from art-gallery openings and church fairs to big tourist events.

SPRING

Late April	Nantucket's **Daffodil Festival** (☎ 508/228–1700 ⊕ www.nantucket.net/daffy) weekend celebrates spring with a flower show, shopwindow displays, and a procession of antique cars adorned with daffodils that ends in tailgate picnics at Siasconset. For about five weeks from mid-April to mid-May, millions of daffodils bloom along Nantucket roadsides and in private gardens.
Mid-May	During the **Nantucket Wine Festival** (⊕ www.nantucketwinefestival.com) when more than 100 international vintners converge on the island to show off—and share—their wares at a series of elegant parties, participants can sign on to sip rare vintages in spectacular private homes to which one might not easily gain access otherwise.

SUMMER

June–Aug.	The islands are all busy with **summer theater, concerts,** and **arts-and-crafts fairs.**
Mid June	The **Nantucket Film Festival** (☎ 508/325–6274 ⊕ www.nantucketfilmfestival.org), begun in 1995, offers four days of independent and art-house films. It's a very low-key event, with a focus on screenwriting.
	The **Taste of the Vineyard** (☎ 508/627–4440), held at the Old Whaling Church in Edgartown, showcases some 75 local restaurants and other food and beverage purveyors, all of whom serve samples.
July 4	Nantucket observes the Fourth of July in spectacular retro style. Children parade down Main Street with their tricolor-decorated bikes, then dig in at watermelon- and blueberry-pie-eating contests. Don't worry about the mess, because next comes a water fight between antique fire trucks. The day winds down with a **fireworks display** over the sound, off Jetties Beach.
July–Aug.	**Martha's Vineyard Chamber Music Society** (☎ 508/696–8055 ⊕ www.mvcms.vineyard.net) performs concerts every Monday and Tuesday for six weeks. Monday concerts are in Edgartown; Tuesday concerts are in Chilmark.
	Edgartown Regatta (☎ 508/627–4364), started in 1923, is three days of yacht racing around Martha's Vineyard.

The **Portuguese Holy Ghost Feast** (☎ 508/693–9875), held the third weekend in July, is a weekend event that includes dance, music, and authentic Portuguese cooking. Held at the Portuguese-American Club's building in Oak Bluffs, it raises funds that the group donates to various island charities and student scholarships.

Early Aug.	Every year, top East Coast dealers bring their wares to Nantucket for the **Annual Antiques Show** (☎ 508/228–1894 ⊕ www.antiquescouncil.com/nant.htm), run by the Nantucket Historical Association and held at the Nantucket High School, 10 Surfside Road.
	At the **Possible Dreams Auction** (☎ 508/693–7900 ⊕ www.possibledreamsauction.org), held the first Monday of August in Edgartown as a benefit for Martha's Vineyard Community Services, a guest auctioneer (Art Buchwald in the past) sells off such starry prizes as a sail with Walter Cronkite and lunch with Carly Simon.
Mid-Aug.	The **Boston Pops Esplanade Orchestra** (☎ 508/825–8248 ⊕ www.bso.org) puts on a sell-out concert on Jetties Beach—piping plovers permitting—to benefit the Nantucket Cottage Hospital.
	Family-friendly Jetties Beach hosts **Sandcastle and Sculpture Day** (☎ 508/228–1700), a tradition started in 1974. Some teams train and plot all year for this contest; others register on a whim. Different categories and age groupings give everyone a good shot at a ribbon, and prizes aside, it makes for a rewarding day of glorified sandbox play.

FALL

Mid-Sept.	**Tivoli Day** (☎ 508/696–7643), an end-of-summer celebration in Oak Bluffs on Martha's Vineyard, has a street fair with live entertainment and crafts.
Mid-Sept.– mid-Oct.	Locals go crazy over the monthlong **Martha's Vineyard Striped Bass and Bluefish Derby** (☎ 508/627–8510 ⊕ www.mvderby.com), one of the East Coast's premier fishing contests, with more than $100,000 in prizes for albacore, bluefish, striped bass, and bonito catches. It raises money for the island's conservation projects and scholarships for Vineyard students pursuing marine sciences.
Early Oct.	The weeklong **Nantucket Arts Festival** (☎ 508/325–8588) offers a chance to partake of the performing, visual, and literary arts.

WINTER

Late Nov.	**Nantucket Noel,** from Thanksgiving to Christmas, is becoming almost as popular as summer for vacationers. Many of the businesses are open and seasonal festivities are celebrated in top New England style.

Early Dec.

Many island towns do up the Christmas season in grand style. But the best-known celebration is the Nantucket **Christmas Stroll** (☎ 508/228–1700), which takes place the first Saturday of the month. Carolers and musicians entertain strollers as they walk the festively decorated cobblestone streets and sample shops' wares and seasonal refreshments. Activities include theatrical performances, art exhibitions, crafts sales, and a tour of historic homes.

On Martha's Vineyard, **Christmas in Edgartown** (☎ 508/693–0085), the second weekend of December, includes tours of historic homes, teas, carriage rides, a parade, caroling, and other entertainment.

PLEASURES & PASTIMES

Beaches Long, dune-backed sand beaches, with both surf and calm water, abound on Martha's Vineyard and Nantucket. Quiet coves, beaches, big waves splashing up against soft white sand, gentle ones lapping up to a shoreline, tide pools, rocky coastlines, dramatic cliffs falling into the ocean, clay pits—they're all here.

Many beaches on Martha's Vineyard are open to the public, and others are owned by the towns they're in and require a pass or sticker, which you can buy from the individual towns' parks and recreation departments (in the town halls). Still others are privately owned by individuals or beach clubs (such as the East Chop Beach Club in Oak Bluffs, Quansoo in Chilmark, and Seven Gates in West Tisbury), requiring you to know people in high places with access to these private paradises.

Nantucket takes pride in keeping all of its beaches open to the public, and any attempt at claiming a stretch in the name of a private residence is frowned upon. Just ½ mi from town, Children's Beach, with placid waves, aims to please families by putting a playground and a concessionaire within reach. Surfside on the south, or Atlantic, shore is the island's most popular beach, although the riptides and undertow can get out of hand. The wide stretch never disappoints, except that it can seem that everybody on the whole island's turned out for a tan and place to plant their beach chair.

Biking Martha's Vineyard and Nantucket are great places for cycling. On Martha's Vineyard, Up-Island roads cross some hilly terrain, and during summer and fall roads islandwide can get very crowded. Still, cycling beats driving as a pleasant and often more practical way to tour the island. Cyclists have access to well-maintained, flat, paved paths along the coast road from Oak Bluffs to Edgartown—very scenic—and inland from Vineyard Haven to Edgartown and South Beach. These connect with sometimes potholed paths that weave through the Manuel F. Correllus State Forest. Middle Road in Chilmark is a lovely, winding country road with less traffic than the main roads.

On Nantucket, bike paths are more significant to transportation and more beloved than roads. These are wide and paved paths—not the gullies between traffic and parked cars that city dwellers endure—that span the island. From Nantucket Town, well-marked paths fan out in all directions, along the newest and scenic Polpis Path to the eastern village of Sconset; south, along Surfside Bike Path, to Surfside Beach; and west, on the Madaket Path, which intersects with the coastal paths at Eel Point/Dionis Beach and Cliff Road, both of which have terrific scenery.

Dining

Influenced by arrivals from Boston and New York, a generation of young chefs—many of whom own their restaurants—is serving eclectic, inventive, cosmopolitan menus, with prices to match. On Martha's Vineyard, first-rate, sophisticated dining is now available everywhere. The latest trend among these smart young chefs is to create menus that range from reasonable burgers to expensive full dinners, blurring the line between hot and haute spots, allowing families and younger diners to enjoy a more upscale ambience.

On Nantucket, dining out is such a popular participatory sport that table talk—and impromptu inter-table talk—is apt to center on discussions of where one ate last, where one is planning to eat next, and what's been the best so far. "So far" is the operative term. With a score of top-tier restaurants intent on outdoing one another, the mantle never settles for long. The cuisine of choice is new-American: classic dishes influenced by the best of other culinary traditions, including French, Mexican, and Japanese. Reservations can be hard to get at the top spots, and even harder is getting an outdoor seat in summer; further, many are not suitable for kids. If you've got a gaggle of hungry little ones with you, choose one of the family-friendly sit-down places or bring something back from one of the island's many excellent take-out spots.

As for a general recommendation on what to order, you don't have to be a graduate of a culinary institute to realize that on an island fish is a smart bet. However, keep in mind that all fish on the menu won't have come from waters surrounding the Vineyard and Nantucket. Some of the more exotic species—mahimahi, for example—are shipped in. Ask your waiter which fish is caught locally. Bluefish, striped bass, swordfish, and bay scallops—each has its own season—are among the local hauls. For those who like to cook their own, the local retail fish shops will guide you to the fresh catches of the day, and the counter people will usually recommend their favorite recipes.

Hiking

The beaches get a lot of press—and deservedly so. Much less heralded are the extensive walking and hiking trails, overseen by various conservation groups. Though the conservation land is primarily set aside to protect native species (some of them rare and even endangered), it's a point of pride that almost all these areas are open for public use. There are hardwood forests, salt marshes, cranberry bogs, freshwater ponds, coastal heathlands, and more. On Martha's Vineyard, the nature preserves and conservation areas are laced with well-marked, scenic trails through varied terrains and ecological habitats.

Especially in summer, but throughout the fall and winter too, many island groups sponsor informative guided walks led by naturalists and other experts. Check the local weekly papers for schedules. For kids, Felix Neck Wildlife Sanctuary on Martha's Vineyard provides an extensive schedule of educational yet entertaining programs aimed at children—and adults, too. The Nantucket Conservation Foundation, Great Point Natural History Tours, and Maria Mitchell Association provide information, maps, and lead guided tours on Nantucket.

Shopping

Art galleries and crafts shops abound on Martha's Vineyard and Nantucket, a reflection of the long attraction the area has held for artists and artisans. Coastal environments and a seafaring past account for the proliferation of sea-related crafts (as well as marine-antiques dealers) on the islands. A craft form that originated on the years-long voyages to whaling grounds is scrimshaw, the etching of finely detailed designs of sailing ships and sea creatures onto a hard surface. In the beginning, the bones or teeth of whales were used; today's ecologically minded (and legally constrained) scrimshanders use a synthetic substitute like Corian, a DuPont countertop material.

Another whalers' pastime was the sailor's valentine: a glass-enclosed wood box, often in an octagonal shape (derived from the shape of the compass boxes that were originally used), containing an intricate mosaic of tiny seashells. The shells were collected on stopovers in the West Indies and elsewhere; sorted by color, size, and shape; and then glued into elaborate patterns during the long hours aboard ship. Exquisite examples can be found in the Nantucket Whaling Museum.

The Nantucket lightship basket was developed in the mid-19th century on a lightship off the island's coast. In good weather there was little to do, and so (the story goes) crew members began weaving intricately patterned baskets of cane, a trade some continued onshore and passed on. Later a woven lid and decoration were added, and the utilitarian baskets were on their way to becoming the handbags that today cost hundreds of dollars. Although Nantucket is still the locus of the craft, antique and new baskets can be found on the Cape and the Vineyard as well.

A specialty of the Martha's Vineyard is *wampum*—beads made from the white and purple shell of the quahog and fashioned into jewelry sold at the Aquinnah Cliffs and elsewhere. Antique and new scrimshaw jewelry, and jewelry incorporating Vineyard and island-specific designs such as lighthouses or bunches of grapes, is also popular. The three main towns have the largest concentrations of shops. In Vineyard Haven, shops line Main Street. Edgartown's are clustered together within a few blocks of the dock, on Main, Summer, and Water streets. Casual clothing and gift shops crowd along Circuit Avenue in Oak Bluffs. At Aquinnah Cliffs, you'll find touristy Native American crafts and souvenirs in season.

On Nantucket, boutiques and galleries in town resemble those along New York City's Madison Avenue. So do their prices. Yes, the island is laid-back—and known for its faded all-cotton wear called "Nantucket reds"—but its shopping district, bounded by Main, Broad, and Centre streets, is thoroughly modern, with upscale home decor shops and designer clothing. In fact, everyone tends to dress up to shop. On the town's waterfront are souvenir, ice-cream, and T-shirt shops, and a mile or two beyond the town limits a few shops, forced out of town by high retail rents, sell necessities and luxuries alike.

FODOR'S CHOICE

Fodor's Choice
★

The sights, restaurants, hotels, and other travel experiences on these pages are our editors' top picks—our Fodor's Choices. They're the best of their type in the area covered by the book—not to be missed and always worth your time. In the chapters that follow, you will find all the details.

LODGING

$$$–$$$$ | **Charlotte Inn**, Edgartown, Martha's Vineyard. In this Edwardian period piece, friendliness and relaxed elegance speak volumes. Go ahead and treat yourself.

$$–$$$$ | **The Wauwinet**, Wauwinet, Nantucket. With its quiet, remote location mere steps from both bay and sea, and its lavishly decorated rooms and cottages, this is far and away Nantucket's most pampering inn, priced accordingly.

$$–$$$$ | **Winnetu**, Edgartown, Martha's Vineyard. You can hear the ocean roaring just 250 yards away and, from some rooms, actually see it at this stylish retreat that's away from it all on the outskirts of Edgartown.

$$–$$$$ | **The Summer House**, Siasconset, Nantucket. This cluster of former fishing shacks, draped in roses, has a quirky, authentic charm. Creature comforts are ample, from the English country furnishings to marble baths, and there's a pool halfway along the short stroll to the beach.

$–$$ | **Seven Sea Street**, Nantucket. This spacious post-and-beam building in town only looks old: it's actually a 1987 replica, custom-built to afford all the comforts expected by modern-day guests.

RESTAURANTS

$$$$ | **L'étoile**, Edgartown, Martha's Vineyard. In the incomparable Charlotte Inn, this longtime contemporary French favorite is one of the finest restaurants outside of major cities on the East Coast.

$$$$ | **the pearl**, Nantucket. With its white onyx bar and white leather banquettes, the pearl is by far the trendiest restaurant in town. It's also among the most accomplished, thanks to chef-owner Seth Raynor's Eastern-leaning finesse.

$$$–$$$$ | **Sweet Life Café**, Oak Bluffs, Martha's Vineyard. Relaxed, gracious, young but not trendy, intimate but not cloying, the Sweet Life serves terrific new American food.

$$–$$$ | **Black-Eyed Susan's**, Nantucket. Decor-wise, this eatery doesn't have much going for it: it's a nominally reconstructed lunch room, complete with counter and stools. But, oh, the luscious breakfasts and daring dinners!

$$-$$$$ | **The Summer House Beachside Bistro,** Nantucket. The terraced potagerie flanking the stairway down to the cluster of white umbrellas attests to the freshness of chef Paul Restrepo's contemporary creations.

$ | **Larsen's,** Menemsha, Martha's Vineyard. There is precious little seating here, but you may find that raw oysters, steamers, lobster, crab cakes, and chowder have never tasted better than they do on the dock outside Larsen's market.

BEACHES

Coatue–Coskata–Great Point reserves, Nantucket. Here, you may see a marsh hawk or an oystercatcher floating in the air or coming and going from stands of cedar and oak, or you might just land a striped bass or bluefish if you brought along a surf-casting pole. Or you could just put your feet in the sand and walk out to the Great Point Light.

Eel Point, Nantucket. At the northwestern end of the island, this beach blossoms summer-long with wild roses, heather, goldenrod, and fragrant bayberry. Great for swimming and surf-casting (the waves are gentle), it's also a terrific birding area: small sandbar islands close to shore serve as inviting perches for shorebirds.

Lucy Vincent Beach, Martha's Vineyard. This Chilmark spot is quite simply the best beach on the island. It is restricted to resident use in summer, at which point you may want to venture out to Aquinnah to take in the sights on the beach under the phenomenal cliffs and lighthouse.

QUINTESSENCE

The **Wednesday-night community sing-along** (in July and August only) at the Tabernacle in the Oak Bluffs Camp Ground on Martha's Vineyard is great old-time fun, as much for the melody as for the sense of community you can't help but feel.

The brick **Aquinnah Lighthouse** overlooking the dramatic cliffs at Aquinnah on Martha's Vineyard quietly speaks, like a time-tested sentinel, of the elemental forces of wind and sea.

In fall, the **moors of Nantucket** morph into a palette of colors so subtle you'll find yourself hypnotized.

Stargazing from Nantucket's Loines Observatory is astonishing because the island's isolation from mainland lights makes the sky virtually blaze with starlight.

Bright crimson cranberries floating on flooded bogs amid fiery foliage are a perfect reminder of the tart pleasures a sere landscape can yield.

Nantucket's **Brant Point** is more than a scenic lighthouse, it's a repository of dreams: ferry passengers heading back to the mainland traditionally toss a penny in the water to ensure a swift return.

One of the most carefully maintained historic repositories in America, Nantucket, with its **cobblestone streets and elegant Greek Revival architecture,** serves as a living monument to the enduring aesthetic enchantments of another age.

SHOPPING

Rafael Osona's auctions, Nantucket. At the American Legion Hall, these auctions are geared to buyers and spectators alike. Even if you never raise a hand to snag a fine antique, the spiel itself is entertaining.

Morning Glory Farm, Martha's Vineyard. From Memorial Day until Thanksgiving, the glistening produce of this 50-acre farm attracts Vineyarders and Vineyard visitors longing for fresh-picked strawberries and corn, lettuce, tomatoes and pumpkins, as well as homemade relishes and jellies.

Bunch of Grapes, Martha's Vineyard. Grapes, in Vineyard Haven, contains an amazing array of books, books, and more books, including island-related titles. Don't be surprised to find yourself browsing through the shelves next to the Hollywood celebs and assorted literati who shop here.

Lightship baskets and scrimshaw on Nantucket continue a crafts tradition—initiated by sailors—which remains unique to the area.

Murray's Toggery, with shops on both islands, is the premier purveyor of "Nantucket reds"—clothes that are actually on the salmon side once they fade—and a universal signifier of preppitude.

Farm stands throughout the islands represent a great way to get close to the land and the rhythm of rural life—while provisioning spectacular feasts.

WILDLIFE

Felix Neck Wildlife Sanctuary, Martha's Vineyard. This wildlife reserve is a Massachusetts Audubon Society jewel, its ponds, marshes, fields, and woods teeming with plant and animal life.

Whales breaching alongside your whale-watch boat create a sense of wonder—the creatures are simply marvelous. It's also quite a treat to see dolphins jumping in and out of the boat's bow waves or in its wake.

SMART TRAVEL TIPS

*Finding out about your destination before
you leave home means you won't squan-
der time organizing everyday minutiae
once you've arrived. You'll be more
streetwise when you hit the ground as
well, better prepared to explore the aspects of Martha's Vineyard and Nantucket that drew you here in the first
place. The organizations in this section
can provide information to supplement
this guide; contact them for up-to-the-
minute details, and consult the A to Z
sections that end each chapter for facts
on the various topics as they relate to the
different regions. Happy landings!*

AIR TRAVEL

BOOKING

When you book, look for nonstop flights
and remember that "direct" flights stop at
least once. Try to avoid connecting flights,
which require a change of plane. Two airlines may operate a connecting flight
jointly, so ask whether your airline operates every segment of the trip; you may
find that the carrier you prefer flies you
only part of the way. To find more booking tips and to check prices and make online flight reservations, log on to www.
fodors.com.

CARRIERS

Cape Air/Nantucket Airlines has direct
flights to Martha's Vineyard and Nantucket from Boston, Hyannis, New Bedford, and Providence; there are also
flights between Nantucket and Provincetown. Colgan Air flies direct to Nantucket and Martha's Vineyard from New
York (year-round for Nantucket, seasonal
for Martha's Vineyard). Continental Express flies from Nantucket to Newark. Island Airlines has regular service between
Nantucket and Martha's Vineyard, as
well as from Hyannis to Nantucket. With
the exception of Cape Air, flights to
Martha's Vineyard are usually chartered.
Chartered flights cost more and leave
from several departure points along the
East Coast. On an annual basis, one or

another major airline may decide to institute scheduled service.

F **Major Airlines Cape Air/Nantucket Airlines** ☎ 800/352-0714 ⊕ www.flycapeair.com. **Colgan Air** Operated by US Airways ☎ 888/265-4267 or 703/368-8880, 800/428-4322 for US Airways ⊕ www.colganair.com. **Island Airlines** ☎ 508/228-7575 or 800/248-7779 ⊕ www.nantucket.net/trans/islandair.

F **Martha's Vineyard Charter Carriers Desert & Island Air Charter** ☎ 800/835-9135 ⊕ www.desertislandair.com. **Eagle Air** ☎ 888/993-2453 ⊕ www.eagleaircharter.com. **Eastern Air Charter** ☎ 800/370-8680 ⊕ www.easternaircharter.com. **Million Air Charters** ☎ 800/882-2333 ⊕ www.millionairteb.com. **Ocean Wings** ☎ 508/693-4646 or 800/253-5039. **Tikal Aviation** ☎ 877/622-3798 ⊕ www.commandshare.com.

F **Nantucket Charter Carriers Century Airlines** ☎ 800/486-2368. **Desert & Island Air Charter** ☎ 800/835-9135 ⊕ www.desertislandair.com. **Green Air** ☎ 800/388-6685 ⊕ www.greenaviation.com. **Million Air Charters** ☎ 800/882-2333 ⊕ www.millionairteb.com. **Nantucket Express** ☎ 800/626-8825 ⊕ www.nantucketexpress.ws. **Primac Air** ☎ 800/247-8699 ⊕ www.primac.com.

CHECK-IN & BOARDING

Always **find out your carrier's check-in policy.** Plan to arrive at the airport about two hours before your scheduled departure time for domestic flights. You may need to arrive earlier if you're flying from one of the busier airports or during peak air-traffic times. Turboprop planes seating up to 19 passengers typically serve the islands. Flights are generally informal and may require slightly less wait time than flights elsewhere else. Be sure to **allow time for your luggage to be weighed upon boarding** and then loaded once you're on the tarmac.

To avoid delays at airport-security checkpoints, try not to wear any metal. Jewelry, belt and other buckles, steel-toe shoes, barrettes, and underwire bras are among the items that can set off detectors.

Always **bring a government-issued photo I.D.** to the airport; even when it's not required, a passport is best.

CUTTING COSTS

The least expensive airfares to Martha's Vineyard and Nantucket are priced for round-trip travel and must usually be purchased in advance. Airlines generally allow you to change your return date for a fee; most low-fare tickets, however, are nonrefundable. It's smart to call a number of airlines and check the Internet; when you are quoted a good price, book it on the spot—the same fare may not be available the next day, or even the next hour. Always check different routings and look into using alternate airports. Also, price off-peak flights, which may be significantly less expensive than others. Travel agents, especially low-fare specialists (⇨ Discounts & Deals), are helpful.

Consolidators are another good source. They buy tickets for scheduled flights at reduced rates from the airlines, then sell them at prices that beat the best fare available directly from the airlines. (Many also offer reduced car-rental and hotel rates.) Sometimes you can even get your money back if you need to return the ticket. Carefully read the fine print detailing penalties for changes and cancellations, purchase the ticket with a credit card, and confirm your consolidator reservation with the airline.

Cape Air commuter books are a good deal if you're planning on making several trips between Boston or Hyannis and Martha's Vineyard or Nantucket within a short period of time.

F **Consolidators AirlineConsolidator.com** ☎ 888/468-5385 ⊕ www.airlineconsolidator.com; for international tickets. **Best Fares** ☎ 800/880-1234 or 800/576-8255 ⊕ www.bestfares.com; $59.90 annual membership. **Cheap Tickets** ☎ 800/377-1000 or 800/652-4327 ⊕ www.cheaptickets.com. **Expedia** ☎ 800/397-3342 or 404/728-8787 ⊕ www.expedia.com. **Hotwire** ☎ 866/468-9473 or 920/330-9418 ⊕ www.hotwire.com. **Now Voyager Travel** ⊠ 45 W. 21st St., Suite 5A New York, NY 10010 ☎ 212/459-1616 📠 212/243-2711 ⊕ www.nowvoyagertravel.com. **Onetravel.com** ⊕ www.onetravel.com. **Orbitz** ☎ 888/656-4546 ⊕ www.orbitz.com. **Priceline.com** ⊕ www.priceline.com. **Travelocity** ☎ 888/709-5983, 877/282-2925 in Canada, 0870/876-3876 in the U.K. ⊕ www.travelocity.com.

ENJOYING THE FLIGHT

State your seat preference when purchasing your ticket, and then repeat it when you confirm and when you check in. For more legroom, you can request one of the few emergency-aisle seats at check-in, if you're capable of moving obstacles comparable in weight to an airplane exit door (usually between 35 pounds and 60 pounds)—a Federal Aviation Administration requirement of passengers in these seats. Seats behind a bulkhead also provide more legroom, but they don't have under-seat storage.

Ask the airline whether a snack or meal is served on the flight. If you have dietary concerns, request special meals when booking. These can be vegetarian, low-cholesterol, or kosher, for example. It's a good idea to pack some healthful snacks and a small (plastic) bottle of water in your carry-on bag. On long flights, try to maintain a normal routine, to help fight jet lag. At night, get some sleep. By day, eat light meals, drink water (not alcohol), and move around the cabin to stretch your legs. For additional jet-lag tips consult *Fodor's FYI: Travel Fit & Healthy* (available at bookstores everywhere).

Smoking policies vary from carrier to carrier. Many airlines prohibit smoking on all of their flights; others allow smoking only on certain routes or certain departures. Ask your carrier about its policy.

FLYING TIMES

Flying time to Martha's Vineyard is one hour from New York, 30 minutes from Boston, and 25 minutes from Providence. It takes 15 minutes longer to get from these points to Nantucket. Flights from Hyannis and between the islands take 15 minutes.

HOW TO COMPLAIN

If your baggage goes astray or your flight goes awry, complain right away. Most carriers require that you file a claim immediately. The Aviation Consumer Protection Division of the Department of Transportation publishes *Fly-Rights,* which discusses airlines and consumer issues and is available online. You can also find articles and information on mytravelrights.com, the Web site of the nonprofit Consumer Travel Rights Center.

7 **Airline Complaints Aviation Consumer Protection Division** ⊠ U.S. Department of Transportation, Office of Aviation Enforcement and Proceedings, C-75, Room 4107, 400 7th St. SW, Washington, DC 20590 ☎ 202/366-2220 ⊕ airconsumer.ost.dot.gov. **Federal Aviation Administration Consumer Hotline** ⊠ for inquiries: FAA, 800 Independence Ave. SW, Washington, DC 20591 ☎ 800/322-7873 ⊕ www.faa.gov.

RECONFIRMING

Check the status of your flight before you leave for the airport. You can do this on your carrier's Web site, by linking to a flight-status checker (many Web booking services offer these), or by calling your carrier or travel agent.

AIRPORTS & TRANSFERS

Nantucket Memorial Airport (often known by its abbreviation, ACK) is 3½ mi southeast of town near Surfside. Martha's Vineyard Airport is in West Tisbury, about 5 mi west of Edgartown.

Boston's Logan International Airport, Providence International Airport, LaGuardia in New York City, and the smaller Hyannis Municipal Airport are the major gateways to the islands.

7 **Airport Information Martha's Vineyard Airport** ⊠ West Tisbury Rd., Edgartown ☎ 508/693-7022 ⊕ www.mvyairport.com. **Nantucket Memorial Airport** ⊠ 30 Macy's La., off Old South Rd., near Surfside ☎ 508/325-5307 operations, 508/325-5300 manager ⊕ www.nantucketairport.com.

AIRPORT TRANSFERS

Taxis meet all arriving flights on both islands.

BIKE TRAVEL

Seeing the islands by bike is the preferred way to travel. (Scooters come in second, although they're accident-prone in Nantucket Town, where streets are cobbled.) Bike paths are everywhere, and there are plenty of bike shops, which have a few types of good-quality bikes for rent and free maps. Note that helmet-wearing is the law for all ages. For bike rentals, *see* the A to Z sections *in* Chapters 1 and 2.

BIKES IN FLIGHT

Most airlines accommodate bikes as luggage, provided they are dismantled and boxed; check with individual airlines about packing requirements. Some airlines sell bike boxes, which are often free at bike shops, for about $20 (bike bags can be considerably more expensive). International travelers often can substitute a bike for a piece of checked luggage at no charge; otherwise, the cost is about $100. Most U.S. and Canadian airlines charge $40–$80 each way.

BOAT & FERRY TRAVEL

Ferries leave for Martha's Vineyard from Wood's Hole on Cape Cod year-round and from Nantucket, New Bedford, and Quonset Point, R.I. in season. Year-round ferries serve Nantucket from Hyannis, on Cape Cod. Ferries connect the islands in season.

See the A to Z sections *in* Chapters 1 and 2 for fares, schedules, and ferry service contact numbers.

BUSINESS HOURS

MUSEUMS & SIGHTS

Hours for attractions are seasonal, so always call ahead. Most museums and historical sights keep daily hours in summer, weekend hours in shoulder season, and very limited hours in winter.

SHOPS

Shops are generally open from 9 or 10 to 5, though in high season many tourist-oriented stores on the Vineyard or stores in Nantucket Town stay open until 10 PM or later. Shops outside these commercial areas are often closed on Sunday. Some may also keep seasonal hours and close during the winter.

BUS TRAVEL

Greyhound serves Boston (and Boston's Logan International Airport) and New York from all over the country, and from there you can connect to a local carrier, such as Bonanza Bus Lines and Plymouth & Brockton, to points on Cape Cod with island-bound ferries. Plymouth & Brockton is the local carrier and serves Boston (and Logan Airport) and the Cape, including Barnstable and Hyannis, all the way to Provincetown. The bus terminals are at most a block and a half from the ferry docks, so travel light or use a suitcase with wheels, and you won't need to call a cab for your luggage. The seven- to nine-hour bus trip from New York's Penn Station via Boston to Woods Hole or Hyannis costs about $80 to $100 round-trip. The three-hour trip from Boston, which includes ferry passage, is about $30 round-trip. As on-board cell-phone use has gotten out of hand, **make your cell phone calls before you board the bus** or you might be asked to comply with increased no-chitchat regulations designed to give all passengers a quiet ride. **Eat before you go,** as no food or beverages are allowed on Plymouth & Brockton coaches.

📋 Bus Information **Bonanza Bus Lines** ☎ 888/751-8800 ⊕ www.bonanzabus.com. **Greyhound** ☎ 800/229-9424, 617/526-1801 Boston terminal, 508/548-5011 in Woods Hole, 508/778-9767 in Hyannis ⊕ www.greyhound.com. **Plymouth & Brockton Street Railway Co.** ☎ 508/746-0378 fares and schedules, 508/771-6191 in Hyannis ⊕ www.p-b.com.

BUS TRAVEL WITHIN MARTHA'S VINEYARD & NANTUCKET

Both islands have local bus service. For local bus information, *see* the A to Z sections *in* Chapters 1 and 2.

CAR RENTAL

Driving on the islands during summer has a number of unique and frustrating aspects. If you really want to relax on your vacation and you're staying in town, **consider not renting a car on the islands.** Unless you're staying in a remote rental property, you won't need it in season, and you will not miss the high rental rates, starting at $80 per day in summer. The towns are infamous for their seasonal parking problems and traffic, too. That said, cars are much less of a problem during the off-season, and you may be better off renting one here, even at the high summer rate, than bringing your own and incurring the steep costs and hassles of the car ferry. For reputable local agencies and four-wheel-drive rental vehicles, *see* the A to Z sections *in* Chapters 1 and 2.

🛂 **Major Agencies Budget** ☎ 800/527-0700, 0870/156-5656 in the U.K. ⊕ www.budget.com. **Hertz** ☎ 800/654-3131, 800/263-0600 in Canada, 0870/844-8844 in the U.K., 02/9669-2444 in Australia, 09/256-8690 in New Zealand ⊕ www.hertz. com. **Thrifty** ☎ 800/847-4389 ⊕ www.thrifty.com.

CUTTING COSTS

For a good deal, book through a travel agent who will shop around. Also, price local car-rental companies—whose prices may be lower still, although their service and maintenance may not be as good as those of major rental agencies—and research rates on the Internet. Consolidators that specialize in air travel can offer good rates on cars as well (⇨ Air Travel). Remember to ask about required deposits, cancellation penalties, and drop-off charges if you're planning to pick up the car in one city and leave it in another. If you're traveling during a holiday period, also make sure that a confirmed reservation guarantees you a car.

INSURANCE

When driving a rented car you are generally responsible for any damage to or loss of the vehicle. You also may be liable for any property damage or personal injury that you may cause while driving. Before you rent, see what coverage you already have under the terms of your personal auto-insurance policy and credit cards.

For about $9 to $25 a day, rental companies sell protection, known as a collision- or loss-damage waiver (CDW or LDW), that eliminates your liability for damage to the car; it's always optional and should never be automatically added to your bill. In Massachusetts the car-rental agency's insurance is primary; therefore, the company must pay for damage to third parties up to a preset legal limit, beyond which your own liability insurance kicks in. However, **make sure you have enough coverage to pay for the car.** If you do not have auto insurance or an umbrella policy that covers damage to third parties, purchasing liability insurance and a CDW or LDW is highly recommended.

REQUIREMENTS & RESTRICTIONS

Most agencies won't rent to you if you're under the age of 21, and many impose strict guidelines about not taking cars off-island.

SURCHARGES

Before you pick up a car in one city and leave it in another, ask about drop-off charges or one-way service fees, which can be substantial. Also inquire about early-return policies; some rental agencies charge extra if you return the car before the time specified in your contract while others give you a refund for the days not used. To avoid a hefty refueling fee, fill the tank just before you turn in the car, but be aware that gas stations near the rental outlet may overcharge. It's almost never a deal to buy the tank of gas that's in the car when you rent it; the understanding is that you'll return it empty, but some fuel usually remains. Surcharges may apply if you're under 25 or if you take the car outside the area approved by the rental agency. You'll pay extra for child seats (about $8 a day), which are compulsory for children under five, and usually for additional drivers (up to $25 a day, depending on location).

CAR TRAVEL

The islands seem to discourage visitors from bringing their cars with the prices they charge to ferry your car and fill up your tank. Expect to pay more than $2.60 a gallon and as much as $3 a gallon if your car has expensive tastes. Unless you *absolutely* need it, **don't bring your car during the summer.** The one-way car-ferry rate is $175 to Nantucket and $57 to Martha's Vineyard, plus the ticket price for passengers. You'll need to **make a reservation far in advance to bring your car on the ferry**—in fact, you may need to plan your trip around when you can get your car transported to the island. The Steamship Authority ferry begins taking car reservations for spring as early as February 1. Gasoline can cost almost $1 more on-island than off. Furthermore, most inns cannot offer you parking, and the onslaught of pedestrians and car traffic in season can be likened to that in Times Square. Off-season is a different story, and ferry rates drop and street parking is more widely available in town. For more information, *see* the A to Z sections *in* Chapters 1 and 2.

FERRY TERMINAL PARKING

If you bring your car as far as the ferry, you'll pay a daily rate of $8 in summer for a space, and signs along Route 28 will indicate which lots are full. A shuttle serves the more remote Woods Hole parking lots and drops you at the ferry. The Steamship Authority ferry provides daily parking and traffic information over the phone and directions to the parking lots on its Web site. Make sure you **arrive an hour before your ferry departs for the island** to allow for unloading, parking, returning to the dock, and boarding.

F Parking Resources Steamship Authority ☎ 508/477-8600 reservations, 617/374-1234 Smart-Traveler parking and traffic information ⊕ www.islandferry.com.

RULES OF THE ROAD

State law requires that you always **strap children who are five years old or younger or weigh 40 pounds or less into approved child-safety seats** that are properly secured and installed. Children who are 12 or under must wear seat belts regardless of where they're seated.

In Massachusetts, you may turn right at a red light after stopping if there is no oncoming traffic. When in doubt, wait for the green. Be alert for one-way streets, "no left turn" intersections, and blocks closed to car traffic. Keep vehicles (and scooters and bikes, for that matter) on roads and paths.

CHILDREN ON MARTHA'S VINEYARD & NANTUCKET

The islands are particularly family-friendly come summer, when the beaches teem with junior architects building their designs in the sand and lines for ice cream slink down town streets. Arts-and-crafts day camps, outdoor music shows, daily story time at libraries, and a slew of other outdoor activities, events, and diversions are available to keep the young and the restless, well, less restless. Also

keep your eyes peeled for kid-friendly restaurants; some offer deals and meals beyond their regular menus and rates. For more information, *see* the A to Z sections *in* Chapters 1 and 2.

For general advice about traveling with children, consult *Fodor's FYI: Travel with Your Baby* (available in bookstores everywhere).

FLYING

If your children are two or older, ask about children's airfares. As a general rule, infants under two not occupying a seat fly at greatly reduced fares or even for free. But if you want to guarantee a seat for an infant, you have to pay full fare. Consider flying during off-peak days and times; most airlines will grant an infant a seat without a ticket if there are available seats. Experts agree that it's a good idea to use safety seats aloft for children weighing less than 40 pounds. Airlines set their own policies: if you use a safety seat, U.S. carriers usually require that the child be ticketed, even if he or she is young enough to ride free, because the seats must be strapped into regular seats. And even if you pay the full adult fare for the seat, it may be worth it, especially on longer trips. Do **check your airline's policy about using safety seats during takeoff and landing.** Safety seats are not allowed everywhere in the plane, so get your seat assignments as early as possible.

When reserving, request children's meals or a freestanding bassinet (not available at all airlines) if you need them. But note that bulkhead seats, where you must sit to use the bassinet, may lack an overhead bin or storage space on the floor.

LODGING

If you're planning to stay at a bed-and-breakfast, be sure to **ask the owners in advance** whether the B&B welcomes children. Some establishments are filled with fragile antiques, and owners may not accept families with children of a certain age. **Families should consider lodging at hotels, condos, and cottages,** which cater to children. These tend to offer more practical furnishings, kitchens, and sometimes laundry facilities. Often cottage or condo communities, such as Duck Inn or Winnetu Inn and Resort on Martha's Vineyard, have play yards and pools, sometimes even full children's programs. On Nantucket, Harbor House Village has babysitting in season, and Wharf Cottages, in town, has kids' programs.

Most hotels on Martha's Vineyard allow children under a certain age to stay in their parents' room at no extra charge, but others charge for them as extra adults; be sure to **find out the cutoff age for children's discounts.** On Nantucket, it's rare to find an inn with two beds in a room.

🛈 Best Choices Duck Inn ✉ Martha's Vineyard ☎ 508/645-9018. **Winnetu Inn and Resort** ✉ Martha's Vineyard ☎ 508/627-4747. **Harbor House Village** ✉ Nantucket ☎ 508/228-1500 or 800/325-9300. **Wharf Cottages** ✉ Nantucket ☎ 508/228-4620 or 800/475-2637.

SIGHTS & ATTRACTIONS

Places that are especially appealing to children are indicated by a rubber-duckie icon (🦆) in the margin.

CONSUMER PROTECTION

Whether you're shopping for gifts or purchasing travel services, **pay with a major credit card** whenever possible, so you can cancel payment or get reimbursed if there's a problem (and you can provide documentation). If you're doing business with a particular company for the first time, contact your local Better Business Bureau and the attorney general's offices in your state and (for U.S. businesses) the company's home state as well. Have any complaints been filed? Finally, if you're buying a package or tour, always consider travel insurance that includes default coverage (⇨ Insurance).

🛈 BBBs Council of Better Business Bureaus ✉ 4200 Wilson Blvd., Suite 800, Arlington, VA 22203 ☎ 703/276-0100 📠 703/525-8277 ⊕ www. bbb.org.

CUSTOMS & DUTIES

IN AUSTRALIA

Australian residents who are 18 or older may bring home A$400 worth of souvenirs and gifts (including jewelry), 250 cigarettes or 250 grams of cigars or other

tobacco products, and 1,125 ml of alcohol (including wine, beer, and spirits). Residents under 18 may bring back A$200 worth of goods. Members of the same family traveling together may pool their allowances. Prohibited items include meat products. Seeds, plants, and fruits need to be declared upon arrival.

🛈 Australian Customs Service ⌖ Regional Director, Box 8, Sydney, NSW 2001 ☎ 02/9213-2000 or 1300/363263, 02/9364-7222 or 1800/020-504 quarantine-inquiry line 📠 02/9213-4043 ⊕ www. customs.gov.au.

IN CANADA

Canadian residents who have been out of Canada for at least seven days may bring in C$750 worth of goods duty-free. If you've been away fewer than seven days but more than 48 hours, the duty-free allowance drops to C$200. If your trip lasts 24 to 48 hours, the allowance is C$50. You may not pool allowances with family members. Goods claimed under the C$750 exemption may follow you by mail; those claimed under the lesser exemptions must accompany you. Alcohol and tobacco products may be included in the seven-day and 48-hour exemptions but not in the 24-hour exemption. If you meet the age requirements of the province or territory through which you reenter Canada, you may bring in, duty-free, 1.5 liters of wine *or* 1.14 liters (40 imperial ounces) of liquor *or* 24 12-ounce cans or bottles of beer or ale. Also, if you meet the local age requirement for tobacco products, you may bring in, duty-free, 200 cigarettes and 50 cigars. Check ahead of time with the Canada Customs and Revenue Agency or the Department of Agriculture for policies regarding meat products, seeds, plants, and fruits.

You may send an unlimited number of gifts (only one gift per recipient, however) worth up to C$60 each duty-free to Canada. Label the package UNSOLICITED GIFT—VALUE UNDER $60. Alcohol and tobacco are excluded.

🛈 Canada Customs and Revenue Agency ✉ 2265 St. Laurent Blvd., Ottawa, Ontario K1G 4K3 ☎ 800/ 461-9999 in Canada, 204/983-3500, 506/636-5064 ⊕ www.ccra.gc.ca.

IN NEW ZEALAND

All homeward-bound residents may bring back NZ$700 worth of souvenirs and gifts; passengers may not pool their allowances, and children can claim only the concession on goods intended for their own use. For those 17 or older, the duty-free allowance also includes 4.5 liters of wine or beer; one 1,125-ml bottle of spirits; and either 200 cigarettes, 250 grams of tobacco, 50 cigars, *or* a combination of the three up to 250 grams. Meat products, seeds, plants, and fruits must be declared upon arrival to the Agricultural Services Department.

🛂 **New Zealand Customs** ✉ Head office: The Customhouse, 17–21 Whitmore St., Box 2218, Wellington ☎ 09/300–5399 or 0800/428–786 ⊕ www.customs. govt.nz.

IN THE U.K.

From countries outside the European Union, including the U.S., you may bring home, duty-free, 200 cigarettes, 50 cigars, 100 cigarillos, or 250 grams of tobacco; 1 liter of spirits or 2 liters of fortified or sparkling wine or liqueurs; 2 liters of still table wine; 60 ml of perfume; 250 ml of toilet water; plus £145 worth of other goods, including gifts and souvenirs. Prohibited items include meat and dairy products, seeds, plants, and fruits.

🛂 **HM Customs and Excise** ✉ Portcullis House, 21 Cowbridge Rd. E, Cardiff CF11 9SS ☎ 0845/010–9000 or 0208/929–0152 advice service, 0208/929–6731 or 0208/910–3602 complaints ⊕ www.hmce. gov.uk.

DINING

For information on the terrific dining scene indigenous to the islands *see* About the Restaurants at the beginning of Chapters 1 and 2.The restaurants we list are the cream of the crop in each price category. Properties indicated by an ✕🏨 are lodging establishments whose restaurant warrants a special trip.

DISABILITIES & ACCESSIBILITY

Travelers who use wheelchairs have access to well-paved sidewalks in towns, even if streets are brick and uneven. For information on accessibility in parks and outdoor activities, consult the Universal Access

Program posted on the Massachusetts Department of Environmental Management Web site. The Cape Organization for Rights of the Disabled supplies information on accessibility of restaurants, hotels, beaches, and other tourist facilities. The Nantucket Chamber of Commerce posts a Guide for Visitors with Special Needs on its Web site. Sight Loss Services provides accessibility and other information and referrals for people with vision impairments.

🛂 **Local Resources Cape Organization for Rights of the Disabled** (CORD) ☎ 508/775–8300 or 800/541–0282 ⊕ www.cordonline.org. **Massachusetts Department of Environmental Management** ✉ Division of Forests and Parks, 251 Causeway St., Suite 600, Boston 02114 ☎ 617/626–1250 ⊕ www. state.ma.us/dem/access.htm. **Massachusetts Directory of Accessible Facilities** ⊕ www.state.ma.us/dem/access.htm. **Sight Loss Services** ☎ 508/394–3904, 800/427–6842 in Massachusetts ⊕ www. geocities.com/sightloss. **Nantucket Chamber of Commerce** Guide for Visitors with Special Needs ✉ 48 Main St., 2nd floor, 02554 ☎ 508/228–1700 ⊕ www.nantucketchamber.org.

LODGING

The Nantucket Island Chamber of Commerce can help find a room to suit your needs. Their *Nantucket Guide* ($7) also indicates a few wheelchair-accessible properties in the index. Despite the Americans with Disabilities Act, the definition of accessibility seems to differ from hotel to hotel. Some properties may be accessible by ADA standards for people with mobility problems but not for people with hearing or vision impairments, for example.

If you have mobility problems, ask for the lowest floor on which accessible services are offered. If you have a hearing impairment, check whether the hotel has devices to alert you visually to the ring of the telephone, a knock at the door, and a fire/emergency alarm. Some hotels provide these devices without charge. Discuss your needs with hotel personnel if this equipment isn't available, so that a staff member can personally alert you in the event of an emergency.

If you're bringing a guide dog, get authorization ahead of time and write down the name of the person with whom you spoke.

RESERVATIONS

When discussing accessibility with an operator or reservations agent, ask hard questions. Are there any stairs, inside *or* out? Are there grab bars next to the toilet *and* in the shower/tub? How wide is the doorway to the room? To the bathroom? For the most extensive facilities meeting the latest legal specifications, opt for newer accommodations. If you reserve through a toll-free number, consider also calling the hotel's local number to confirm the information from the central reservations office. Get confirmation in writing when you can.

TRANSPORTATION

All Martha's Vineyard and Nantucket shuttles (May–October) are wheelchair accessible. Fares are half price (25¢–$1) for persons with disabilities on both islands.
71 Complaints Aviation Consumer Protection Division (⇨ Air Travel) for airline-related problems. **Departmental Office of Civil Rights** ✉ for general inquiries, U.S. Department of Transportation, S-30, 400 7th St. SW, Room 10215, Washington, DC 20590 ☎ 202/366-4648 📠 202/366-9371 ⊕ www.dot. gov/ost/docr/index.htm. **Disability Rights Section** ✉ NYAV, U.S. Department of Justice, Civil Rights Division, 950 Pennsylvania Ave. NW, Washington, DC 20530 ☎ ADA information line 202/514-0301, 800/514-0301, 202/514-0383 TTY, 800/514-0383 TTY ⊕ www.ada.gov. **U.S. Department of Transportation Hotline** ☎ for disability-related air-travel problems, 800/778-4838 or 800/455-9880 TTY.

TRAVEL AGENCIES

In the United States, the Americans with Disabilities Act requires that travel firms serve the needs of all travelers. Some agencies specialize in working with people with disabilities.
71 Travelers with Mobility Problems Access Adventures/B. Roberts Travel ✉ 206 Chestnut Ridge Rd., Scottsville, NY 14624 ☎ 585/889-9096 ⊕ www. brobertstravel.com, run by a former physical-rehabilitation counselor. **Accessible Vans of America** ✉ 9 Spielman Rd., Fairfield, NJ 07004 ☎ 877/282-8267, 888/282-8267, 973/808-9709 reservations 📠 973/808-9713 ⊕ www.accessiblevans.com. **Flying Wheels Travel** ✉ 143 W. Bridge St., Box 382, Owatonna, MN 55060 ☎ 507/451-5005 📠 507/451-1685 ⊕ www.flyingwheelstravel.com.

DISCOUNTS & DEALS

Bus and airline carriers both have commuter priced tickets, which may be worth your while if you're staying all summer (⇨ *see* Bus Travel *or* Air Travel for contact information).

Be a smart shopper and compare all your options before making decisions. A plane ticket bought with a promotional coupon from travel clubs, coupon books, and direct-mail offers or purchased on the Internet may not be cheaper than the least expensive fare from a discount ticket agency. And always keep in mind that what you get is just as important as what you save.

DISCOUNT RESERVATIONS

To save money, look into discount reservations services with Web sites and toll-free numbers, which use their buying power to get a better price on hotels, airline tickets (⇨ Air Travel), even car rentals. When booking a room, always **call the hotel's local toll-free number** (if one is available) rather than the central reservations number—you'll often get a better price. Always ask about special packages or corporate rates.
71 Airline Tickets Air 4 Less ☎ 800/AIR4LESS; low-fare specialist.
71 Hotel Rooms Accommodations Express ☎ 800/444-7666 or 800/277-1064 ⊕ www.acex.net. **Hotels. com** ☎ 800/246-8357 ⊕ www.hotels.com. **Quikbook** ☎ 800/789-9887 ⊕ www.quikbook.com. **Turbotrip.com** ☎ 800/473-7829 ⊕ www.turbotrip.com.

PACKAGE DEALS

Don't confuse packages and guided tours. When you buy a package, you travel on your own, just as though you had planned the trip yourself. Fly/drive packages, which combine airfare and car rental, are often a good deal. In cities, ask the local visitor's bureau about hotel and local transportation packages that include tickets to major museum exhibits or other special events.

EMERGENCIES

Dial **911** for emergencies. Vineyard Medical Services provides walk-in care; call for days and hours. Leslie's Drug Store is open daily and has a pharmacist on 24-hour call for emergencies. Nantucket Cottage Hospital has a 24-hour medical and dental emergency room.

7 Hospital & Emergency Service Martha's Vineyard Hospital ⊠ Linton La., Oak Bluffs ☎ 508/693-0410. Nantucket Cottage Hospital ⊠ 57 Prospect St. ☎ 508/228-1200 ⊕ www.nantuckethospital.org. Vineyard Medical Services ⊠ State Rd., Vineyard Haven ☎ 508/693-4400.
7 Late-Night Pharmacy Leslie's Drug Store ⊠ 65 Main St., Vineyard Haven ☎ 508/693-1010.

GAY & LESBIAN TRAVEL

Although it is common for gay and lesbian travelers to bypass the islands for Provincetown, at the end of the Cape, they will find Martha's Vineyard and Nantucket to be welcoming seaside destinations, too. The Vineyard is a tad more cosmopolitan, with a handful of gay-friendly establishments. Nantucket has a bit more of a reserved air, and gays and lesbians here keep a lower profile than elsewhere on the Cape.

For details about the gay and lesbian scene, consult *Fodor's Gay Guide to the USA* (available in bookstores everywhere).
7 Gay- & Lesbian-Friendly Travel Agencies Different Roads Travel ⊠ 8383 Wilshire Blvd., Suite 520, Beverly Hills, CA 90211 ☎ 323/651-5557 or 800/429-8747 (Ext. 14 for both) 🖷 323/651-5454. Kennedy Travel ⊠ 130 W. 42nd St., Suite 401, New York, NY 10036 ☎ 212/840-8659, 800/237-7433 🖷 212/730-2269 ⊕ www.kennedytravel.com. Now, Voyager ⊠ 4406 18th St., San Francisco, CA 94114 ☎ 415/626-1169 or 800/255-6951 🖷 415/626-8626 ⊕ www.nowvoyager.com. Skylink Travel and Tour/Flying Dutchmen Travel ⊠ 1455 N. Dutton Ave., Suite A, Santa Rosa, CA 95401 ☎ 707/546-9888 or 800/225-5759 🖷 707/636-0951; serving lesbian travelers.

HEALTH

PESTS & OTHER HAZARDS

A troublesome problem on the islands is Lyme disease (named after Lyme, Connecticut, where it was first diagnosed). This bacterial infection is transmitted by deer ticks and can be very serious, leading to chronic arthritis and worse if left untreated. Pregnant women are advised to **avoid areas of possible deer tick infestation,** such as wooded areas or places with tall grasses (including dunes). Deer ticks are most prevalent April through October but can be found year-round. They are about the size of a pinhead. Anyone planning to explore these areas should **wear long pants, socks drawn up over pant cuffs, and a long-sleeve shirt with a close-fitting collar**; boots are also recommended. The National Centers for Disease Control recommends that DEET repellent be applied to skin (not face!) and that permethrin be applied to clothing directly before entering infested areas; **use repellents very carefully** and conservatively with small children. Always closely **check yourself within 12 hours** of nature excursions for any ticks you might have attracted.

Ticks also attach themselves to pets. If you plan to bring your dog or cat, the best prevention is to **visit a veterinarian for a prophylactic medication** that is applied monthly. Reliable brands are Revolution and Front Line; despite advertising claims, supermarket brands are not as effective. While here and after your return, you should **check your pet frequently for infestation,** running your hands along your pet's legs and face and combing through his fur to check visually. If the ticks are not yet engorged, they may be more difficult to spot but may be visible when crawling around looking for a good place to bite. Once they have attached themselves, you can **remove them yourself,** but be sure you get the entire tick, not just the body; tweezers are very helpful for this operation. If you don't want to remove the tick yourself, take your pet to a vet immediately.

If you wander into the woods or stray off a bike path, **be on the lookout for poison ivy,** a pervasive vinelike plant that has three shiny green leaves together. In spring, poison-ivy leaves are red; likewise, they can take on a reddish tint as fall approaches. The oil from these leaves produces an itchy skin rash that spreads with scratching. If you think you may have touched some leaves, **wash as soon as you can** with soap and cool water; calamine lotion can help calm the itch.

Although many public beaches have life-guards on duty throughout the summer, **beware of riptides and heavy undertows,** especially before or after a storm.

Be careful if you rent a scooter on Nantucket. Even if you have experience with such things, the cobblestone streets in town are not at all conducive to smooth riding, and there are many distractions on the road. Accidents, many of them serious, are all too common.

HOLIDAYS

Major national holidays are New Year's Day (Jan. 1); Martin Luther King Day (3rd Mon. in Jan.); Presidents' Day (3rd Mon. in Feb.); Memorial Day (last Mon. in May); Independence Day (July 4); Labor Day (1st Mon. in Sept.); Columbus Day (2nd Mon. in Oct.); Thanksgiving Day (4th Thurs. in Nov.); Christmas Eve and Christmas Day (Dec. 24 and 25); and New Year's Eve (Dec. 31).

INSURANCE

The most useful travel-insurance plan is a comprehensive policy that includes coverage for trip cancellation and interruption, default, trip delay, and medical expenses (with a waiver for preexisting conditions).

Without insurance you'll lose all or most of your money if you cancel your trip, regardless of the reason. Default insurance covers you if your tour operator, airline, or cruise line goes out of business—the chances of which have been increasing. Trip-delay covers expenses that arise because of bad weather or mechanical delays. Study the fine print when comparing policies.

Always **buy travel policies directly from the insurance company**; if you buy them from a cruise line, airline, or tour operator that goes out of business you probably won't be covered for the agency or operator's default, a major risk. Before making any purchase, review your existing health and home-owner's policies to find what they cover away from home.

⊓ **Travel Insurers** In the U.S.: **Access America** ⊠ 2805 N. Parham Rd., Richmond, VA 23294 ☎ 800/284-8300 ☐ 804/673-1491 or 800/346-9265 ⊕ www.accessamerica.com. **Travel Guard In-**ternational ⊠ 1145 Clark St., Stevens Point, WI 54481 ☎ 715/345-0505 or 800/826-1300 ☐ 800/955-8785 ⊕ www.travelguard.com.

FOR INTERNATIONAL TRAVELERS

For information on customs restrictions, *see* Customs & Duties.

CAR RENTAL

When picking up a rental car, non-U.S. residents need a reservation voucher for any prepaid reservations that were made in the traveler's home country, a passport, a driver's license, and a travel policy that covers each driver.

CAR TRAVEL

Driving in the United States is on the right. Do obey speed limits posted along roads and highways. Watch for lower limits in small towns and on back roads. On weekdays between 6 and 10 AM and again between 4 and 7 PM expect heavy traffic. To encourage carpooling, some freeways have special lanes for so-called high-occupancy vehicles (HOV)—cars carrying more than one passenger.

Gas stations are plentiful. Most stay open late (24 hours along large highways and in big cities), except in rural areas, where Sunday hours are limited and where you may drive long stretches without a refueling opportunity. Highways are well paved. Interstate highways—limited-access, multilane highways whose numbers are prefixed by "I-"—are the fastest routes. Interstates with three-digit numbers encircle urban areas, which may have other limited-access expressways, freeways, and parkways as well. Tolls may be levied on limited access highways. So-called U.S. highways and state highways are not necessarily limited-access but may have several lanes.

Along larger highways, roadside stops with restrooms, fast-food restaurants, and sundries stores are well spaced. State police and tow trucks patrol major highways and lend assistance. If your car breaks down on an interstate, pull onto the shoulder and wait for help, or have your passengers wait while you walk to an emergency phone (available in most states). If you carry a cell phone, dial *55, noting your location, which is listed on the small green roadside mileage markers.

Bookstores, gas stations, convenience stores, and rest stops sell maps (about $3) and multiregion road atlases (about $10).

CURRENCY

The dollar is the basic unit of U.S. currency. It has 100 cents. Coins are the copper penny (1¢); the silvery nickel (5¢), dime (10¢), quarter (25¢), and half-dollar (50¢); and the golden $1 coin, replacing a now-rare silver dollar. Bills are denominated $1, $5, $10, $20, $50, and $100, all mostly green and identical in size; designs and background tints vary. In addition, you may come across a $2 bill, but the chances are slim.

ELECTRICITY

The U.S. standard is AC, 110 volts/60 cycles. Plugs have two flat pins set parallel to each other.

INSURANCE

Britons and Australians need extra medical coverage when traveling overseas.

⑦ Insurance Information In the U.K.: **Association of British Insurers** ✉ 51 Gresham St., London EC2V 7HQ ☎ 020/7600-3333 ⊟ 020/7696-8999 ⊕ www. abi.org.uk. In Australia: **Insurance Council of Australia** ✉ Insurance Enquiries and Complaints, Level 12, Box 561, Collins St. W, Melbourne, VIC 8007 ☎ 1300/780808 or 03/9629-4109 ⊟ 03/9621-2060 ⊕ www.iecltd.com.au. In Canada: **RBC Insurance** ✉ 6880 Financial Dr., Mississauga, Ontario L5N 7Y5 ☎ 800/668-4342 or 905/816-2400 ⊟ 905/813-4704 ⊕ www.rbcinsurance.com. In New Zealand: **Insurance Council of New Zealand** ✉ Level 7, 111-115 Customhouse Quay, Box 474, Wellington ☎ 04/472-5230 ⊟ 04/473-3011 ⊕ www.icnz.org.nz.

MAIL & SHIPPING

You can buy stamps and aerograms and send letters and parcels in post offices. Stamp-dispensing machines can occasionally be found in airports, bus and train stations, office buildings, drugstores, and the like. You can also deposit mail in the stout, dark blue, steel bins at strategic locations everywhere and in the mail chutes of large buildings; pickup schedules are posted. You can deposit packages at public collection boxes as long as the parcels are affixed with proper postage and weigh less than one pound. Packages weighing one or more pounds must be taken to a post office or handed to a postal carrier.

For mail sent within the United States, you need a 37¢ stamp for first-class letters weighing up to 1 ounce (23¢ for each additional ounce) and 23¢ for postcards. You pay 80¢ for 1-ounce airmail letters and 70¢ for airmail postcards to most other countries; to Canada and Mexico, you need a 60¢ stamp for a 1-ounce letter and 50¢ for a postcard. An aerogram—a single sheet of lightweight blue paper that folds into its own envelope, stamped for overseas airmail—costs 70¢.

To receive mail on the road, have it sent c/o General Delivery at your destination's main post office (use the correct five-digit ZIP code). You must pick up mail in person within 30 days and show a driver's license or passport.

PASSPORTS & VISAS

When traveling internationally, carry your passport even if you don't need one (it's always the best form of I.D.) and **make two photocopies of the data page** (one for someone at home and another for you, carried separately from your passport). If you lose your passport, promptly call the nearest embassy or consulate and the local police.

Visitor visas aren't necessary for Canadian or European Union citizens, or for citizens of Australia who are staying fewer than 90 days.

⑦ Australian Citizens **Passports Australia** ☎ 131-232 ⊕ www.passports.gov.au. **United States Consulate General** ✉ MLC Centre, Level 59, 19-29 Martin Pl., Sydney, NSW 2000 ☎ 02/9373-9200, 1902/941-641 fee-based visa-inquiry line ⊕ usembassy-australia.state.gov/sydney.

⑦ Canadian Citizens **Passport Office** ✉ to mail in applications: 200 Promenade du Portage, Hull, Québec J8X 4B7 ☎ 819/994-3500, 800/567-6868, 866/255-7655 TTY ⊕ www.ppt.gc.ca.

⑦ New Zealand Citizens **New Zealand Passports Office** ✉ For applications and information, Level 3, Boulcott House, 47 Boulcott St., Wellington ☎ 0800/22-5050 or 04/474-8100 ⊕ www. passports.govt.nz. **Embassy of the United States** ✉ 29 Fitzherbert Terr., Thorndon, Wellington

☎ 04/462-6000 ⊕ usembassy.org.nz. **U.S. Consulate General** ✉ Citibank Bldg., 3rd floor, 23 Customs St. E, Auckland ☎ 09/303-2724 ⊕ usembassy. org.nz.

🛈 **U.K. Citizens U.K. Passport Service** ☎ 0870/ 521-0410 ⊕ www.passport.gov.uk. **American Consulate General** ✉ Danesfort House, 223 Stranmillis Rd., Belfast, Northern Ireland BT9 5GR ☎ 028/ 9032-8239 🖷 028/9024-8482 ⊕ usembassy.org.uk. **American Embassy** ✉ for visa and immigration information or to submit a visa application via mail (enclose an SASE), Consular Information Unit, 24 Grosvenor Sq., London W1 1AE ☎ 09055/444-546 for visa information (per-minute charges), 0207/ 499-9000 main switchboard ⊕ usembassy.org.uk.

TELEPHONES

All U.S. telephone numbers consist of a three-digit area code and a seven-digit local number. Within many local calling areas, you dial only the seven-digit number. Within some area codes, you must dial "1" first for calls outside the local area. To call between area-code regions, dial "1" then all 10 digits; the same goes for calls to numbers prefixed by "800," "888," "866," and "877"—all toll free. For calls to numbers preceded by "900" you must pay—usually dearly.

For international calls, dial "011" followed by the country code and the local number. For help, dial "0" and ask for an overseas operator. The country code is 61 for Australia, 64 for New Zealand, 44 for the United Kingdom. Calling Canada is the same as calling within the United States. Most local phone books list country codes and U.S. area codes. The country code for the United States is 1.

For operator assistance, dial "0." To obtain someone's phone number, call directory assistance at 555-1212 or occasionally 411 (free at many public phones). To have the person you're calling foot the bill, phone collect; dial "0" instead of "1" before the 10-digit number.

At pay phones, instructions often are posted. Usually you insert coins in a slot (usually 25¢–50¢ for local calls) and wait for a steady tone before dialing. When you call long-distance, the operator tells you how much to insert; prepaid phone

cards, widely available in various denominations, are easier. Call the number on the back, punch in the card's personal identification number when prompted, then dial your number.

LODGING

Because the islands are incredibly popular, with quaint B&Bs, refined inns, beachside cottages, and even an affordable seaside hostel, **make your lodging arrangements months in advance**—as much as a year ahead if you're planning to visit in the busy summer season, or during such popular weekends as the Nantucket Daffodil Festival or Christmas Stroll. Most inns require prepayment or a nonrefundable deposit, as well as a three-night minimum in summer—and rates are steep, with inns commanding $225 a night on average.

In this book, properties are assigned price categories based on the range from their least-expensive standard double room at high season (excluding holidays) to the most expensive. The lodgings we list are the cream of the crop in each price category. We always list the facilities that are available, but we don't specify whether they cost extra; when pricing accommodations, always ask what's included and what costs extra.

Properties marked ✕🏨 are lodging establishments whose restaurants warrant a special trip. Assume that hotels operate on the European Plan (no meals) unless we specify that they use the **Continental Plan** (CP; Continental breakfast) or **Breakfast Plan** (BP; full breakfast). All hotels listed have private bath unless otherwise noted.

Meal services vary greatly from inn to inn. Several of the larger hotels have excellent in-house restaurants. Some B&Bs offer gourmet sit-down breakfasts or breakfast in bed; others lay out a "Continental" spread, which will often encompass exquisite home-baked pastries. Some offer vouchers to nearby restaurants. If you plan to stay at a bed-and-breakfast, **check in advance whether your B&B welcomes children.** Some establishments are filled with fragile antiques, and owners may not accept children of a certain age.

If you prefer to be self-sufficient and appliances such as coffeemakers and mini-refrigerators are essential to your comfort, **inquire before reserving a room**; they're far from standard here. Some inns have air-conditioning, but many do not. As the innkeepers will tell you, it's usually not an issue: even on hot summer days, cool ocean breezes tend to keep temperatures within a comfortable range.

For island-specific lodging information, including hotels and B&Bs, see the About the Hotels and Where to Stay sections in Chapters 1 and 2.

BED-AND-BREAKFAST RESERVATION AGENCIES

These agencies can do more than find you a great B&B: they can also arrange any and all details of your visit. Fees vary.

🚹 **Martha's Vineyard Bed-and-Breakfast Contacts Martha's Vineyard and Nantucket Reservations** ☎ 508/693-7200 ⊕ www.mvreservations.com. 🚹 **Nantucket Bed-and-Breakfast Contacts Heaven Can Wait Accommodations** ✍ Box 622, Siasconset 02564 ☎ 508/257-4000. **Martha's Vineyard and Nantucket Reservations** ✍ 73 Lagoon Pond Rd. ✍ Box 1322, Vineyard Haven 02568 ☎ 508/693-7200, 800/649-5671 in Massachusetts. **Nantucket Accommodations** ✉ 4 Dennis Dr. ✍ Box 217, 02554 ☎ 508/228-9559 ⊕ www. nantucketaccommodation.com. **Nantucket Concierge** ✍ Box 1257, 02554 ☎ 508/228-8422 🖷 508/228-8422 ⊕ www.nantucketconcierge.com.

HOME EXCHANGES

If you would like to exchange your home for someone else's, join a home-exchange organization, which will send you its updated listings of available exchanges for a year and will include your own listing in at least one of them. It's up to you to make specific arrangements.

🚹 **Exchange Clubs HomeLink International** ✍ Box 47747, Tampa, FL 33647 ☎ 813/975-9825 or 800/638-3841 🖷 813/910-8144 ⊕ www.homelink. org; $110 yearly for a listing, online access, and catalog; $70 without catalog. **Intervac U.S.** ✉ 30 Corte San Fernando, Tiburon, CA 94920 ☎ 800/756-4663 🖷 415/435-7440 ⊕ www.intervacus.com; $125 yearly for a listing, online access, and a catalog; $65 without catalog.

HOSTELS

No matter what your age, you can save on lodging costs by staying at hostels. In some 4,500 locations in more than 70 countries around the world, Hostelling International (HI), the umbrella group for a number of national youth-hostel associations, offers single-sex, dorm-style beds and, at many hostels, rooms for couples and family accommodations. The Nantucket hostel, on the south Atlantic shore, is one of the country's most scenic. Membership in any HI national hostel association, open to travelers of all ages, allows you to stay in HI-affiliated hostels at member rates; one-year membership is about $28 for adults (C$35 for a two-year minimum membership in Canada, £14 in the U.K., A$52 in Australia, and NZ$40 in New Zealand); hostels charge about $10–$30 per night. Members have priority if the hostel is full; they're also eligible for discounts around the world, even on rail and bus travel in some countries.

🚹 **Organizations Hostelling International–USA** ✉ 8401 Colesville Rd., Suite 600, Silver Spring, MD 20910 ☎ 301/495-1240 🖷 301/495-6697 ⊕ www. hiusa.org. **Hostelling International–Canada** ✉ 205 Catherine St., Suite 400, Ottawa, Ontario K2P 1C3 ☎ 613/237-7884 or 800/663-5777 🖷 613/ 237-7868 ⊕ www.hihostels.ca. **YHA England and Wales** ✉ Trevelyan House, Dimple Rd., Matlock, Derbyshire DE4 3YH, U.K. ☎ 0870/870-8808, 0870/ 770-8868, 0162/959-2600 🖷 0870/770-6127 ⊕ www.yha.org.uk. **YHA Australia** ✉ 422 Kent St., Sydney, NSW 2001 ☎ 02/9261-1111 🖷 02/9261-1969 ⊕ www.yha.com.au. **YHA New Zealand** ✉ Level 1, Moorhouse City, 166 Moorhouse Ave., Box 436, Christchurch ☎ 03/379-9970 or 0800/278-299 🖷 03/365-4476 ⊕ www.yha.org.nz.

HOUSE RENTALS

Martha's Vineyard Vacation Rentals and Sandcastle Vacation Home Rentals can help you find rentals for long-term visits. In Nantucket, a number of real-estate agents (complete lists are provided by the Chamber of Commerce and the Nantucket Information Bureau) have rentals ranging from in-town apartments in lovely old buildings to new waterfront houses.

🚹 **Martha's Vineyard Vacation Rentals** ☎ 800/ 556-4225 ⊕ www.mvvacationrentals.com. **Sandcas-**

tle Vacation Home Rentals ☎ 508/627–5665 ⊕ www.sandcastlemv.com.

MAIL & SHIPPING

Post office hours vary from city to city in Martha's Vineyard. Weekdays the Nantucket post office is open 8:30–5 and Saturday 8:30–12:30. Overnight service may actually take an extra day to and from the islands.

🚺 **Martha's Vineyard Post Offices Edgartown Post Office** ⊠ 236B Edgartown-Vineyard Haven Rd., Edgartown, MA 02539 ☎ 508/627–7318. **Oak Bluffs Post Office** ⊠ 24E Kennebec Ave., Oak Bluffs, MA 02557 ☎ 508/693–1049. **Vineyard Haven Post Office** ⊠ 1 Lagoon Pond Rd., Vineyard Haven, MA 02568 ☎ 508/693–2815. **West Tisbury Post Office** ⊠ State Rd., West Tisbury, MA 02575 ☎ 508/693–7899.

🚺 **Nantucket Post Office Nantucket Post Office** ⊠ 5 Federal St., Nantucket, MA 02554 ☎ 508/228–1067.

MEDIA

NEWSPAPERS & MAGAZINES

The *Martha's Vineyard Times* (⊕ www.mvtimes.com) and *Vineyard Gazette* (⊕ www.mvgazette.com) are the island's two main news sources, and between them you'll have a good idea of island events and happenings. On Nantucket, look for the free tabloid-size weekly, *Yesterday's Island* (⊕ www.yesterdaysisland.com), and the regular island newspaper, the *Inquirer and Mirror,* whose Web site (⊕ www.ack.net)—named for the island's airport code—lists events. The *Cape Cod Times* (⊕ www.capecodonline.com), printed in Hyannis, is also available on the islands and often carries news of local interest. Local magazines include *Vineyard Home & Garden* and *Times of the Islands* (⊕ www.timesoftheislands.com/Nantucket/begin.htm), covering Nantucket as well as the Vineyard. You can find these at any bookstore, convenience store, supermarket, or pharmacy on the islands.

RADIO & TELEVISION

The local radio station on Martha's Vineyard is **WMVY** (92.7 on the dial ⊕ www.mvyradio.com), an FM album music station, also a good source for concert and nightlife news. **WNAN 91.1** (☎ 508/548–

9600 ⊕ www.cainan.org) is Nantucket's own NPR station, a thrilling millennial addition to the island's cultural discourse. Interspersed amid the standard NPR fare are local vignettes and coverage of island-specific issues.

Channel 17 Television (⊠ 25 Liberty St. [Box 1042, 02554] ☎ 508/825–8817 ⊕ www.genotv.com), is a community-access cable channel run by local independent filmmaker Geno Geng; it's simulcast online. **Nantucket Plum Channel 22** (⊠ 9 Amelia Dr. ☎ 508/228–8001), majority-owned by Nantucket Juice Guy partner Tom Scott, is considered must-viewing by many. Several islanders have their own shows with a devoted following.

MONEY MATTERS

Nantucket and Martha's Vineyard are expensive, plain and simple, but there are things you can do to cut costs—riding a bike around the island and eating simply at lunch counters or at your rental house can help. Free outdoor concerts and art galleries are also at your disposal, as are the beaches and wildlife areas. Sightseeing and commuter passes are available and are a good deal, especially for those staying longer than a weekend or going back and forth. Prices throughout this guide are given for adults. Substantially reduced fees are almost always available for children, students, and senior citizens. For information on taxes, *see* Taxes.

ATMS

For exact ATM location, *see* the A to Z sections *in* Chapters 1 and 2.

CREDIT CARDS

Throughout this guide, the following abbreviations are used: **AE,** American Express; **D,** Discover; **DC,** Diners Club; **MC,** MasterCard; and **V,** Visa.

🚺 **Reporting Lost Cards American Express** ☎ 800/992–3404. **Diners Club** ☎ 800/234–6377. **Discover** ☎ 800/347–2683. **MasterCard** ☎ 800/622–7747. **Visa** ☎ 800/847–2911.

PACKING

Pack a sweater or jacket, even in summer, as the island breezes can really cool things off. Even the fanciest restaurants no longer require formal dress, though you're still expected to dress nicely. In general, the area prides itself on its informality. Perhaps most important of all, **don't forget a swimsuit** or two.

In your carry-on luggage, pack an extra pair of eyeglasses or contact lenses and enough of any medication you take to last a few days longer than the entire trip. You may also ask your doctor to write a spare prescription using the drug's generic name, as brand names may vary from country to country. In luggage to be checked, **never pack prescription drugs, valuables, or undeveloped film.** And don't forget to carry with you the addresses of offices that handle refunds of lost traveler's checks. Check *Fodor's How to Pack* (available at online retailers and bookstores everywhere) for more tips.

To avoid customs and security delays, carry medications in their original packaging. Don't pack any sharp objects in your carry-on luggage, including knives of any size or material, scissors, nail clippers, and corkscrews, or anything else that might arouse suspicion.

To avoid having your checked luggage chosen for hand inspection, don't cram bags full. The U.S. Transportation Security Administration suggests packing shoes on top and placing personal items you don't want touched in clear plastic bags.

CHECKING LUGGAGE

You're allowed to carry aboard one bag and one personal article, such as a purse or a laptop computer. Make sure what you carry on fits under your seat or in the overhead bin. Get to the gate early, so you can board as soon as possible, before the overhead bins fill up.

Baggage allowances vary by carrier, destination, and ticket class. On international flights, you're usually allowed to check two bags weighing up to 70 pounds (32 kilograms) each, although a few airlines allow checked bags of up to 88 pounds (40 kilograms) in first class. Some international carriers don't allow more than 66 pounds (30 kilograms) per bag in

business class and 44 pounds (20 kilograms) in economy. On domestic flights, the limit is usually 50 to 70 pounds (23 to 32 kilograms) per bag. In general, carry-on bags shouldn't exceed 40 pounds (18 kilograms). Most airlines won't accept bags that weigh more than 100 pounds (45 kilograms) on domestic or international flights. Expect to pay a fee for baggage that exceeds weight limits. Check baggage restrictions with your carrier before you pack.

Airline liability for baggage is limited to $2,500 per person on flights within the United States. On international flights it amounts to $9.07 per pound or $20 per kilogram for checked baggage (roughly $640 per 70-pound bag), with a maximum of $634.90 per piece, and $400 per passenger for unchecked baggage. You can buy additional coverage at check-in for about $10 per $1,000 of coverage, but it often excludes a rather extensive list of items, shown on your airline ticket.

Before departure, itemize your bags' contents and their worth, and label the bags with your name, address, and phone number. (If you use your home address, cover it so potential thieves can't see it readily.) Include a label inside each bag and **pack a copy of your itinerary.** At check-in, make sure each bag is correctly tagged with the destination airport's three-letter code. Because some checked bags will be opened for hand inspection, the U.S. Transportation Security Administration recommends that you leave luggage unlocked or use the plastic locks offered at check-in. TSA screeners place an inspection notice inside searched bags, which are re-sealed with a special lock.

If your bag has been searched and contents are missing or damaged, file a claim with the TSA Consumer Response Center as soon as possible. If your bags arrive damaged or fail to arrive at all, file a written report with the airline before leaving the airport.

7 Complaints U.S. Transportation Security Administration Contact Center ☎ 866/289-9673 ⊕ www.tsa.gov.

SENIOR-CITIZEN TRAVEL

Deals for seniors are less likely here than elsewhere, because there is no short supply of customers willing to pay for the islands' *chère* dining and lodging experience. Furthermore, most restaurants and inns are fairly small and privately owned and are unable to grant the kind of discounts available to chains. It doesn't hurt to **ask if discounts are available,** especially for off-season trips, and **keep your eye open for early-bird specials and deals** around town.To qualify for age-related discounts, mention your senior-citizen status up front when booking hotel reservations (not when checking out) and before you're seated in restaurants (not when paying the bill). Be sure to have identification on hand. When renting a car, ask about promotional car-rental discounts, which can be cheaper than senior-citizen rates.

🚩 Educational Programs **Elderhostel** ✉ 11 Ave. de Lafayette, Boston, MA 02111-1746 ☎ 877/426-8056, 978/323-4141 international callers, 877/426-2167 TTY 🖨 877/426-2166 ⊕ www.elderhostel.org.

SIGHTSEEING TOURS

Summer has the greatest selection of boat, bike, bus, and guided walking tours—including island sightseeing, historical and architectural walks, and guided nature excursions. For information on tours and local outfitters, *see* the A to Z sections *in* Chapters 1 or 2.

STUDENTS IN MARTHA'S VINEYARD & NANTUCKET

Discounts for students are not prevalent, although the seaside hostel on Nantucket is one of the country's most beautifully set and costs a fraction of even the least expensive inn. Those on a budget should visit during the off-season, when rates on almost everything drop.

🚩 I.D.s & Services **STA Travel** ✉ 10 Downing St., New York, NY 10014 ☎ 212/627-3111, 800/777-0112 24-hr service center 🖨 212/627-3387 ⊕ www.sta.com. **Travel Cuts** ✉ 187 College St., Toronto, Ontario M5T 1P7, Canada ☎ 800/592-2887 in the U.S., 416/979-2406 or 866/246-9762 in Canada 🖨 416/979-8167 ⊕ www.travelcuts.com.

TAXES
SALES TAX

Massachusetts state sales tax is 5%. Clothing is not taxed until its price reaches $175 for a single item; then it is subject to a luxury tax.

TAXIS

Taxis meet all scheduled ferries and flights on both islands. For taxi phone numbers on each island and limousine services, *see* the A to Z sections *in* Chapters 1 and 2.

TIME

The islands are in the Eastern time zone.

TIPPING

At restaurants a tip of 15%–20% is standard for food servers and bartenders. The same goes for taxi drivers. Coat-check operators usually expect $1 per coat. Give inn staff and porters $1 per bag carried to your room, and leave about $2–$5 per night of your stay for maid service—more if extra service, like shoe shines, warrants it. Tour guides and naturalists may also be tipped up to $10 (less for half-day tour) depending upon the size of the group, whether it's already been figured in, and personalized attention.

TOURS & PACKAGES

Because everything is prearranged on a prepackaged tour or independent vacation, you spend less time planning—and often get it all at a good price.

BOOKING WITH AN AGENT

Travel agents are excellent resources. But it's a good idea to collect brochures from several agencies, as some agents' suggestions may be influenced by relationships with tour and package firms that reward them for volume sales. If you have a special interest, find an agent with expertise in that area; the American Society of Travel Agents (ASTA; ⇨ Travel Agencies) has a database of specialists worldwide. You can log on to the group's Web site to find an ASTA travel agent in your neighborhood.

Make sure your travel agent knows the accommodations and other services of the place being recommended. Ask about the hotel's location, room size, beds, and whether it has a pool, room service, or programs for children, if you care about these. Has your agent been there in person or sent others whom you can contact?

Do some homework on your own, too: local tourism boards can provide information about lesser-known and small-niche operators, some of which may sell only direct.

BUYER BEWARE

Each year consumers are stranded or lose their money when tour operators—even large ones with excellent reputations—go out of business. So check out the operator. Ask several travel agents about its reputation, and try to **book with a company that has a consumer-protection program.** (Look for information in the company's brochure.) In the United States, members of the United States Tour Operators Association are required to set aside funds ($1 million) to help eligible customers cover payments and travel arrangements in the event that the company defaults. It's also a good idea to choose a company that participates in the American Society of Travel Agents' Tour Operator Program; ASTA will act as mediator in any disputes between you and your tour operator.

Remember that the more your package or tour includes, the better you can predict the ultimate cost of your vacation. Make sure you know exactly what is covered, and beware of hidden costs. Are taxes, tips, and transfers included? Entertainment and excursions? These can add up.

7 Tour-Operator Recommendations **American Society of Travel Agents** (⇨ Travel Agencies). **National Tour Association** (NTA) ⊠ 546 E. Main St., Lexington, KY 40508 ☎ 859/226-4444 or 800/682-8886 ⊟ 859/226-4404 ⊕ www.ntaonline.com. **United States Tour Operators Association** (USTOA) ⊠ 275 Madison Ave., Suite 2014, New York, NY 10016 ☎ 212/599-6599 ⊟ 212/599-6744 ⊕ www.ustoa.com.

TRAIN TRAVEL

There is no Amtrak service to Cape Cod. Service ends at Boston.

TRANSPORTATION AROUND THE ISLANDS

Shuttles, buses, and bikes are the best way to get around the traffic-jammed islands in season—unless you're staying in the outskirts or have small children to tote, who might be better transported in a car. You'll see many visitors on scooters, too, although these are not recommended on Nantucket's cobblestone streets in town, where accidents are common. Off-season parking and town traffic are much less of a problem.

TRAVEL AGENCIES

A good travel agent puts your needs first. Look for an agency that has been in business at least five years, emphasizes customer service, and has someone on staff who specializes in your destination. In addition, **make sure the agency belongs to a professional trade organization.** The American Society of Travel Agents (ASTA)—the largest and most influential in the field with more than 20,000 members in some 140 countries—maintains and enforces a strict code of ethics and will step in to help mediate any agent-client disputes involving ASTA members if necessary. ASTA (whose motto is "Without a travel agent, you're on your own") also maintains a Web site that includes a directory of agents. (If a travel agency is also acting as your tour operator, *see* Buyer Beware *in* Tours & Packages.)

7 Local Agent Referrals **American Society of Travel Agents** (ASTA) ⊠ 1101 King St., Suite 200, Alexandria, VA 22314 ☎ 703/739-2782 or 800/965-2782 24-hr hotline ⊟ 703/684-8319 ⊕ www.astanet.com. **Association of British Travel Agents** ⊠ 68-71 Newman St., London W1T 3AH ☎ 020/7637-2444 ⊟ 020/7637-0713 ⊕ www.abta.com. **Association of Canadian Travel Agencies** ⊠ 130 Albert St., Suite 1705, Ottawa, Ontario K1P 5G4 ☎ 613/237-3657 ⊟ 613/237-7052 ⊕ www.acta.ca. **Australian Federation of Travel Agents** ⊠ Level 3, 309 Pitt St., Sydney, NSW 2000 ☎ 02/9264-3299 or 1300/363-416 ⊟ 02/9264-1085 ⊕ www.afta.com.au. **Travel Agents' Association of New Zealand** ⊠ Level 5, Tourism and Travel House, 79 Boulcott St., Box 1888, Wellington 6001 ☎ 04/499-0104 ⊟ 04/499-0786 ⊕ www.taanz.org.nz.

VISITOR INFORMATION

7 Visitor Information **Martha's Vineyard Chamber of Commerce** ⊠ Beach Rd. ⊕ Box 1698, Vineyard Haven 02568 ☎ 508/693-4486 or 800/505-4815 ⊕ www.mvy.com. **Martha's Vineyard Online**

⊕ www.mvol.com. **Massachusetts Office of Travel & Tourism** ☎ 617/973-8500 or 800/227-6277 ⊕ www.massvacation.com. **Nantucket Chamber of Commerce** ✉ 48 Main St., 2nd floor, 02554 ☎ 508/228-1700 ⊕ www.nantucketchamber.org. **Nantucket Visitor Services and Information Bureau** ✉ 25 Federal St., 02554 ☎ 508/228-0925 ⊕ nantucketonline.com.

WEB SITES

Do check out the World Wide Web when planning your trip. You'll find everything from weather forecasts to virtual tours of famous cities. Be sure to visit Fodors.com (⊕ www.fodors.com), a complete travel-planning site. You can research prices and book plane tickets, hotel rooms, rental cars, vacation packages, and more. In addition, you can post your pressing questions in the Travel Talk section. Other planning tools include a currency converter and weather reports, and there are loads of links to travel resources.

For more island-specific Web sites, *see* the A to Z sections *in* Chapters 1 and 2.

MARTHA'S VINEYARD

1

TAKE IN A FIERY SUNSET
from the West Chop Lighthouse ➪ *p.13*

UNWIND BY YOUR OWN FIREPLACE
in a room at the Thorncroft Inn ➪ *p.14*

LINGER OVER A LATE BREAKFAST
at Linda Jean's ➪ *p.25*

SEEK OUT AN ISLAND LANDSCAPE
at the Gardner-Colby Gallery ➪ *p.41*

TASTE A VARIETY OF GRAPES
on a visit to Chicama Vineyards ➪ *p.49*

SAVOR SUCCULENT OYSTERS
at Larsen's ➪ *p.61*

Updated by
Phyllis Meras

BARTHOLOMEW GOSNOLD CHARTED Martha's Vineyard for the British Crown in 1602 and is credited with naming it, supposedly after his infant daughter or mother-in-law (or both) and after the wild grapes he found growing in profusion. Later, Massachusetts Bay Colony businessman Thomas Mayhew was given a grant to the island, along with Nantucket and the Elizabeth Islands, from King Charles of England. Mayhew's son, Thomas Jr., founded the first European settlement here in 1642 at Edgartown, finding the resident Wampanoags good neighbors. The Wampanoags called their island Noepe, thought to mean "Island in the Streams." They taught the settlers, among other survival skills, to kill whales on shore. When moved out to sea, this practice would bring the island great prosperity, for a time. Historians estimate a Wampanoag population of 3,000 upon Mayhew's arrival. Today approximately 350 members of the tribe live on the island, with another 650 Wampanoags living off-island. The tribe is now working hard to reclaim and perpetuate its cultural identity, and it has managed to take back nearly 500 acres of ancestral lands in the town of Aquinnah (from Acquiadene-auke, for "Land Under the Hill"), formerly called Gay Head.

Europeans settled as a community of farmers and fishermen, and both occupations continue to flourish. In the early 1800s, the basis of the island's economy made a decided shift to whaling. Never as influential as Nantucket or New Bedford, Martha's Vineyard nonetheless held its own, and many of its whaling masters returned home wealthy men. Especially during the industry's golden age, between 1830 and 1845, captains built impressive homes with their profits. These, along with many graceful houses from earlier centuries, still line the streets of Vineyard Haven and Edgartown, both former whaling hubs. The industry went into decline after the Civil War, but by then revenue from tourism had picked up, and those dollars just keep flooding in.

The story of the Vineyard's development as a resort begins in 1835, when the first Methodist Camp Meeting—a two-week gathering of far-flung parishes for group worship and a healthy dose of fun—was held in the Oak Bluffs area, barely populated at the time. From the original meeting's 9 tents, the number grew to 250 by 1857. Little by little, returning campers built permanent platforms arranged around the central preachers' tent. Then the odd cottage popped up in place of a tent. By 1880, Wesleyan Grove, named for Methodism's founder, John Wesley, was a community of about 500 tiny cottages, most built in Gothic Revival styles. Lacy filigree insets of jigsaw-cut detail work—known as gingerbread—began to appear on cottage facades, and the ornamented look came to be known as Carpenter Gothic.

Meanwhile, burgeoning numbers of cottagers coming to the island each summer helped convince speculators of its desirability as a resort destination, and in 1867 they laid out a separate secular community alongside the Camp Ground. Steamers from New Bedford, Boston, New York, and elsewhere brought in fashionable folk for bathing and taking in the sea air, for picking berries, or for playing croquet. Grand hotels sprang up around Oak Bluffs Harbor. A railroad followed, connecting

The outings below cover all the towns on the island, but you don't have to. You might want to spend a short time in Vineyard Haven before getting rural Up-Island or heading for a beach. Or you might prefer to go straight to Edgartown to stroll past the antique white houses, pop into a museum or two, and shop. If you just want to have fun, Oak Bluffs, with its harbor scene and nearby beaches, is the place to go. In essence, pick and choose what you like best from what follows. The Vineyard is small enough, too, that you can pick one town as your base and explore other areas easily.

1

a perfect day down island

Start your day in Vineyard Haven. Historic houses line William Street, and you'll find shops and eateries along Main Street. Take a quick jaunt out to **West Chop** for a great view over Vineyard Sound from the lighthouse; then head back through town toward Oak Bluffs via Beach Road. Spend some time wandering the streets of the **Oak Bluffs Camp Ground,** where tightly packed pastel-painted Victorian cottages vie with one another for the fanciest gingerbread trim. Then head into the center of Oak Bluffs for a ride on the Flying Horses, the oldest continuously operating carousel in the country.

Instead of going to Oak Bluffs from Vineyard Haven, you could head straight to **Edgartown,** where you can spend the afternoon browsing the shops and visiting museums. Take the On-Time ferry to **Chappaquiddick Island** to visit the Mytoi preserve or have a picnic at Three Ponds Preserve. If conservation areas are your thing, the Cape Pogo Wildlife Refuge on the island is a must. You'll need a few hours on Chappaquiddick to make the visit worthwhile.

a perfect day up island

Begin your day with a visit to the **West Tisbury** farms, some of which have pony rides for kids. The Mayhew Chapel and Indian Burial Ground are interesting and give an almost eerie look into the past.

Then drive out to **Aquinnah Cliffs** (formerly Gay Head), one of the most spectacular spots on the island. Go to the lookout at the cliffs for the view, or take the boardwalk to the beach and walk back to see the cliffs and Aquinnah Light from below. Spend some time sunning and swimming at this breathtaking spot. (A note to the modest: the beach attracts nude sunbathers; though it's illegal, the officials usually look the other way.)

On your way back from the cliffs, stop in the fishing village of **Menemsha.** You could also stop at the **Winery at Chicama Vineyards** in West Tisbury for a tasting. As the day comes to an end, pick up some seafood and take it to Menemsha Beach for a sunset picnic.

a perfect rainy day

After you've assessed that gray skies and steady downpour do not constitute beach weather, start your day curled up with a good book. Lacking reading material, get up early and visit **Edgartown Books** in Edgartown or **Bunch of Grapes** in Vineyard Haven. **Book Den East,** in a converted barn in Oak Bluffs, is full of rare and fascinating used books. Or drop by one of the six island libraries.

By late morning, with cabin fever setting in, visit the small handful of island museums. The **Martha's Vineyard Historical Society** houses exhibits in the Captain Pease House, the Gale Huntington Library of History, and the Foster Gallery—all in Edgartown. The **Vincent House Museum,** also in Edgartown, contains displays of early island life. While in Edgartown, have lunch at the cozy, wood-paneled **Newes from America**; if it's chilly, there may be a blaze in the fireplace (even in summer).

After lunch, head to the video arcade in Oak Bluffs and, across the street, the **Flying Horses** carousel, both for kids and kids-at-heart. The whole family can unwind at the **Offshore Ale** brewpub, also in Oak Bluffs, where dart enthusiasts can find formidable foes.

By late afternoon and into evening, movies can distract you from the downpour. However, island theaters rarely show matinees earlier than 4 PM. If you're renting a house that has a TV and a VCR or DVD, you're set. There are great video rental shops in the Down-Island towns. Up-Island try Alley's General Store in West Tisbury and the Harbor Craft Shop in Menemsha. The libraries also have videos for overnight loan, though, depending on the town, you may have to purchase a library card first. Other than that, there's no better place than an island to stare out a window on a rainy day and daydream . . . of sunny days.

---

the town with the beach at Katama. The Victorian seaside resort was called Cottage City before its name changed to Oak Bluffs.

More than 300 of the Camp Ground cottages remain. And just as Edgartown and Vineyard Haven reflect their origins as whaling ports, so Oak Bluffs—with its porch-wrapped beach houses and a village green where families still gather to hear the town band play in the gazebo—evokes the days of Victorian summer ease, of flowing white dresses and parasols held languidly against the sun.

Far less developed than Cape Cod—thanks to a few local conservation organizations—yet more cosmopolitan than neighboring Nantucket, Martha's Vineyard is an island with a double life. From Memorial Day through Labor Day the quieter, some might say real, Vineyard quickens into a vibrant, star-studded place. Edgartown floods with people who come to wander narrow streets flanked with elegant boutiques, stately whaling captains' homes, and charming inns. The busy main port, Vineyard Haven, welcomes day-trippers fresh off ferries and private yachts to browse in its own array of shops. Oak Bluffs, where pizza and ice cream emporiums reign supreme, attracts diverse crowds with its boardwalk-town air and nightspots that cater to high-spirited, carefree youth.

Summer regulars include a host of celebrities, among them William Styron, Art Buchwald, Walter Cronkite, Beverly Sills, Patricia Neal, Spike Lee, and Diane Sawyer. Former president Clinton and his wife, Senator Hillary Clinton, are frequent visitors. Concerts, theater, dance performances, and lecture series draw top talent to the island; a county agricultural fair, weekly farmers' markets, and miles of walking trails provide earthier pleasures.

Most people know the Vineyard's summer persona, but in many ways its other self has even more appeal, for the off-season island is a place of peace and simple beauty. Drivers traversing country lanes through the agricultural center of the island find time to linger over pastoral and ocean vistas, without being pushed along by a throng of other cars, bicycles, and mopeds. In nature reserves, the voices of summer are gone, leaving only the sounds of birdsong and the crackle of leaves underfoot. Private beaches open to the public, and the water sparkles under crisp, blue skies.

Locals are at their convivial best off-season. After the craziness of their short moneymaking months, they reestablish contact with friends and take up pastimes temporarily crowded out by work. The result for visitors—besides the extra dose of friendliness—is that cultural, educational, and recreational events continue year-round.

About the Restaurants

From fried fish at roadside stands to boiled lobster and foie gras at fancy French restaurants and a growing array of international influences—Thai, Brazilian, Japanese, Mexican, to name just a few—the Vineyard serves an amazing variety of culinary choices.The majority of eating establishments, both take-out and sit-down, are concentrated in the three Down-Island towns of Vineyard Haven, Oak Bluffs, and Edgartown. As you travel Up-Island—to West Tisbury, Chilmark, and Aquinnah—choices dwindle, especially when it comes to sit-down dinners. Sadly, Vineyard diners—all-American institutions where you can get an honest, no-frills meal at reasonable prices—are a dying breed. Notable for their willingness to serve simple but good dishes such as bacon and eggs with home fries, meat loaf, or tuna melt are the Main Street Diner in Edgartown and island favorite Linda Jean's in Oak Bluffs. Luckily, you can pick up a sandwich or pastry and other to-go specialties at a number of places around the island, and with good planning you can eat well on a modest budget and splurge for an elegant dinner.

Part of how the Vineyard maintains its charm—and part of what makes it somewhat frustrating as well—is that alcoholic beverages are sold in retail stores and in restaurants in only two towns: Edgartown and Oak Bluffs. At restaurants in the so-called "dry" towns of Vineyard Haven, West Tisbury, Chilmark, and Aquinnah you can BYOB, but only if you've had the foresight to visit a "wet" town for provisions first. Also, once at the restaurant, expect to be charged up to $6 for corkage fees (this includes the opening of the bottle and the provision of glasses).

Most restaurants begin to open for the season in late spring, with weekend openings. By Memorial Day weekend, most eateries are open daily. Although the season seems to stretch longer each year, most restaurants remain open full time through Columbus Day weekend, then only weekends through Thanksgiving. A small handful of die-hard restaurants, however, remain open year-round. Dress, even for the upscale spots, is casual. A man in a sport jacket is a rare sight. Reservations are highly recommended in the summer months; however, you may find some people make reservations at their favorite restaurants weeks ahead of time. Dinner reservations are more easily secured for the earlier hours.

WHAT IT COSTS				
$$$$	**$$$**	**$$**	**$**	**¢**
AT DINNER over $28	$20–$28	$12–$20	$8–$12	under $8

Prices are for per person for a main course at dinner.

About the Hotels

The variety of lodging on Martha's Vineyard ranges from historic whaling captains' mansions filled with antiques to sprawling modern oceanfront hotels to cozy cottages in the woods. When choosing your accommodations, keep in mind that each town has a different personality: Oak Bluffs tends to cater to a younger, active, nightlife-oriented crowd; Edgartown is more subdued and dignified. Chilmark has beautiful beaches and miles of conservation lands but not much of a downtown shopping area. Vineyard Haven provides a nice balance of downtown bustle and rustic charm. Bear in mind that many of the island's B&Bs, set in vintage homes filled with art and antiques, have age restrictions—call ahead if you're traveling with a family. And remember that in July and August, the height of the summer season, minimum stays of as many as four nights may be required. If you're planning to visit for a week or more, consider renting a house. For more lodging information, including rental properties and B&Bs, *see* Lodging *in* Smart Travel Tips.

You should make reservations for summer stays as far in advance as possible; late winter is not too early. Rates in season are very high but can fall by as much as 50% in the off-season. The Martha's Vineyard Chamber of Commerce (⇨ Visitor Information) maintains a listing of availability in the peak tourist season, from mid-June to mid-September.

WHAT IT COSTS				
$$$$	**$$$**	**$$**	**$**	**¢**
HOTELS over $450	$325–$450	$225–$325	$150–$225	under $150

Prices are for a standard double room in high season, excluding gratuities and a 5.7% state tax plus an additional 4% room tax levied locally. Some inns add a 15% service charge.

Exploring Martha's Vineyard

The island is roughly triangular, with maximum distances of about 20 mi east to west and 10 mi north to south. The west end of the Vineyard, known as Up-Island—from the nautical expression of going "up"

Beaches

The north shore of the island faces Vineyard Sound. The beaches on this side have more gentle waters; they're also often slightly less chilly. On a clear day you can see across the sound to the chain of Elizabeth Islands, Cape Cod, and sometimes even all the way to New Bedford, Massachusetts.

1

On the Vineyard's south shore—18 mi from the Aquinnah Cliffs east to South Beach in Katama, said to be among the longest continuous uninterrupted stretches of white-sand beach from Georgia to Maine—the Atlantic Ocean side, surf crashes in refreshingly chilly waves—a great place for bodysurfing. The more protected beaches on the Nantucket and Vineyard sounds tend to have slightly warmer and calmer waters, perfect for swimmers and for families. A few freshwater beaches at inland ponds provide a change of pace from the salty sea.

Note that public beaches are split between free beaches such as the Joseph A. Sylvia State Beach, for which no parking fees are required, and several open to the public for which parking fees are collected, such as Moshup Beach in Aquinnah. Private beaches are reserved for permanent and summer residents, who must obtain parking or resident stickers from the appropriate town hall.

Biking

The downside first: you'll be sharing some winding roads with wide trucks and tour buses cruising right by your elbow, inexperienced moped riders, and automobile drivers unfamiliar with the island roads, not to mention other cyclists of various levels of experience. In addition, the roads are winding and most are bordered by sand—even those not near the beaches. The bottom line is this: pay attention at all times. And if ever there was a place to commit to wearing a helmet, this would be that place.

That said, the Vineyard is also a cyclist's paradise, and you don't have to be an experienced rider to enjoy the paths and roads here. With the highest elevation about 300 feet above sea level, this is relatively easy uphill and downhill biking with well-paved bike paths both Down-Island and Up. There are a couple of fun roller-coaster-like dips on the state-forest bike path. Watch out for the occasional in-line skater on these paths. Quiet country roads wind up and down gentle hills covered by low-hanging trees that make you feel as though you're riding through a lush green tunnel. The views—across open fields to the Atlantic Ocean, alongside ponds with floating swans, or of sun-flecked meadows where handsome horses graze—will nearly knock you off your bike seat. There is another benefit: you'll be helping environmentalists who would rather see more non-polluting bikes here than carbon monoxide–spewing, fossil fuel–guzzling vehicles.

Two of the quietest and most scenic roads without paths are North Road, from North Tisbury center all the way to Menemsha; and Middle Road, from its start at Music Street west to Beetlebung Corner, where South Road and Menemsha Cross Road intersect. The ride from there Up-Island to the western tip of the island in Aquinnah is challenging—winding and sandy roads with a steep hill or two—but worth the rewards of spectacular views.

Fishing

Huge trawlers unload abundant daily catches at the docks in Vineyard Haven and Menemsha, attesting to the richness of the waters surrounding the island. But some of the most zealous fishing is done by amateurs—the striped bass and bluefish derby in the fall is serious business. One of the most popular spots for sport anglers is Wasque Point on Chappaquiddick. Two others are South Beach and the jetty at the mouth of the Menemsha Basin. Striped bass and bluefish are island stars. Several outfits operate deep-sea fishing trips if surf fishing is not your thing.

Hiking & Walking

The nature preserves and conservation areas are laced with well-marked, scenic trails through varied terrains and ecological habitats, and the island's miles of uninterrupted beaches are perfect for stretching your legs. At the trailheads of most are small parking areas and bulletin boards with maps and other posted instructions, restrictions, directions, and information. Note that some prohibit dogs; some allow them on a leash.

Shopping

Martha's Vineyard is a shopper's paradise, with a plethora of unique shops lining picturesque streets and nary a chain store in sight (strict zoning laws make this possible). The three main towns have the largest concentrations of shops: in Vineyard Haven, most of the stores line Main Street; Edgartown's stores are clustered together within a few blocks of the dock, on Main, Summer, and Water streets; and casual clothing and gift shops crowd along Circuit Avenue in Oak Bluffs. At the Aquinnah Cliffs, touristy Native American crafts and souvenirs abound during the season, and cottage industries and the odd shop or gallery appear off the main roads in many locations.

A different, more modest shopping experience unfolds at the West Tisbury Farmers' Market, the largest farmers' market in Massachusetts. Elsewhere, some of the antiques stores hidden along back roads brim with the interesting and the unusual.

A specialty of the island is wampum—beads made from black, white, or purple shells and fashioned into jewelry sold at the cliffs and elsewhere. Antique and new scrimshaw jewelry, and jewelry incorporating Vineyard and island-specific designs such as lighthouses or bunches of grapes, are also popular. Many island shops carry the ultraexpensive Nantucket lightship baskets, tightly woven creations of wood and rattan that were originally made by sailors but are now valued collectibles made by artisans. A good number of Vineyard shops close for the winter, though quite a few in Vineyard Haven and some stores in other locations remain open—call ahead before making a special trip.

---

in degrees of longitude as you sail west—is more rural and wild than the eastern Down-Island end, comprising Vineyard Haven, Oak Bluffs, and Edgartown. Conservation land claims almost a quarter of the island, with preservationist organizations acquiring more all the time. The Land Bank, funded by a tax on real-estate transactions, is a leading group,

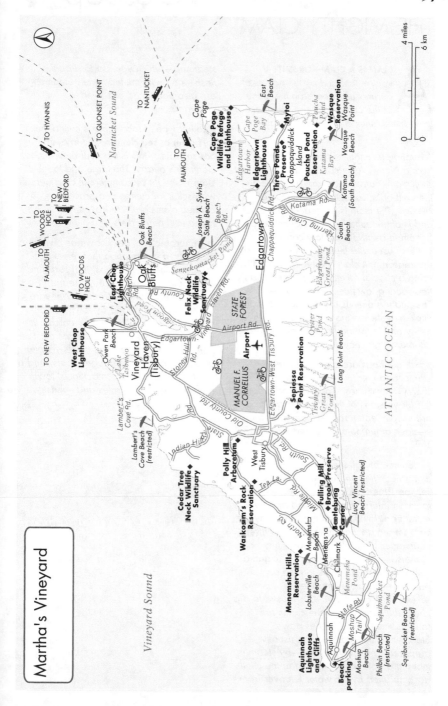

Martha's Vineyard

TO NEW BEDFORD

TO WOODS HOLE

TO FALMOUTH

FALMOUTH

NEW BEDFORD

TO WOODS HOLE

TO HYANNIS

TO QUONSET POINT

TO NANTUCKET

Nantucket Sound

TO FALMOUTH

Vineyard Sound

West Chop Lighthouse

East Chop Lighthouse

Oak Bluffs

Oak Bluffs Beach

Felix Neck Wildlife Sanctuary

Joseph A. Sylvia State Beach

Cape Pogo

Cape Poge Wildlife Refuge and Lighthouse

East Beach

Edgartown Harbor

Cape Poge Bay

Mytoi

Wasque Reservation

Wasque Point

Edgartown Lighthouse

Three Ponds Preserve

Chappaquiddick Island

Poucha Pond Reservation

Poucha Pond

Katama Bay

Wasque Beach

Owen Park Beach

Vineyard Haven (Tisbury)

Lake Tashmoo

Lambert's Cove Rd.

Lambert's Cove Beach (restricted)

Indian Hill Rd.

State Rd.

Stoney Hill Rd.

Airport Rd.

Edgartown–Vineyard Haven Rd.

Sengekontacket Pond

Lagoon Pond

Beach Rd.

County Rd.

Edgartown

Chappaquiddick Rd.

Katama Rd.

Herring Creek Rd.

Katama (South Beach)

South Beach

STATE FOREST

MANUEL F. CORRELLUS

Airport

Edgartown–West Tisbury Rd.

Sepiessa Point Reservation

Tisbury Great Pond

Oyster Pond

Edgartown Great Pond

Long Point Beach

ATLANTIC OCEAN

Cedar Tree Neck Wildlife Sanctuary

Polly Hill Arboretum

West Tisbury

Waskosim's Rock Reservation

Tea La.

South Rd.

Old County Rd.

Fulling Mill Brook Preserve

Beetlebung Corner

Lucy Vincent Beach (restricted)

North Rd.

Middle Rd.

Menemsha Hills Reservation

Lobsterville Beach

Menemsha Beach

Menemsha

Chilmark

Menemsha Pond

State Rd.

Squibnocket Pond

Aquinnah Lighthouse and Cliffs

Beach parking

Aquinnah

Moshup Trail

Moshup Beach

Philbin Beach (restricted)

Squibnocket Beach (restricted)

0   4 miles

0   6 km

CloseUp

THE MIGHTY CLAM

A CLAM IS A CLAM—OR IS IT? If you're confused by the names of our mollusk friends on the menu at the chowder house, then take a look at this quick clam primer, a guide to local shellfish:

A **quahog** (pronounced ko-hog, derived from a Native American word) is a hard-shell clam, native in coastal areas from the Gulf of St. Lawrence to the Gulf of Mexico. The clam is not a deep burrower and is often found lying along the ocean bottom in relatively shallow coastal waters, just under the low-tide mark. For this reason, the clam is often harvested by using a special rake to scrape the ocean floor during low tide, or near to low tide. The quahog gets as big as your fist, with a thickened shell in the middle. Due to their fleshy and tough body, large quahogs are often used for chowder.

Small quahogs are called **littleneck** clams, and medium quahogs are called **cherrystones.** These younger and more tender versions of the chowder quahog are usually eaten raw, accompanied by wedges of lemon or lime and various sauces.

A **steamer,** or soft-shell clam, has an elongated shell and flattened middle section. This clam is a burrower and is found in intercoastal soft sand and tidal marshes at low tide—many locals say the best time to go clamming is two to three hours after high tide. Look for a tiny hole in the sand, where the clam's elongated "neck," or siphon, waits to feed on passing microscopic marine life. Special rakes with elongated tines are used to dig under the sand, where the clams are found some 6 to 12 inches down. Steamers are tender and are usually prepared—no surprise here—by steaming them in a pot. They're served in the shell, accompanied by the water left over from steaming—which you use to rinse the flesh—and with melted butter. Steamers are also deep-fried or served in chowders.

Another type of local clam is called the **surf clam** or **sea clam.** Found in deep ocean waters, this is not your recreational clammer's quarry. The large and tough clam is sought by commercial clammers, who sell it for cutting and processing as canned clams or those frozen clam strips found in supermarkets.

In general, clams are known as bivalve mollusks, a designation that refers to their two shells, or valves, that surround and protect the body. They are not endangered, but on Martha's Vineyard clamming is managed by towns—clams must be of a certain size, the catch per week is regulated, and clammers must hold licenses. If you want to get yourself a rake, a pair of big rubber boots, and a pot full of steamers, contact local town halls for the proper rules and licenses.

— Karl Luntta

set up to preserve as much of the island in its natural state as is possible and practical.

Numbers in the text correspond to numbers in the margin and on the Vineyard Haven, Oak Bluffs, Edgartown, and Up-Island maps.

When to Go

Summer is the most popular season on the Vineyard, the time when everyone is here and everything is open and happening. With weather perfect for all kinds of activities, the island hosts special events from the Martha's Vineyard Agricultural Fair to the Edgartown Regatta. Another busy season, fall brings cool weather, harvest celebrations, and fishing derbies. Tivoli Day, an end-of-summer/start-of-fall celebration, includes a street fair. The island does tend to curl up in winter, when many shops and restaurants close. However, for the weeks surrounding the Hanukkah–Christmas–New Year's holidays, the Vineyard puts bells on for all kinds of special events and celebrations, most notably in Edgartown and Vineyard Haven. Spring sees the island awaken from its slumber in a burst of garden and house tours as islanders warm up for the busy season.

DOWN-ISLAND

Characterizing Martha's Vineyard is a bit like characterizing the taste of milk; it's a complete and unique experience, unlike any other. The three towns that compose Down-Island (the east end of Martha's Vineyard)—Vineyard Haven, Oak Bluffs, and Edgartown—are the most popular and the most populated. Here you'll find the ferry docks, the shops, and a concentration of things to do and see, including the centuries-old houses and churches that document the island's history. A stroll through any one of these towns allows you to look into the past while enjoying the pleasures of the present.

Vineyard Haven (Tisbury)

3½ mi west of Oak Bluffs, 8 mi northwest of Edgartown by the inland route.

Most people call this town Vineyard Haven for the name of the port where the ferry pulls in, but its official name is Tisbury. Not as high-toned as Edgartown or as honky-tonk as Oak Bluffs, Vineyard Haven blends the past and the present with a touch of the bohemian. Settled in the mid-1600s when the island's first governor-to-be purchased rights to the land from local Wampanoags, it is the busiest year-round community on Martha's Vineyard. Visitors arriving here step off the ferry right into the bustle of the harbor, a block from the shops and restaurants of Main Street.

1 If you need to stock up on maps or information on the island, **Martha's Vineyard Chamber of Commerce** is a good place to get your bearings. The office is around the corner from the steamship terminal (where you'll find a small information booth, open daily 8–8 in season) on Beach Road. ⊠ *24 Beach Rd.* ☎ *508/693–0085* ⊕ *www.mvy.com* ☉ *Weekdays 9–5 (plus abbreviated weekend hrs in season).*

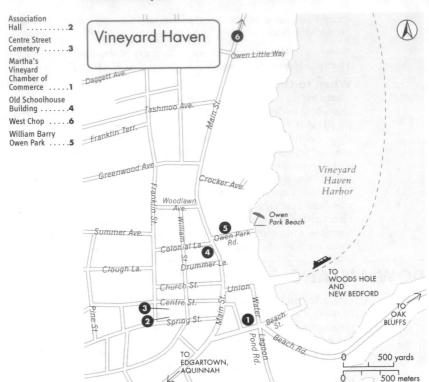

need a break?

The delicious breads, pastries, and quick-lunch items at **Black Dog Bakery** (⊠ 11 Water St. ☎ 508/693–4786) are simply not to be missed—it's a popular stop for good reason.

2 The stately, neoclassic 1844 **Association Hall** houses the town hall and the Katharine Cornell Memorial Theatre, created in part with funds that Cornell (1898–1974)—one of America's foremost stage actresses in the 1920s, '30s, and '40s and a longtime summer resident—donated in her will. The walls of the theater on the second floor are painted with murals depicting whaling expeditions and a Native American gathering, and the ceiling resembles a blue sky with seagulls overhead. Island artist Stan Murphy painted the murals on the occasion of the town's tercentenary in 1971. The theater holds performances of plays, concerts, and dances. ⊠ *51 Spring St.* ☎ *508/696–4200.*

3 At the **Centre Street Cemetery,** tall pine trees shade grave markers dating as far back as 1817. Some stones are simple gray slate slabs, and others are carved with such motifs as the death's-head—a skull, common on tombstones of the era. Actress Katharine Cornell, who died in 1974 and whose largesse helped build the theater named for her (housed in the Association Hall), is buried here. ⊠ *Centre St., between William and Franklin Sts.*

A stroll down **William Street,** a quiet stretch of white picket fences and Greek Revival houses, many of them built for prosperous sea captains, lets you imagine the town as it was in the 19th century. Now part of a National Historic District, the street was spared when the Great Fire of 1883 claimed much of the old whaling and fishing town.

❹ Built in 1829, the **Old Schoolhouse Building** was the first town school and today houses Sail Martha's Vineyard, a program teaching Vineyard children how to sail. Out front, the Liberty Pole was erected by the Daughters of the American Revolution in honor of three patriotic girls who blew up the town's liberty pole in 1776 to prevent it from being taken for use on a British warship. ⊠ *110 Main St.*

❺ For a little relaxation, try the tree-shaded benches in **William Barry Owen Park** (⊠ Off Owen Park Rd.), a lovely spot for a picnic and for summer concerts held at the bandstand. At the end of the lawn is a public beach with a swing set and a close-up view of the boats sailing in and out of the harbor. In the 19th century this harbor was one of the busiest ports in the world, welcoming thousands of vessels each year. Lighthouses still stand at the headlands—West Chop in Vineyard Haven and East Chop in Oak Bluffs—to help bring ships safely into port.

❻ Beautiful and green, **West Chop** retains its exclusive air and claims some of the island's most distinguished residents. This area, as well as East Chop across the harbor, was largely settled in the late 19th to early 20th century, when the very rich from Boston and Newport built expansive bluff-top "summer cottages." The shingle-style houses, characterized by broad gable ends, dormers, and natural shingle siding that weathers to gray, were meant to eschew pretense, though they were sometimes gussied up with a turret or two. A 2-mi walk, drive, or bike ride along Vineyard Haven's Main Street—which becomes increasingly residential on the way—will take you there.

One of two lighthouses that mark the opening to the harbor, the 52-foot white-and-black **West Chop Lighthouse** was built in 1838 of brick to replace an 1817 wood building. It has been moved back twice from the edge of the eroding bluff. (It is not open to the public.) Just beyond the lighthouse, on the point, is a scenic overlook with a landscaped area and benches. ⊠ *W. Chop Rd. (Main St.)* ⊕ *www.marthasvineyardhistory.com.*

West Chop Woods is an 85-acre conservation area with marked walking trails through pitch pine and oak. The area is just south and west of the West Chop lighthouse, with entrances on Main Street and Franklin Street and parking on Franklin.

Martha's Vineyard Shellfish Group grows seed clams, scallops, and oysters to stock lagoons and beds throughout the county. From spring through fall, tours of the solar shellfish hatchery on Lagoon Pond in Vineyard Haven can be arranged with advance notice. ⊠ *Weaver La.* ☎ *508/ 693–0391* ✉ *$5 donation suggested* ☉ *Call for appointment.*

Where to Eat

$$$–$$$$ ✕ **Le Grenier.** Up narrow stairs, above the M.V. Bagel Authority at the upper end of Vineyard Haven's downtown, owner–chef Jean Dupon has been serving classic French food since the late 1970s. Although some island restaurants have come and gone, and others shifted with the newest trends, Dupon has been consistently loyal to the French standards: frogs' legs, sweetbreads, and tournedos are among the entrées. The decor is hardly stuffy in the French tradition; rather, it's almost backyard casual, with a string of lightbulbs and souvenir wine-bottle corks lining the walls. Open year-round, the restaurant serves a hot chocolate bread pudding that warms the cockles of your heart. ⊠ *Upper Main St.* ☎ *508/693–4906* ⊟ *AE, MC, V* ⏱ *BYOB* ⊘ *No lunch.*

$$–$$$$ ✕ **Cafe Moxie.** Open year-round, this classy restaurant has a handsome wooden bar (though it's a dry town) and island artists' work on the walls. A lunchtime favorite is Chef Austin Racine's mussels steamed in garlic and ginger served over noodles. Something fancier for dinner is duck breast wrapped in Swiss chard over a white bean and duck ragout. You can eat lunch here for under $15. ⊠ *Main St. at Centre St.* ☎ *508/693–1484* ⊟ *D, MC, V* ⏱ *BYOB* ⊘ *Closed Mon. No lunch.*

$$–$$$$ ✕ **Zephrus.** Mansion House owners Sherman and Susan Goldstein have created a new and exciting restaurant beside their hotel. Chefs here prepare such fish dishes as halibut in horseradish crust with fresh rock crab hash. And there's a Chocaholic's Platter of assorted cakes, chocolate mousse, and fresh strawberries to dip into warm caramel and roll in shaved chocolate. ⊠ *Main St.* ☎ *508/693–3416* ⊟ *AE, MC, V* ⏱ *BYOB.*

$$–$$$ ✕ **Tropical Restaurant.** The house specialty in this roadside restaurant is *rodizio,* a Brazilian style of barbecue where slow-roasted meat—in this case beef, chicken, sausage, pork, and lamb—are carved table-side and served continuously throughout your meal. Along with rice and beans, side dishes include collard greens and yucca. ⊠ *Five Corners* ☎ *508/696–0715* ⊟ *MC, V* ⏱ *BYOB.*

$–$$$ ✕ **Black Dog Tavern.** This island landmark, just steps from the ferry terminal in Vineyard Haven, remains a hangout for year-rounders in winter (when the lines aren't a mile long). In July and August, the wait can be as much as an hour as early as 8 AM or so. Why? Partly because the ambience inside—roaring fireplace, dark wood walls, maritime memorabilia, and a grand view of the water—makes them feel so at home, as it has since its founding in 1971. The menu is heavy on local fish, chowders, and burgers. Breakfast is the best, winning points for perhaps the largest assortment of omelets (with goofy island names) of any restaurant on the island. ⊠ *Beach St.* ☎ *508/693–9223* ⚑ *Reservations not accepted* ⊟ *AE, D, MC, V* ⏱ *BYOB.*

¢–$$ ✕ **Artcliff Diner.** Since 1943, this vintage diner has been a year-round breakfast and lunch meeting place for locals. Owner–chef Gina Stanley, who once lived in Washington, D.C. and was on call to make desserts for Blair House, serves anything but ordinary diner fare today. She whips up pecan pancakes with real rum raisins for breakfast, and lunch crepes with chèvre or arugula or almost anything you ask for. But if some of the old crowd still want steak 'n eggs, she'll cook that, too. ⊠ *39 Beach Rd.* ☎ *508/693–1224* ⊟ *No credit cards* ⊘ *Closed Wed. No dinner.*

Where to Stay

★ $$–$$$$ ▥ **Thorncroft Inn.** On 3½ wooded acres about 1 mi from the ferry, this inn's main building, a 1918 Craftsman bungalow, combines fine colo-

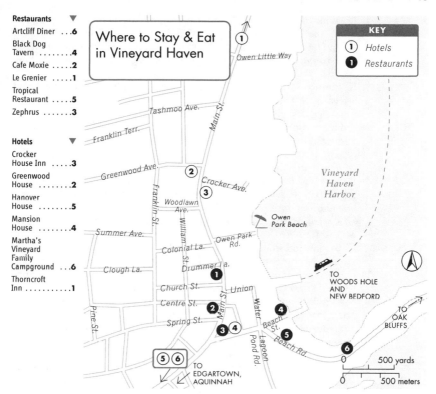

Where to Stay & Eat
in Vineyard Haven

KEY

① *Hotels*

❶ *Restaurants*

nial and richly carved Renaissance Revival antiques with tasteful re-productions to create a somewhat formal environment. Ten of the rooms have working fireplaces. Most rooms have canopy beds; three rooms have two-person whirlpool baths, and two have private hot-tub spas. Rooms in the carriage house are more secluded and set apart from the main house via a breezeway; a private, ultradeluxe cottage has a king-size bed and a whirlpool tub and is wheelchair accessible. A full break-fast is served in bed on request or up in the main dining room (also the site of afternoon tea). ✉ *460 Main St.* ✇ *Box 1022, 02568* ☎ *508/693–3333 or 800/332–1236* 🖷 *508/693–5419* ⊕ *www.thorncroft.com* ⤳ *14 rooms, 1 cottage* ⚸ *Dining room, some in-room hot tubs, some refrigerators, in-room VCRs, library; no kids under 13, no smoking* ▤ *AE, D, DC, MC, V* ⏍ *BP.*

$$–$$$ 🏠 **Crocker House Inn.** This 1924 farmhouse-style inn is tucked into a quiet lane off Main Street, minutes from the ferries and Owen Park Beach. The rooms are decorated casually with understated flair—pastel-painted walls, softly upholstered wing-back chairs, white-wicker nightstands. Each contains a small, wall-mounted "honor bar" with such items as disposable camera, sun lotion, and other useful sundries. Three rooms have soothing whirlpool tubs, and two have fireplaces. No. 6, with a small porch and a private entrance, has the best view of the harbor.

Breakfast is served at a large farmer's table inside the small common room and kitchen area. ⊠ *12 Crocker Ave.* ☎ *Box 1658, 02568* ☎ *508/693–1151 or 800/772–0206* ⊕ *www.crockerhouseinn.com* ⮡ *8 rooms* ⚬ *Some in-room hot tubs; no kids under 12, no smoking* ⊟ *MC, V* ⦿ *CP.*

$–$$$ 🏨 **Mansion House.** Since 1794, there has been a hostelry on this Main Street site just above Vineyard Haven Harbor. Today's Mansion House, following designs of the past, opened in 2003. Apart from the cheerful, summery rooms—some with balconies, some with gas fireplaces, some with soaking tubs—the cupola deck provides a pleasant spot for a respite. It affords sweeping views of the harbor, the town, and the lagoon that stretches between Vineyard Haven and Oak Bluffs. Afternoon cookies and lemonade are served there or you can BYOB. ⊠ *9 Main St.* ☎ *Box 428, 02568* ☎ *509/693–2200 or 800/332–4112* ⊕ *www. mvmansionhouse.com* ⮡ *32 rooms, 11 suites* ⚬ *Restaurant, room service, refrigerators, pool, health club, spa, cable TV, Internet* ⊟ *AE, D, MC, V* ⦿ *CP.*

$–$$ 🏨 **Greenwood House.** A low-key bed-and-breakfast on a quiet lane around the corner from Vineyard Haven's public library, the Greenwood House is one of the better values in town. Affable innkeepers Kathy Stinson and Larry Gomez own this homey, three-story Arts and Crafts–style cottage with classic shingle siding and a shaded yard. Rooms are decorated with a mix of antiques and contemporary pieces, including brass and four-poster beds, island artwork, and functional but attractive nightstands and bureaus. It's a 10- to 15-minute walk from the ferry and even closer to many shops and restaurants. ⊠ *40 Greenwood Ave.* ☎ *Box 2734, 02568* ☎ *508/693–6150 or 866/693–6150* ☎ *508/696– 8113* ⊕ *www.greenwoodhouse.com* ⮡ *4 rooms* ⚬ *Refrigerators, library; no smoking* ⊟ *AE, D, MC, V* ⦿ *BP.*

¢–$$ 🏨 **Hanover House.** Set on ½ acre of landscaped lawn on a busy road but within walking distance of the ferry, this three-property inn consists of a classic, home-style bed-and-breakfast, a country inn, and a carriage house. Rooms are decorated with a combination of antiques and reproduction furniture. Each room has individual flair. In one, an antique sewing machine serves as the TV stand. The three carriage house suites have private decks or patios and two have kitchenettes. Homemade breads and muffins are served at breakfast. ⊠ *28 Edgartown Rd.* ☎ *Box 2108, 02568* ☎ *508/693–1066 or 800/696–863* ⊕ *www. hanoverhouseinn.com* ⮡ *12 rooms, 3 suites* ⚬ *Some kitchenettes, Internet* ⊟ *AE, D, MC, V* ⊗ *Closed Dec.–Mar.* ⦿ *CP.*

★ ¢ 🏕 **Martha's Vineyard Family Campground.** Wooded sites, a ball field, camp store, bicycle rentals, and electrical and water hookups are among the facilities at this 20-acre campsite a couple of miles from Vineyard Haven. A step up from tents are 21 rustic one- or two-room cabins, which come with combinations of double and bunk beds (but bring your own bedding) and with electricity, refrigerators, and gas grills. The campground also has hookups for trailers. This is the only campsite on the island, so book early. Discounts are available for extended stays. No dogs or motorcycles are allowed. ⊠ *569 Edgartown Rd.* ☎ *Box 1557, 02568* ☎ *508/693–3772* ☎ *508/693–5767* ⊕ *www.campmvfc.com*

A PERFECT HOLIDAY

TIME YOUR VISIT RIGHT, and a perfect holiday starts on the dock where you can greet Santa as he arrives on the morning ferry in Vineyard Haven. After you've seen Santa, you can shop along the town's Main Street—one of the nicest perks of being on the Vineyard during the holidays is the peaceful and relaxed pace of shopping as compared to the frenetic mainland. Keep an eye out for holiday fairs and bazaars, sponsored by local groups and benefiting island charities, where island-made crafts are featured. Continue in the shopping mode along Circuit Avenue in Oak Bluffs and Main Street in Edgartown. In both towns many of the island's best inns and B&Bs don their gayest apparel over the holidays and open their doors for tours; check the papers for times and dates and make sure to visit a few for a quick peek and a glass of cider.

In the afternoon, though it may be a bit nippy, revive yourself with a brisk walk on an island beach. Or, check with the **Felix Neck Wildlife Sanctuary** (☎ 508/627–4850) for seasonal guided nature walks.

In the early evening, treat yourself to a festive meal. Dressed in holiday lights and colors, the Coach House at the Harbor View Hotel in Edgartown is a lovely, traditional setting for a holiday dinner. Come evening, catch a holiday show at the Vineyard Playhouse in Vineyard Haven. Past performances have included "The Snow Queen," "Arthur's Christmas," and Jean Shepherd's "A Christmas Story." Or attend a holiday concert by the highly regarded Martha's Vineyard Regional High School singing group, the Minnesingers, or the Island Community Chorus's Christmas concert. For a late repast, a nibble from the bar menu at Alchemy in Edgartown, washed down with some warm holiday drinks, is the perfect way to end the day and fill your holiday heart.

➥ 130 tent sites, 50 RV sites, 21 cabins ♨ Picnic area, some refrigerators, bicycles, recreation room, shop, playground, laundry facilities ▤ D, MC, V ☉ Closed mid-Oct.–mid-May.

Nightlife & the Arts

Island Theatre Workshop (☎ 508/693–5290) is the island's oldest year-round company. Under the direction of Lee Fierro, the group performs at various venues and has a summer theater arts program for children.

The **Martha's Vineyard Festival Orchestra** (☎ 508/645–2745 ⊕ www. mvfo.org), a 70-member all-star ensemble of Boston's best musicians, performs a gala summer-ending concert the third weekend of August at the Tabernacle in Oak Bluffs.

At **Nathan Mayhew Seminars** (✉ N. William St. ☎ 508/696–8428) you can master the mambo, rhumba, waltz, fox-trot, and cha-cha. Basic steps are taught at 7:30 PM and dancing continues till 9:30 PM. A donation of $3 is requested.

The **Vineyard Haven Town Band** (☎ 508/645–3458) is the oldest continuing performing arts band on the island. Hear the group in concert at 8 PM every Sunday during the summer, alternating between Owen Park in Vineyard Haven and at the gazebo in Ocean Park on Beach Road in Oak Bluffs. Bring a blanket or beach chair and a picnic if you'd like. The concerts are free.

The **Vineyard Playhouse** (✉ 24 Church St. ☎ 508/693–6450 or 508/696–6300) has a year-round schedule of professional productions. From mid-June through early September, a troupe performs drama, classics, and comedies on the air-conditioned main stage, as well as summer Shakespeare and other productions at the natural amphitheater at Tashmoo Overlook on State Road in Vineyard Haven—bring insect repellent and a blanket or lawn chair. Children's programs and a summer camp are also scheduled, as well as local art exhibitions throughout the year. The theater is wheelchair-accessible and provides hearing devices.

Shopping

ANTIQUES **A. E. Kirkpatrick** (✉ 30 Main St. ☎ 508/693–1632) carries vintage and estate jewelry and a wide array of compacts and cigarette cases. It also sells contemporary wampum and sea-glass jewelry.

Menagerie (✉ 10 Union St. ☎ 508/696–7650) is a great source of authentic vintage chenille and original clothes for children and women made from other vintage fabrics.

ART **Shaw Cramer Gallery** (✉ 76 Main St., 2nd floor ☎ 508/696–7323) carries one-of-a-kind and limited-edition crafts and paintings by nationally known artists and top island artists.

BOOKS **Bunch of Grapes** (✉ 44 Main St. ☎ 508/693–2291) carries a wide se-
Fodor'sChoice lection of fiction and nonfiction, including many island-related titles,
★ and sponsors book signings—watch the papers for announcements.

CLOTHES **Alley Cat and Shoes by Arche** (✉ 38 Main St. ☎ 508/693–6970) is worth a stop just for its clever display windows. Inside there's great women's clothing in a cool, comfortable atmosphere.

Brickman's (✉ 8 Main St. ☎ 508/693–0047) sells sportswear, surf-style clothing, and major-label footwear for the whole family. It also carries beach and sports gear, such as camping, fishing, and snorkeling equipment, and boogie boards and lots of toys and games for those occasional rainy days.

Lorraine Parish (✉ 18 S. Main St. ☎ 508/693–9044) designs and sells sophisticated women's dresses, suits, and blouses in natural fibers; and, just in case you forgot that dress you planned to wear for an island wedding, she carries lots of floaty chiffons. She also designed Carly Simon's wedding dress.

Mystic Martha (✉ 3 Centre St. ☎ 508/693–5828) is a clothing consignment shop for women with great buys on previously owned designer wear. This shop also sells "mystical gifts" such as rune books and candles.

FOOD **Cronig's Market** (✉ State Rd. ☎ 508/693–4457) supports local farmers and specialty-item producers and sells a great selection of produce and other edibles.

Vineyard Gourmet (✉ Main St. ☎ 508/693–5181) stocks foods produced on-island and from around the world.

HOME **All Things Oriental** (✉ 123 Beach Rd. ☎ 508/693–8375) sells new and
ACCESSORIES antique jewelry, porcelains, paintings, furniture, and more, all with an Asian theme.

The **Beach House** (✉ 30 Main St. ☎ 508/693–6091) stocks a large assortment of Italian pottery, linens, and party supplies. It's a great source for bridal and shower gifts.

Bowl and Board (✉ 35 Main St. ☎ 508/693–9441) is summer-home central. It carries everything you need to cozy up in a summer rental.

Bramhall & Dunn (✉ 19 Main St. ☎ 508/693–6437) sells fine crafts, linens, and housewares including outstanding quilts and innovative rag rugs by Judi Boisson. It also carries hand-knit sweaters and unique women's accessories and shoes.

JEWELRY **C. B. Stark Jewelers** (✉ 53A Main St. ☎ 508/693–2284 ✉ N. Water St., Edgartown ☎ 508/627–1260) creates one-of-a-kind pieces for both women and men, including island charms and custom work in 14- and 18-karat gold and platinum. It also carries other fine jewelry and watches. The Edgartown shop is smaller but has a more upscale inventory.

Moonstone (✉ 12 Main St. ☎ 508/693–3367) sells estate jewelry and unique designs incorporating colorful and unusual stones. Artisans create many original pieces with nautical and island themes, and both a gemologist and jeweler are on staff. Ask about the cuff links, tie tacks, pendants, and rings cast from the jacket buttons of the last civilian West Chop lighthouse keeper.

Sioux Eagle Designs (✉ 29 Main St. ☎ 508/693–6537) sells unusual handmade jewelry from around the world. This is the place for quality wampum jewelry by Joan LeLacheur and striking designs by Paul d' Olympia.

ODDS & ENDS **Church Street** (✉ off Main St.) is a little enclave of shops including **Fleece Dreams** (☎ 508/693–6141), which sells handmade clothes in sumptuous fabrics; **Good Impressions** (☎ 508/693–7682), which carries rubber stamp supplies and has classes in stamp art and fabric embossing; and **Beadnicks** (☎ 508/693–7650), a bead lover's paradise.

Martha's Vineyard Craft Cooperative (✉ Woodland Business Center, State Rd. ☎ 508/693–2314) carries island-made crafts and stocks all-cotton handwoven place mats, sculpture and pierced lamp shades by Ayn Chase, Jeffrey Borr pottery, wampum jewelry, island-shape baskets, and antiques.

Midnight Farm (✉ 18 Water-Cromwell La. ☎ 508/693–1997) is co-owned by Carly Simon and Tamara Weiss and stocks furniture, clothes, shoes, jewelry, linens, dinnerware, books, soaps, candles, garden supplies, snack foods, and, of course, Carly's books and CDs.

Nothing extends the feeling of vacation like viewing your snapshots on the way home. **Mosher Photo** (⊠ 25 Main St. ☎ 508/693–9430) carries a full line of cameras—both disposable and non—and can process your pictures within three hours. Best of all, it's close to the ferry.

Paper Tiger (⊠ 29 Main St. ☎ 508/693–8970) sells a wide array of hand-made paper, cards, and gift items, plus wind chimes, pottery, writing utensils, and works by local artists. Check out the minimobiles over the counter.

Wind's Up! (⊠ 199 Beach Rd. ☎ 508/693–4340) sells swimwear, windsurfing and sailing equipment, boogie boards, and other outdoor gear.

Sports & the Outdoors

BEACHES **Lake Tashmoo Town Beach** (⊠ end of Herring Creek Rd.) invites swimming in the warm, relatively shallow, brackish lake or in the cooler, gentle Vineyard Sound. There is a lifeguarded area and some parking.

Owen Park Beach (⊠ off Main St.), a small, sandy harbor beach, has a children's play area, lifeguards, and a harbor view. The beach straddles a dock that juts into the harbor and is just steps away from the ferry terminal in Vineyard Haven, making it a great spot for some last rays and a dip before you have to kiss the island good-bye.

Tisbury Town Beach (⊠ end of Owen Little Way off Main St.) is a public beach next to the Vineyard Haven Yacht Club. As at Owen Park Beach, its proximity to the town makes it a perfect out-of-the-way yet near-everything spot for a quick escape from the crowds and a dip.

BIKING **Cycle Works** (⊠ 351 State Rd. ☎ 508/693–6966) sells all variety of bikes, rents and sells fitness equipment, and has an excellent repair shop.

Martha's Bike Rentals (⊠ 4 Lagoon Pond Rd., at Five Corners ☎ 508/693–6593) rents bicycles, helmets, baby seats, and trailer bikes that attach to the rear of adult bikes to carry kids. It also handles repairs and will deliver and pick up your bike free anywhere on the island.

Martha's Vineyard Strictly Bikes (⊠ 24 Union St. ☎ 508/693–0782) rents a variety of bicycles and baby trailers. It also sells bikes and does repairs.

BOATING **Martha's Vineyard Ocean Sports** (⊠ 86 Beach St., Vineyard Haven ☎ 508/693–2838) rents equipment for a variety of water sports, including wakeboarding, knee boarding, and tubing.

Wind's Up! (⊠ 199 Beach Rd. ☎ 508/693–4252 or 508/693–4340) rents day sailers, catamarans, surfboards, sea kayaks, canoes, and Sunfish, as well as Windsurfers and boogie boards; the shop also gives lessons.

GOLF The semiprivate **Mink Meadows Golf Club** (⊠ Golf Club Rd. at Franklin St. ☎ 508/693–0600), on West Chop, has 9 holes and ocean views. Reservations can be made 48 hours in advance.

HEALTH & **Fitness Firm of Martha's Vineyard** (⊠ 155 State Rd. ☎ 508/693–5533)
FITNESS CLUBS has Lifecycle bikes and Precor EFX cross-training and Icarian strength equipment, as well as a full array of free weights. Personal trainers are on staff. Day, weekly, monthly, and yearly memberships are available.

The **Health Club at the Mansion House** (⌗ 9 Main St. ☎ 508/693–7400) has Lifecycle, Nautilus, Universal, and StairMaster machines; bikes; free-weight rooms; tanning facilities; aerobics classes; and personal trainers. The club also has a large heated pool, a hot tub, and a sauna. Short-term memberships, from one day to a month, are available.

MINIATURE GOLF   At **Island Cove Mini Golf** (⌗ State Rd. ☎ 508/693–2611) you golf on an 18-hole course with bridges, a cave, sand traps, and a stream that powers a waterfall. The island's only rock-climbing wall is also here.

TENNIS   The public clay courts on Church Street are open between July 1 and Labor Day. Two asphalt courts on Lake Street (heading toward Lake Tashmoo, to the left of a large rock painted blue at the curve) are available for free on a first-come, first-served basis Monday and Wednesday when town recreation programs are not under way.

Oak Bluffs

3½ mi east of Vineyard Haven, 6 mi northwest of Edgartown, 22 mi northeast of Aquinnah.

Purchased from the Wampanoags in the 1660s, Oak Bluffs was a farming community that did not come into its own until the 1830s, when Methodists began holding summer revivalist meetings in a stand of oaks known as Wesleyan Grove, named for Methodism's founder, John Wesley. As the camp meetings caught on, attendees built small cottages in place of tents. Then the general population took notice and the area became a popular summer vacation spot. Hotels, a dance hall, a roller-skating rink, and other shops and amusements were built to accommodate the flocks of summer visitors.

Today Circuit Avenue is the center of action in Oak Bluffs, the address of most of the town's shops, bars, and restaurants. Oak Bluffs Harbor, once the setting for a number of grand hotels—the 1879 Wesley Hotel on Lake Avenue is the last of them—is still crammed with gingerbread-trimmed guesthouses and food and souvenir joints. With its whimsical cottages, long beachfront, and funky shops, the small town is more high-spirited than haute, more fun than refined.

East Chop is one of two points of land that jut out into the Nantucket–Vineyard sound, creating the sheltered harbor at Vineyard Haven and some fine views. From Oak Bluffs, take East Chop Drive, or you can loop out to the point on your way from Vineyard Haven by taking Highland Drive off Beach Road after crossing the drawbridge.

❼ The **East Chop Lighthouse** was built of cast iron in 1876 to replace an 1828 tower—used as part of a semaphore system of visual signaling between the island and Boston—that burned down. The 40-foot structure stands high atop a 79-foot bluff with spectacular views of Nantucket Sound. East Chop is one of three island lighthouses open to the public. ⌗ *E. Chop Dr.* ☎ *508/627–4441* ⌗ *$3* ⊘ *Late June–mid Sept., 1 hr before sunset–1 hr after sunset, Sundays only.*

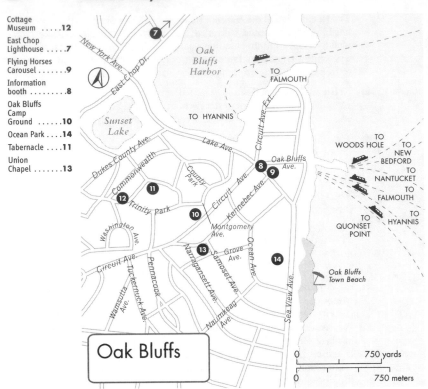

Oak Bluffs

| 0 | 750 yards |
| 0 | 750 meters |

8 The **information booth** will help you get your bearings and point the way to the not-to-be-missed spots in Oak Bluffs, with some good tips for gingerbread-trim lovers. ✉ *Lake and Oak Bluffs Aves.* ☎ *508/693–4266* ⏱ *Mid-May–mid-Oct., daily 9–5.*

9 A National Historic Landmark, the **Flying Horses Carousel** is the nation's oldest continuously operating carousel. Handcrafted in 1876 (the horses have real horse hair and glass eyes), the ride gives children a taste of entertainment from a TV-free era. On summer evenings or rainy days, however, the carousel can get crowded; you can avoid the crunch by going early in the day. While waiting in line (the wait is rarely longer than 20 minutes or so), you can munch on popcorn or cotton candy or slurp a slush. The waiting area has a number of arcade games. ✉ *Oak Bluffs Ave.* ☎ *508/693–9481* 🎟 *Rides $1.50; $10 for a book of 8 tickets* ⏱ *Late May–early Sept., daily 10–10; Easter–late May, weekends 10–5; early Sept.–mid-Oct., weekdays 11–4:30, weekends 10–5.*

need a break? The **Coop de Ville** (✉ Dockside Marketplace, Oak Bluffs Harbor ☎ 508/693–3420) often teems with people eager to sample the delectables from the raw bar and the simple fried seafood. Eat out on the patio deck overlooking the water—the oysters are fantastic. It's open May–mid-October.

★ ⑩ Don't miss a look at **Oak Bluffs Camp Ground,** a 34-acre warren of streets tightly packed with more than 300 Carpenter Gothic Victorian cottages with wedding-cake trim, gaily painted in pastels. As you wander through this fairy-tale setting, imagine it on a balmy summer evening, lit by the warm glow of hundreds of Japanese paper lanterns hung from every cottage porch. This describes the scene on Illumination Night at the end of the Camp Meeting season—attended these days by some fourth- and fifth-generation cottagers. Attendees mark the occasion as they have for more than a century, with lights, song, and open houses for families and friends. Note that because of overwhelming crowds of onlookers in seasons past, the date is not announced until the week before. Two-hour tours are conducted Tuesday and Thursday at 10 AM. ⊠ *Off Circuit Ave.* 🚌 *Tour $10.*

⑪ The **Tabernacle,** an impressive open-air structure of iron and wood at the center of Trinity Park, is the original site of the Methodist services. On Wednesdays at 8 PM in season, visitors are invited to join in on an old-time community sing-along. If you know tunes like "The Erie Canal" or just want to listen in, drop by the Tabernacle and take a seat. Music books are available for a donation. Sunday services are held in summer at 9:30 AM. The 1878 **Trinity Methodist Church** also stands in the park and is open for visits during daylight hours (no tours however) and, of course, for services on Sunday.

⑫ For a glimpse at life in Cottage City during its heyday, visit the **Cottage Museum,** in an 1868 Creamsicle-hue cottage near the Tabernacle. The two-story museum exhibits cottage furnishings from the early days, including photographs, hooked rugs, quilts, and old Bibles. The gift shop sells Victorian and nautical items. ⊠ *1 Trinity Park* 🕾 *508/693–7784* 🚌 *$1.50 donation requested* ⊙ *Mid-June–Sept., Mon.–Sat. 10–4.*

⑬ An octagonal, nonsectarian house of worship, **Union Chapel** was constructed in 1870 for the Cottage City resort folk who lived outside the Camp Ground's 7-foot-high fence. In summer, concerts are held here, as are 10 AM Sunday services. ⊠ *Kennebec and Samoset Aves.* 🕾 *508/693–5350.*

⑭ A long stretch of green facing the sea, **Ocean Park** fronts a crescent of large shingle-style cottages with numerous turrets, breezy porches, and pastel façades. Band concerts take place at the gazebo here on summer nights, and in August the park hosts hordes of island families and visitors for a grand fireworks display over the ocean. ⊠ *Sea View Ave.*

Where to Eat

$$$–$$$$ ✕ **Jimmy Sea's.** The irresistible fragrance of sautéed garlic wafting out its doors beckons lovers of the "stinking rose." Most dishes come in the pan they're cooked in and are among the biggest portions you'll find on the island. Classic Italian dishes include *vongole* (whole littleneck clams) marinara, and linguine puttanesca. A brightly colored porch and painted ceilings add to the charm of the place. ⊠ *32 Kennebec Ave.* 🕾 *508/696–8550* 🍴 *Reservations not accepted* 🖃 *MC, V.*

$$$–$$$$ ✕ **Lola's.** This spot draws a party crowd. On one side, a spirited bar hosts live music; on another side is an enclosed patio for dining and a large

separate dining room. Ribs and Louisiana standards such as jambalaya with swordfish, tuna, salmon, sausage, and crawfish fill the long menu; Sunday mornings are reserved for an all-you-can-eat buffet brunch, often with live gospel or jazz. This is more of a scene than a relaxing dining spot. However, the bar is big and welcoming, and the wall mural is full of familiar local faces. ⊠ *Beach Rd., just over 1 mi from Oak Bluffs* ☎ *508/693–5007* ⊟ *DC, MC, V.*

$$$–$$$$
Fodor'sChoice
★

✕ **Sweet Life Café.** Housed in a charming Victorian house, this island favorite, with its warm tones, low lighting, and handsome antique furniture, will make you feel like you've entered someone's home, but the cooking is more sophisticated than home-style. Dishes on the menu are prepared in inventive ways. The duck breast is roasted with a lavender honey-and-rosemary glaze. The desserts remain superb; try the warm chocolate fondant (a sort of soufflé) with toasted almond ice cream. There's outdoor dining by candlelight in a shrub-enclosed garden, with heaters for when it turns cold. ⊠ *Upper Circuit Ave., at far end of town* ☎ *508/ 696–0200* ⌖ *Reservations essential* ⊟ *AE, D, MC, V* ⊘ *Closed Jan.–Mar.*

★ $$–$$$$

✕ **Tsunami.** In a quaint converted gingerbread house overlooking the harbor, this restaurant delivers an exclusively Asian-influenced menu. Chef Ricardo Reno focuses on Thai flavors but also samples from Japan, China, Burma, and France. The small upstairs dining room is decorated with a minimalist's touch; downstairs is a handsome mahogany bar with several small tables. The dinner menu, which includes sushi and sake, is available on both levels. A favorite entrée is the filet mignon, served with pungent wasabi mashed potatoes. All the spring-roll appetizers (vegetable, mango and crab, tuna and avocado) are delicate and subtle. ⊠ *6 Circuit Ave.* ☎ *508/696–8900* ⊟ *AE, MC, V* ⊘ *Closed mid-Oct.–mid-May.*

$–$$$$

✕ **Offshore Ale Company.** Since opening in 1997, the island's first and only microbrewery restaurant has become quite popular. There are private wooden booths, dark wood throughout, a dartboard in the corner, and live music throughout the year (Wednesday-night Irish music jams are a hoot). Take your own peanuts from a barrel by the door and drop the shells on the floor; then order from a menu that includes steaks and burgers, chicken, gumbo, and fish. However, to truly appreciate the beer, try it with one of the wood-fired brick-oven pizzas. ⊠ *30 Kennebec Ave.* ☎ *508/693–2626* ⌖ *Reservations not accepted* ⊟ *AE, MC, V.*

$$–$$$

✕ **Smoke 'n Bones.** This is the island's only rib joint, with its own smoker out back and a cord of hickory, apple, oak, and mesquite wood stacked up around the lot. The place has a cookie-cutter, prefab feeling, with all the appropriate touches such as neon flames around the kitchen and marble bones for doorknobs. If you're a true ribs aficionado from the South, this may not satisfy you, but on the Vineyard it's an offbeat treat. ⊠ *Siloam Rd., about 7 blocks from Oak Bluffs* ☎ *508/696–7427* ⌖ *Reservations not accepted* ⊟ *MC, V.*

$$–$$$

✕ **Zapotec Cafe.** Southwest meets gingerbread at one of the island's most unpretentious restaurants. The crowded quarters, dressed in warm Caribbean and fruit colors and strung with chili-pepper Christmas

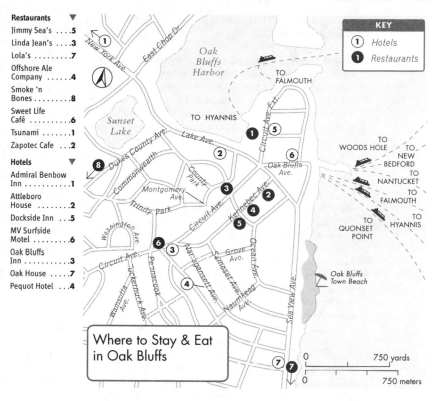

Where to Stay & Eat in Oak Bluffs

Restaurants ▼

Jimmy Sea's **5**

Linda Jean's **3**

Lola's **7**

Offshore Ale
Company **4**

Smoke 'n
Bones **8**

Sweet Life
Café **6**

Tsunami **1**

Zapotec Cafe . . .**2**

Hotels ▼

Admiral Benbow
Inn **1**

Attleboro
House **2**

Dockside Inn . . .**5**

MV Surfside
Motel **6**

Oak Bluffs
Inn **3**

Oak House **7**

Pequot Hotel . . .**4**

lights, add to its character. On the menu are original versions of classic Mexican-American fare. *Tacos de pescado* lays barbecued swordfish over a creamy yogurt sauce in soft flour tortillas. Don't pass up the outstanding mussels Oaxaca, a big bowlful steamed with wine, chipotle peppers, lime, cilantro, and cream. ⊠ *Kennebec Ave.* ☎ *508/693–6800* ⚇ *Reservations not accepted* ▤ *AE, MC, V* ☉ *Closed mid-fall–mid-spring; call for exact months.*

★ **$–$$** ✕ **Linda Jean's.** This is a classic local hangout, a diner the way diners should be: hearty helpings, inexpensive prices. Want breakfast at 6 AM? No problem. Want breakfast at 11:30 AM? No problem. Tired of the gourmet world and want comfortable booths, friendly waitresses, and few frills? No problem. The only problem: you may have to wait—even at 6 AM. ⊠ *34 Circuit Ave.* ☎ *508/693–4093* ⚇ *Reservations not accepted* ▤ *No credit cards.*

Where to Stay

$–$$ ▦ **Oak Bluffs Inn.** A tan octagonal viewing tower dominates this rosy-hued Victorian B&B with a veranda on Oak Bluffs' main street, a stroll from the beach. Victorian and country pieces fill the rooms, all of which have private baths and gauzy white curtains, and one has a four-poster bed. ⊠ *64 Circuit Ave., at the corner of Pequot Ave.* ⌂ *Box 2546, 02557*

☎ *508/693–7171 or 800/955–6235* 🖨 *508/693–8787* ⊕ *www.oakbluffsinn.com* 🗺 *9 rooms* ⚬ *No smoking* ☰ *AE, MC, V* ⊙ *Closed Nov.–early Apr.* ⊠ *CP.*

★ **$–$$** 🖼 **Oak House.** The wraparound veranda of this courtly pastel-painted 1872 Victorian looks across a busy street to the beach and out across Nantucket Sound. Several rooms have private terraces or balconies; if you're bothered by noise, ask for a room at the back. Inside you will see richly painted oak in ceilings, wall paneling, wainscoting, and furnishings. All this well-preserved wood creates an appropriate setting for the choice antique furniture and nautical-theme accessories. An elegant afternoon tea with cakes and cookies is served in a glassed-in sunporch. With its white wicker, plants, floral-print pillows, and original stained-glass window accents, it's a lovely place to while away the end of the day. It's close enough to walk into town yet far enough to avoid the madding crowds. ⊠ *75 Sea View Ave.* ⊕ *Box 299, 02557* ☎ *508/693–4187 or 800/245–5979* 🖨 *508/696–7385* ⊕ *www.vineyardinns.com/oakhouse.html* 🗺 *10 rooms, 2 suites* ⚬ *No kids under 10, no smoking* ☰ *AE, D, MC, V* ⊙ *Closed mid-Oct.–mid-May* ⊠ *CP.*

$ 🖼 **Dockside Inn.** Just yards from the Oak Bluffs ferry and in the thick of the town's bustle, this gingerbread Victorian inn decked with broad porches sits right by the dock, steps from the ferry landing and downtown shops, restaurants, and bars. Kids are welcome, and they'll have plenty to do in town and at nearby beaches. Some rooms open onto building-length balconies; a small cottage at the back of the main building, the inn's quiet spot, houses two suites (both with private decks and room for four guests) and a rooftop widow's walk. ⊠ *9 Circuit Ave. Exit* ⊕ *Box 1206, 02557* ☎ *508/693–2966 or 800/245–5979* 🖨 *508/696–7293* ⊕ *www.vineyardinns.com* 🗺 *19 rooms, 5 suites, 2 apartments* ⚬ *Some in-room hot tubs, some kitchens, some kitchenettes, cable TV* ☰ *AE, MC, V* ⊙ *Closed late Oct.–mid-May* ⊠ *CP.*

$ 🖼 **Martha's Vineyard Surfside Motel.** These two buildings stand right in the thick of things, so it tends to get noisy in summer. Rooms are spacious and bright (corner rooms more so), with smartly decorated rooms with contemporary furnishings, carpets, stylish wallpaper, and tile floors; each has fairly standard but attractive chain-style hotel furnishings and a table and chairs. Deluxe rooms have water views. Four suites have whirlpool baths, and two are wheelchair-accessible. The staff is helpful and courteous. ⊠ *70 Oak Bluffs Ave.* ⊕ *Box 2507, 02557* ☎ *508/693–2500 or 800/537–3007* 🖨 *508/693–7343* ⊕ *www.mvsurfside.com* 🗺 *34 rooms, 4 suites* ⚬ *Restaurant, in-room hot tubs, refrigerators, some pets allowed (fee)* ☰ *AE, D, MC, V.*

¢–$ 🖼 **Admiral Benbow Inn.** On a busy road between Vineyard Haven and Oak Bluffs Harbor, the Benbow is endearing. The small B&B was built for a minister in 1885, and it is decked out with elaborate woodwork, a comfortable hodgepodge of antique furnishings, and a Victorian parlor with a stunning tile-and-carved-wood fireplace. The rooms are much the same, an eclectic mix of antiques and your grandmother's favorite comfy furniture. You have access to an ice machine and refrigerator in the kitchen. Next door to the rather drab yard is a gas station, but the price is right, and the location a few blocks from the harbor is convenient and children are welcome. ⊠ *81 New York Ave., 02557* ☎ *508/693–6825* 🖷 *508/693–7820* ⊕ *www.admiral-benbow-inn.com* 🛏 *7 rooms* ▭ *AE, D, MC, V* ⦿¶ *CP.*

¢–$ 🏨 **Pequot Hotel.** All the bustle of downtown Oak Bluffs is a pleasant five-minute walk past Carpenter Gothic houses from this casual cedar-shingle inn on a tree-lined street. The furniture is quirky but comfortable; the old wing has the most atmosphere. In the main section of the building, the first floor has a wide porch with rocking chairs—perfect for enjoying coffee or tea with the cookies that are set out in the afternoon—and a small breakfast room where you help yourself to bagels, muffins, and cereal in the morning. The hotel is one block from the beaches that line the Oak Bluffs–Edgartown Road. ⊠ *19 Pequot Ave., 02557* ☎ *508/693–5087 or 800/947–8704* 🖷 *508/696–9413* ⊕ *www.pequothotel.com* 🛏 *29 rooms, one 3-bedroom apartment* ♨ *Dining room; no room phones, no TV in some rooms* ▭ *AE, MC, V* ⊘ *Closed mid-Oct.–Apr.* ⦿¶ *CP.*

¢ 🏨 **Attleboro House.** This guesthouse, part of the Methodist Association Camp Grounds, is across the street from bustling Oak Bluffs Harbor. The big 1874 gingerbread Victorian, an inn since its construction, has wraparound verandas on two floors and small, simple rooms with powder-blue walls, lacy white curtains, and a few antiques. Some rooms have sinks. Singles have three-quarter beds, and every room is provided linen exchange but no chambermaid service during a stay. The five shared baths are rustic and old but clean. ⊠ *42 Lake Ave.* ✉ *Box 1564, 02557* ☎ *508/693–4346* 🛏 *11 rooms with shared bath* ▭ *AE, D, MC, V* ⊘ *Closed Oct.–May* ⦿¶ *CP.*

Nightlife & the Arts

NIGHTLIFE At the far end of Circuit Ave., **Bar None** (⊠ 57 Circuit Ave., at Balance Restaurant ☎ 508/696–3000) is the only club on the island with a pub-food menu that is served till midnight. The lighting is nice, the music's not too loud, and the service is friendly. It's a nice getaway from the craziness of the Oak Bluffs weekend bar scene.

Dark and crowded, the **Island House** (⊠ 11 Circuit Ave. ☎ 508/693–4516) hosts a mixture of rock, blues, and reggae for a younger crowd whose ears crave volume.

The **Lampost** (⊠ 6 Circuit Ave. ☎ 508/696–9352) is a good, old-fashioned neighborhood bar with a DJ and dancing. In addition to events such as an '80s night, a Brazilian night, and a Hawaiian night, there are also swing nights. The bar is popular with a young crowd.

Lola's (⊠ Beach Rd. ☎ 508/693–5007), a popular restaurant, has a lively bar that hosts local musicians and a great pub menu year-round. You can also get regular restaurant cuisine at the bar.

The island's only family brewpub, **Offshore Ale** (⊠ Kennebec Ave. ☎ 508/693–2626) hosts live Latin, folk, and blues year-round and serves its own beer and ales and a terrific pub menu. Cozy up to the fireplace with a pint on cool nights.

The **Rare Duck** (✉ 6 Circuit Ave. ☎ 508/696–9352), next to the Lampost, is a dark cocktail lounge with live rock, blues, and acoustic music.

The **Ritz Café** (✉ 4 Circuit Ave. ☎ 508/693–9851) is a popular year-round bar with a pool table that's removed in the summer to make way for dancing. From Monday through Saturday in summer and on weekends in the off-season there's an eclectic mix of live performances including rock, blues, and reggae.

Enjoy the harbor view at **Tsunami** (✉ 6 Circuit Ave. Exit ☎ 508/696–8900) while you sip a fabulous sake martini—a blend of passionfruit juice, sake, and plum wine—and listen to DJs spinning house music on Friday and Saturday nights. The bartenders are friendly and professional.

THE ARTS At the **Featherstone Meetinghouse for the Arts** (✉ Barnes Rd. ☎ 508/693–1850), classes are available in photography, watercolor, pottery, printmaking, drawing, stained glass, weaving, music, and more. During the summer, the Musical Mondays program (6:30 to 8 PM) hosts off- and on-island talent. Admission is $5, free for well-behaved kids; performances are on the lawn, so bring a blanket or lawn chair.

Fodor'sChoice The **Tabernacle** (✉ Trinity Park at the Methodist Camp Grounds behind
★ Circuit Ave.) is the scene of a popular, old-fashioned-style, Wednesday-evening community sing-along at 8 PM, as well as other family-oriented entertainment, including the Martha's Vineyard Festival Orchestra in August. For a schedule, contact the **Camp Meeting Association** (✆ Box 1176, Oak Bluffs 02557 ☎ 508/693–0525).

Union Chapel (✉ Kennebec Ave. ☎ 508/693–5350) presents occasional music recitals during the summer.

Sunday-night summer **Vineyard Haven Town Band concerts** (☎ 508/645–3458) alternate weekly locations between the gazebo in Ocean Park on Beach Road in Oak Bluffs and Owen Park in Vineyard Haven. Admission is free.

Shopping
ANTIQUES **Tuckernuck Antiques** (✉ 79 Tuckernuck, off Upper Circuit Ave., ☎ 508/696–6392) carries oak Victorian and early American pine furniture, as well as an extensive collection of old island postcards and other memorabilia.

ART **Cousen Rose Gallery** (✉ 71 Circuit Ave. ☎ 508/693–6656) displays works by many island artists including Myrna Morris, John Breckenridge, Marietta Cleasby, Deborah Colter, Lynn Hoefs, Ray Prosser, and Renee Balter. During the summer months, be sure to inquire about art classes held especially for children.

Dragonfly Gallery (✉ Dukes County and Vineyard Aves. ☎ 508/693–8877) changes shows weekly and holds artist receptions every other Saturday during the summer from 4 to 7 PM, featuring jazz pianist John Alaimo. Check the local papers for a schedule of artists.

The **Firehouse Gallery** (✉ 635 Dukes County Ave., at Vineyard Ave. ☎ 508/693–9025) is home to the Martha's Vineyard Center for the Visual Arts. It holds weekly shows throughout the summer, featuring island and off-island artists. Check the local paper for receptions and featured artists.

BOOKS **Book Den East** (✉ 71 New York Ave. ☎ 508/693–3946) is an amazing place to browse and buy, with 20,000 out-of-print, antiquarian, and paperback books housed in an old barn.

CLOTHES **Island Outfitters** (✉ Post Office Sq., off Circuit Ave. ☎ 508/693–5003) will blind you with its extensive line of tropical prints by Lilly Pulitzer and Tommy Bahama.

The gorgeous dresses hanging in the window of **Laughing Bear** (✉ 33 Circuit Ave. ☎ 508/693–9342) will lure you into the store. Inside you'll find women's wear made of cool silk, soft linen, and Moroccan fabrics, plus jewelry and accessories from around the world. Although the goods are pricey, there's a great sales rack.

Slight Indulgence (✉ Post Office Sq. ☎ 508/693–8194) is best known for its sterling jewelry from all over the world and moderately-priced fashionable summer wear.

ODDS & ENDS If you're looking for out-of-the-ordinary, **Craftworks** (✉ 42 Circuit Ave. ☎ 508/693–7463) carries outrageous painted furniture, ceramic figures, and home accessories—all handmade by American artists.

Good Dog Goods (✉ 79 Circuit Ave. ☎ 508/696–7100) is doggy heaven. You'll find all-natural dog foods and homemade biscuits, as well as dog-related items for humans. The back room is the "Bakery," where an old-fashioned display case houses healthy doggy pastries that look so enticing they'll make your own mouth water. Four-legged shoppers are welcome.

The **Secret Garden** (✉ 41 Circuit Ave. ☎ 508/693–4759), set in a yellow gingerbread cottage, has a complete line of Shelia collectibles—miniature wooden versions of Camp Ground houses and other island landmarks.

Sports & the Outdoors

BEACHES **Eastville Beach** (✉ over the bridge on Beach Rd. leading from Vineyard Haven to Oak Bluffs) is a small beach where children can swim in the calm waters and dive off the pilings under the drawbridge. From the shore you can watch boats of all sizes passing under the bridge between the lagoon and the harbor.

Joseph A. Sylvia State Beach (✉ between Oak Bluffs and Edgartown, off Beach Rd.) is a 6-mi-long sandy beach with a view of Cape Cod across Nantucket Sound. The calm, warm water and food vendors make it popular with families. There's parking along the roadside, and the beach is accessible by bike path or shuttle bus. Across the street from this barrier beach is Sengekontacket Pond, a popular fishing and shellfishing spot. Even if you don't love beaches, the drive and the expansive vista of the sound and the pond alone will make you at least develop a severe case of infatuation.

Oak Bluffs Town Beach (⊠ between steamship dock and state beach, off Sea View Ave.) is a crowded, narrow stretch of calm water on Nantucket Sound, with snack stands, lifeguards, roadside parking, and restrooms at the steamship office. One section has been nicknamed Inkwell Beach by the generations of African-Americans who summer on the Vineyard and have been enjoying this stretch for more than a century. There's a changing area and showers in this section as well.

BIKING **Anderson's** (⊠ Circuit Ave. Exit ☎ 508/693–9346), on the harbor, rents several different styles of bicycle.

DeBettencourt's (⊠ Circuit Ave. Exit ☎ 508/693–0011) rents bikes, mopeds, scooters, and Jeeps.

Ride-On Mopeds and Bikes (⊠ Circuit Ave. Exit ☎ 508/693–2076) rents bicycles and mopeds.

Sun 'n' Fun (⊠ 28 Lake Ave. ☎ 508/693–5457) rents bikes, cars, and Jeeps.

BOATING **My Ocean Sports** (⊠ Dockside Marketplace, Oak Bluffs Harbor ☎ 508/693–8476) rents a variety of personal watercraft.

FISHING **Dick's Bait and Tackle** (⊠ New York Ave. ☎ 508/693–7669) rents gear, sells accessories and bait, and keeps a current copy of the fishing regulations.

GOLF **Farm Neck Golf Club** (⊠ County Rd. ☎ 508/693–3057), a semiprivate club on marsh-rimmed Sengekontacket Pond, has 18 holes in a championship layout and a driving range. Reservations are required 48 hours in advance.

HEALTH & **Muscle Discipline** (⊠ 29 Kennebec Ave. ☎ 508/693–5096) has Lifecy-
FITNESS CLUB cle, Nautilus, StairMaster, treadmill, and cross-training machines and free weights. All staff are certified trainers. Eight TVs are located throughout the gym. Daily, weekly, monthly, and three-month summer memberships are available.

ICE-SKATING **Martha's Vineyard Arena** (⊠ Edgartown–Vineyard Haven Rd. ☎ 508/693–4438) is open mid-July–March. Open public skating is weekdays 11 AM–1 PM, weekends 4–5:30 PM.

SCUBA DIVING Vineyard waters hold a number of sunken ships, among them several schooners and freighters off East Chop and Aquinnah. Visibility is decent, though the water clarity isn't in the same league as that of the Caribbean. Guided dives are the norm.

Vineyard Scuba (⊠ 110 S. Circuit Ave. ☎ 508/693–0288) has diving information and equipment rentals and is the only full-service dive shop on the island. Certification classes are given.

TENNIS Tennis is very popular on the island, and at all times reservations are strongly recommended.

Farm Neck Golf Club (⊠ County Rd. ☎ 508/693–9728) is a semiprivate club with four clay tennis courts, lessons, and a pro shop. It's open mid-April through mid-November; reservations are required.

Island Country Club Tennis (⊠ Beach Rd. ☎ 508/693–6574) is a semiprivate club with three Har-Tru courts and a pro shop. It's open May–mid-October.

Hard-surface courts in **Niantic Park** (☎ 508/693–6535) cost $10 per hour and are open 8 AM–7 PM.

Edgartown

6 mi southeast of Oak Bluffs, 9 mi southeast of Vineyard Haven via Beach Rd., 8½ mi east of West Tisbury.

Edgartown has long been the Vineyard's toniest spot. Ever since Thomas Mayhew, Jr., landed here in 1642 as the Vineyard's first governor, the town has served as the county seat. Plenty of settlers inhabited the area, making it the island's first colonial settlement, but the town was not officially named until 1652. First called Great Harbour, it was renamed for political reasons some 30 years later, after the three-year-old son of the Duke of York.

Once a well-to-do whaling port, Edgartown has managed to preserve the elegance of that wealthy era. Lining the streets are 18th- and 19th-century sea captains' houses, many painted white with black shutters, set among well-manicured gardens and lawns. Plenty of shops as well as other sights and activities here occupy the crowds who walk the streets. A stroll is definitely the best way to absorb it all.

★ ⓵⑤ To orient yourself historically before making your way around town, stop off at a complex of buildings and lawn exhibits that constitutes the **Martha's Vineyard Historical Society.** The opening hours and admission listed below apply to all the buildings and exhibits—including the Thomas Cooke House, the Francis Foster Museum, the Capt. Francis Pease House, and the Carriage Shed—and the Huntington Reference Library of Vineyard History, which contains archives of oral history, letters, and law documents. The museum sells an excellent Edgartown walking-tour booklet full of anecdotes and the history of the people who have lived in the old houses over the past three centuries. You can purchase it at the entrance gatehouse in summer or at the library in winter. ⊠ *Cooke and School Sts.* ☎ *508/627–4441* ☎ *$6* ☉ *Mid-June–mid-Oct., Tues.–Sat. 10–5; mid-Oct.–mid-June, Wed.–Fri. 1–4, Sat. 10–4.*

⓵⑥ The one Vineyard Museum property open only from mid-June to mid-October is the **Thomas Cooke House,** set in the 1765 home of a customs collector. The house itself is part of the display, evoking the past with its low doorways, wide-board floors, original raised-panel woodwork with fluted pilasters, and hearths in the summer and winter kitchens. Docents answer questions about the 12 rooms, whose exhibits reveal the island's history with furniture, tools, costumes, portraits, toys,

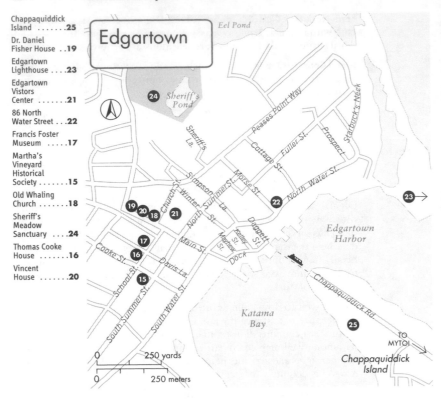

crafts, and various household objects. One room is set up as a 19th-century parlor, illustrating the opulence of the golden age of whaling with such period pieces as a pianoforte. Upstairs are ship models, whaling paraphernalia, old customs documents, and a room tracing the evolution of the Camp Meeting through photographs and objects. ⊠ *School St.* ☎ *508/627–4441.*

⓱ The **Francis Foster Museum** houses a small collection of whaling implements, scrimshaw, navigational instruments, and many old photographs. Among them are images of 110 19th-century Edgartown whaling masters. The **Dale Huntington Reference Library and Foster Maritime Gallery** is also in the building, with genealogical records, rare island books, and ships' logs from the whaling days, as well as some publications for sale. ⊠ *School St.* ☎ *508/627–4441.*

☙ The **Capt. Francis Pease House,** an 1850s Greek Revival, houses a permanent exhibit of Native American, prehistoric, pre-Columbian, and later artifacts, including arrowheads and pottery, plus changing exhibits from the collection. The Children's Gallery presents changing exhibits created by children, and the museum shop sells books, maps, jewelry, and island crafts. ⊠ *School St.* ☎ *508/627–4441.*

The **Carriage Shed** displays a number of vessels and vehicles, among them a whaleboat, a snazzy 1855 fire engine with stars inlaid in wood, and an 1830 hearse, considerably less ornate than the fire engine. The shed also houses some peculiar gravestones that mark the eternal resting places of an eccentric poet's strangely beloved chickens. In the yard outside are a replica of a 19th-century brick tryworks, used to process whale oil from blubber aboard ship, and the 1,008-prism Fresnel lens installed in the Aquinnah Lighthouse (⇨ *see* Aquinnah) in 1854 and removed when the light was automated in 1952. Each evening the lens lamp is lighted briefly after sundown. The toolshed contains harvesting tools used both on land and at sea in the early 19th century. ⊠ *School St.* ☎ *508/627–4441.*

⓲ The **Old Whaling Church,** which opened in 1843 as a Methodist church and is now a performing-arts center, is a massive building with a six-column portico, unusual triple-sash windows, and a 92-foot clock tower that can be seen for miles. The simple, graceful interior is brightened by light from 27-foot-tall windows and still contains the original box pews and lectern. Aside from attending performances, you can get inside only if you join one of the historical walking tours run by Vineyard History Tours (⇨ Martha's Vineyard A to Z). ⊠ *89 Main St.* ☎ *508/627–8619 for tour.*

⓳ A truly elegant sight is the graceful **Dr. Daniel Fisher House,** with a wraparound roof walk and a small front portico with fluted Corinthian columns. It was built in 1840 for one of the island's richest men, who was a doctor, the first president of the Martha's Vineyard National Bank, and the owner of a whale-oil refinery, a spermaceti (whale-oil) candle factory, and a gristmill, among other pursuits. The good doctor came to a portion of his fortune through marriage—as a wedding gift, his generous but presumably eccentric father-in-law presented him with the bride's weight in silver. The house is now used for functions and office space, and you can gain access only on Liz Villard's Vineyard History Tours (⇨ Martha's Vineyard A to Z). ⊠ *99 Main St.*

⓴ The island's oldest dwelling is the 1672 **Vincent House.** It was moved to its present location behind the Dr. Daniel Fisher House in 1977, restored, and furnished with pieces that date from the 17th to the 19th century. A tour of this weathered-shingle farmhouse takes you along a time line that starts with the sparse furnishings of the 1600s and ends in a Federal-style parlor of the 1800s. ⊠ *Main St.* ☎ *508/627–4440* 🖼 *Museum $3* 🕐 *Late May–Oct., Mon.–Sat. 10–3.*

㉑ A good place to stop for directions or suggestions is the **Edgartown Visitors Center,** which has information, restrooms, and snacks in season. ⊠ *Church St.* ☎ *No phone.*

need a break? If you need a pick-me-up, pop into **Espresso Love** (⊠ 3 S. Water St. ☎ 508/627–9211) for a cappuccino and a homemade raspberry scone or blueberry muffin. If you prefer something cold, the staff makes fruit smoothies. Light lunch fare is also served: bagel sandwiches, soups, and delicious pastries and cookies—all homemade, of course.

The architecturally pristine, much-photographed upper part of North Water Street is lined with many fine captains' houses. You can seemingly always discover an interesting detail on this stretch that you never noticed before—like a widow's walk with a mannequin poised, spyglass in hand, watching for her seafaring husband to return. The 1832 house **22** where this piece of whimsy can be seen stands at **86 North Water Street,** which the Society for the Preservation of New England Antiquities maintains as a rental property.

23 The **Edgartown Lighthouse,** surrounded by a public beach, provides a great view (but seaweedy bathing). The original light guarding the harbor was built in 1828 and set on a little island made of granite blocks. The island was later connected to the mainland by a bridge. By the time the 1938 hurricane made a new light necessary, sand had filled in the gap between the island and the mainland. The current white cast-iron tower was floated by barge from Ipswich, Massachusetts, in 1938. At this area, called Starbuck's Neck, you can wander about and take in views of the ocean, harbor, a little bay, and moorland. ⊠ *Off N. Water St.* ☉ *Closed to the public.*

24 A pleasant walking trail circles an old ice pond at the center of **Sheriff's Meadow Sanctuary,** 17 acres of marsh, woodland, and meadow. One of the area's many wildlife preserves, Sheriff's Meadow contains a variety of habitats. ⊠ *Planting Field Way* ☎ *508/693–5207.*

★ ♻ The Vineyard's conservation areas are a good way to get acquainted with local flora and fauna. The 350-acre **Felix Neck Wildlife Sanctuary,** a Massachusetts Audubon Society preserve 3 mi out of Edgartown toward Oak Bluffs and Vineyard Haven, has 6 mi of hiking trails traversing marshland, fields, oak woods, seashore, and waterfowl and reptile ponds. Nesting ospreys and barn owls also call the sanctuary home. A full schedule of events unfolds throughout the year, including sunset hikes along the beach, explorations of the salt marsh, stargazing, snake or bird walks, snorkeling, canoeing, and more, all led by trained naturalists. An exhibit center has trail maps, aquariums, snake cages, and a gift shop. A bit of summer fun and learning experience combined, the sanctuary's **Fern & Feather Day Camp** is a great way for children to learn about wildlife, plants, and the stars. It runs one- or two-week summer sessions that include overnight camping expeditions. Early registration is advised and begins in February. ⊠ *Off Edgartown–Vineyard Haven Rd.* ☎ *508/ 627–4850* 🖼 *$4* ☉ *Center June–Sept., daily 8–4; Oct.–May, Tues.–Sun. 9–4. Trails daily sunrise–7 PM.*

Where to Eat

$$$$ ✕ **L'étoile.** Perhaps the Vineyard's finest traditional French restaurant,
Fodor's Choice   L'étoile carries on a long history of excellent dining. Both the food and
★   the setting in the stunningly appointed Charlotte Inn are unforgettable. The glass-enclosed dining room reminds you why hunter green, dark wood, and glass became so popular—and imitated. Preparations are at once classic and creative. Not to be missed are spice-crusted foie gras with sauteed nectarines and a "trilogy" of Chilmark lamb that includes a rack chop, a leg filet, and homemade sausage with a warm chèvre-

and-sunchoke Napoleon. The outstanding wine list has selections from California and Europe that are solid, if a little pricey. During the shoulder seasons (May–mid-June, September) the restaurant's weekday schedule varies. ⊠ *27 S. Summer St.* ☎ *508/627–5187* ⌕ *Reservations essential* ▭*AE, MC, V* ⊗ *Closed Jan.–mid-Feb., and weekdays Oct.–Dec. and late Feb.–Apr. No lunch.*

$$$–$$$$ ✕ **Alchemy Bistro and Bar.** According to the menu, the dictionary meaning of *alchemy* is "a magic power having as its asserted aim the discovery of a panacea and the preparation of the elixir of longevity"—lofty goals for yet another French-style bistro. This high-class version has elegant gray wainscoting, classic paper-covered white tablecloths, old wooden floors, and an opening cut into the ceiling to reveal the second-floor tables. The only things missing are the patina of age, experience, cigarette smoke—and French working folk's prices, but you can expect quality and imagination. One example is a mustard-braised pork tenderloin with Gorgonzola grits and marinated figs and pine nuts. The alcohol list, long and complete, includes cognacs, grappas, and beers. ⊠*71 Main St.* ☎*508/627–9999* ▭ *AE, MC, V.*

$$–$$$$ ✕ **The Grill on Main.** The space between the tables is what strikes you first in this low-key restaurant. Chef–owner Tony Saccoccia not only aims to provide some intimacy for his patrons but also creates inventive takes on seafood. For a starter, try the lobster turnover with a shrimp and lemon cream, then the baked codfish with a lump crab and smoked scallop sauce for the entrée. If you want to see how it's all prepared, ask for a seat with a view of the kitchen. ⊠ *227 Upper Main St.* ☎ *508/627–8344* ▭ *AE, D, DC, MC, V.*

$$–$$$ ✕ **The Square Rigger.** Locals are loyal to this comfort food spot because it tends to stay open seven days a week until January. Grilled lamb chops, pork chops, and swordfish are on the menu along with other hearty fare; prime rib with a popover is served Thursday through Sunday. It's just right for a night out with the family. ⊠ *The Triangle* ☎ *508/627–9968* ▭ *AE, MC, V.*

$–$$ ✕ **Lattanzi's Pizzeria.** Albert and Cathy Lattanzi's big brick oven gets fired up by 2:30 PM, and the pizza that slides out come evening is delicious—baby clams with plum tomatoes, oregano, spinach, roasted garlic, and Asiago cheese is just one example. ⊠ *Old Post Office Sq.* ☎ *508/627–9084* ▭ *D, DC, MC, V* ⊗ *No lunch.*

$–$$ ✕ **Newes from America.** Sometimes a nearly subterranean, darkened scene feels right on a hot summer afternoon, in which case the Newes is the perfect spot for an informal lunch or dinner. Inside, there's plenty of wood and greenery and many things "olde." The food is mostly Americana (burgers and fries), though some dishes like Roquefort Stilettos (French bread, Roquefort cheese, and bacon) have made their way onto the menu. There's a massively inclusive list of microbrewed beers, and the staff is well equipped to make recommendations. The Newes is open from 11 AM until midnight every day of the year except Christmas. ⊠ *23 Kelly St.* ☎ *508/627–4397* ⌕ *Reservations not accepted* ▭ *AE, D, MC, V.*

¢–$ ✕ **Edgartown Deli.** A no-frills place with a down-home, happy feeling, this deli has walls and a glass counter plastered with specials written on

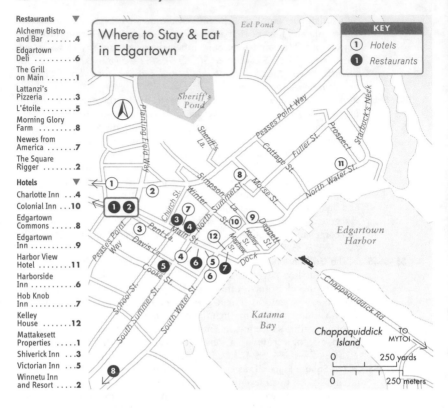

multicolored paper. Brightly lit booths fill one side of the room, while customers line up at the counter for orders to go. Breakfast specials are served from 8 until 10:45 and include egg, cheese, and *linguiça* (garlicky Portuguese sausage) on a roll. Lunch sandwiches include corned beef and Swiss, roast beef, turkey, pastrami, or steak and cheese. ⊠ *52 Main St.* ☎ *508/627–4789* ⚠ *Reservations not accepted* ▭ *No credit cards* ☉ *Closed Nov.–Apr. No dinner.*

¢–$
Fodor'sChoice
★

✕ **Morning Glory Farm.** Fresh farm greens in the salads and vegetables in the soups; homemade pies, cookies, and cakes; and a picnic table and grass to enjoy them on make this an ideal place for a simple country lunch. ⊠ *West Tisbury Rd.* ☎ *508/627–9003* ▭ *No credit cards.*

Where to Stay

$$$$
🏠 **Mattakesett Properties.** This attractive resort complex, which lies just down the road from its sister resort, the Winnetu, sits close to South Beach. Mattakesett differs from the Winnetu in that all of its units are owner-furnished town houses and condominiums with three to four bedrooms; guests at either property use the amenities at both. All homes have fireplaces and decks. The children's programs are extensive, and the pool and barbecue grills make this a favorite for families. Bookings at Mattakesett are taken on a per-week basis only. A vintage fire truck

and livery are used to shuttle you around the area. ✉ *Katama Rd.* 🕾 *RFD 270, 02539* ☎ *508/627–4747 or 978/443–1733* ⊕ *www. winnetu.com/mattakesett.htm* ➷ *92 units* ⚒ *Kitchens, 10 tennis courts, pool, theater, children's programs (ages 3–12), laundry facilities* ▭ *AE, MC, V* ☺ *Mattakesett closed Nov.–Apr.*

$$$–$$$$
Fodor'sChoice
★
🏨 **Charlotte Inn.** From the moment you walk up to the dark-wood Scottish barrister's desk at check-in you'll be surrounded by the trappings and customs of a bygone era. Guests' names are handwritten into the register by the dignified and attentive staff. Beautiful antique furnishings, *objets,* and paintings fill the property—the book you pick up in your room might be an 18th-century edition of Voltaire, and your bed could be a hand-carved four-poster. All rooms have hair dryers and robes. This elegant atmosphere extends to the outstanding restaurant L'étoile. ✉ *27 S. Summer St., 02539* ☎ *508/627–4751* 🖷 *508/627–4652* ⊕ *www. relaischateaux.com* ➷ *21 rooms, 2 suites* ⚒ *Restaurant, library; no kids under 14* ▭ *AE, MC, V* ⦿ *CP.*

★ $$$–$$$$
🏨 **Harbor View Hotel.** The centerpiece of this historic hotel is a gray-shingle, 1891 Victorian building with wraparound veranda and a gazebo. Accommodations are also in a complex of nearby buildings in a residential neighborhood. The contemporary town houses have cathedral ceilings, decks, kitchens, and large living areas with sofa beds. Rooms in other buildings, however, resemble upscale motel rooms, so ask for main-building or town-house rooms. A beach, good for walking, stretches ¾ mi from the hotel's dock, and the sheltered bay is a great place for kids to swim. Packages and theme weekends are available. The hotel is also home to the Coach House restaurant. ✉ *131 N. Water St.* 🕾 *Box 7, 02539* ☎ *508/627–7000 or 800/225–6005* 🖷 *508/742–1042* ⊕ *www.harbor-view.com* ➷ *102 rooms, 22 suites* ⚒ *2 restaurants, room service, some kitchenettes, refrigerators, 2 tennis courts, pool, dock, laundry service, concierge, business services* ▭ *AE, DC, MC, V.*

★ $$–$$$$
🏨 **Hob Knob Inn.** This 19th-century Gothic Revival inn a short walk from the harbor blends the amenities and service of a luxury hotel with the ambience and charm of a small B&B. Rooms are gracious and quite large by island standards; the upper floors have dormer windows. Art and antiques help capture the island's rural, seaside charm. Many rooms overlook the spectacular gardens. It's on the main road into town but far enough out to avoid crowds. The inn also runs fishing trips and charters on its 27-foot Boston Whaler. Full breakfast and lavish afternoon tea are included. ✉ *128 Main St., 02539* ☎ *508/627–9510 or 800/696–2723* 🖷 *508/627–4560* ⊕ *www.hobknob.com* ➷ *20 rooms* ⚒ *In-room data ports, gym, massage, sauna, bicycles, meeting rooms; no kids under 10* ▭ *AE, MC, V* ⦿ *BP.*

$$–$$$$
🏨 **Kelley House.** In the center of town, this sister property of the Harbor View combines services and amenities with a country-inn feel. The 1742 white clapboard main house and the adjacent Garden House are surrounded by pink roses. Large suites in the Chappaquiddick House and the two spacious town houses in the Wheel House have porches (most with harbor views) and living rooms. The Newes from America, with original hand-hewn timbers and ballast-brick walls, serves light

fare and microbrewed beers on tap. ✉ *23 Kelley St.* ☎ *Box 37, 02539* ☎ *508/627–7900 or 800/225–6005* 🖷 *508/627–8142* ⊕ *www.kelley-house.com* 🖘 *42 rooms, 9 suites, 2 town-house units* ♢ *Restaurant, some kitchens, cable TV, 2 tennis courts, pool, pub, babysitting, laundry service, business services* ▭ *AE, DC, MC, V* ☉ *Closed mid-Oct.–Apr.* ⫪ *CP.*

$$–$$$$
Fodor'sChoice
★

🏨 **Winnetu Inn and Resort.** A departure from most properties on the island, the contemporary Winnetu—styled after the grand multistory resorts of the gilded age—both encourages families and provides a contemporary seaside-resort experience for couples. This all-suite property has units that can sleep up to 11 guests. All have kitchens, and decks or patios with views. Room decor is stylish and modern but casual enough so that kids feel right at home. The resort arranges bicycling and kayaking trips, lighthouse tours, and other island activities. The General Store carries snacks, and Lure, the only restaurant on the island with a south-facing water view, prepares tasty box lunches for the beach. (It is also open to the public and specializes in gourmet fish fare.) The staff will stock your kitchen in advance of your arrival on request. Clambakes are held on the grounds on Wednesday evening. In summer, all stays must be a minimum of three nights. ✉ *Katama Rd.* ☎ *RFD 270, 02539* ☎ *508/627–4747 or 978/443–1733* ⊕ *www.winnetu.com* 🖘 *22 suites* ♢ *Restaurant, snack bar, kitchens, in-room VCRs, putting green, 10 tennis courts, pool, gym, croquet, Ping-Pong, library, children's programs (ages 3–12), laundry facilities, concierge, Internet, business services, meeting rooms* ▭ *MC, V* ☉ *Closed Dec.–mid-Apr.*

★ $$–$$$

🏨 **Colonial Inn.** The inn is perfect if you like having modern conveniences and being at the center of the action. It was built in 1911 but doesn't have the same antique quality as the sea captains' houses. Still, rooms are immaculate and attractively decorated with white pine furniture and wall-to-wall carpeting in most rooms. Several common upper-floor decks are great for relaxing, and the fourth-floor deck has a superb view of the harbor. An adjoining day spa and salon are a great place to pamper yourself. ✉ *38 N. Water St.* ☎ *Box 68, 02539* ☎ *508/627–4711 or 800/627–4701* 🖷 *508/627–5904* ⊕ *www.colonialinnmvy.com* 🖘 *39 rooms, 2 suites, 2 efficiencies* ♢ *Restaurant, in-room data ports, some kitchenettes, some refrigerators, some in-room VCRs, gym, spa, library* ▭ *AE, MC, V* ☉ *Closed Dec.–Apr.* ⫪ *CP.*

$–$$$

🏨 **Harborside Inn.** Right on the harbor, with boat docks at the end of a nicely landscaped lawn, the large inn provides a central town location, harbor-view decks, and plenty of amenities. Seven two- and three-story buildings sprawl around formal rose beds, brick walkways, a brick patio, and a heated pool. Rooms have colonial-style but modern furnishings, brass beds and lamps, and textured wallpapers. ✉ *3 S. Water St.* ☎ *Box 67, 02539* ☎ *508/627–4321 or 800/627–4009* 🖷 *508/627–7566* ⊕ *www.theharborsideinn.com* 🖘 *89 rooms, 3 suites* ♢ *Refrigerators, cable TV, pool, hot tub, sauna, dock* ▭ *AE, MC, V* ☉ *Closed mid-Nov.–mid-Apr.*

★ $–$$$

🏨 **Victorian Inn.** White with the classic black shutters of the town's historic homes and fronted by ornate columns, this appropriately named inn a block from the downtown harbor was built as the home of

19th-century whaling captain Lafayette Rowley. Today the inn's three floors are done in dark woods and bold floral wallpapers, with rugs over wood floors. Several rooms hold handmade reproduction four-poster beds. Breakfast, served in season in the brick-patio garden, includes creative muffins and breads. ⊠ *24 S. Water St., 02539* ☎ *508/627–4784* ⊕ *www.thevic.com* ⤙ *14 rooms* ♿ *No kids under 8* ⊟ *MC, V* ⍩ *BP.*

$$ ⊡ **Shiverick Inn.** This inn is set in a striking 1840 former doctor's home with mansard roof and cupola. Rooms are airy and bright, with high ceilings, lots of windows, eclectic American and English antiques and Oriental rugs. Beds are mostly queen-size with canopies or carved four-posters. Nine rooms have fireplaces or woodstoves. A full breakfast and tea are served. There's a second-floor library with cable TV and a stereo, as well as a terrace and a first-floor flagstone garden patio. It's about a five-minute walk to downtown. ⊠ *5 Pease's Point Way, at Pent La.* ⍋ *Box 640, 02539* ☎ *508/627–3797 or 800/723–4292* 🖷 *508/627–8441* ⊕ *www.shiverickinn.com* ⤙ *11 rooms* ♿ *No room phones* ⊟ *AE, D, MC, V* ⍩ *BP.*

$ ⊡ **Edgartown Commons.** This condominium complex of seven buildings, which includes an old house and motel rooms around a busy pool, is just a couple of blocks from town. Studios and one- or two-bedroom condos all have full kitchens, and some are very spacious. Each has been decorated by its individual owner, so the decor varies—some have an older look, and some are new and bright. Definitely family-oriented, the place buzzes with lots of kids; rooms away from the pool are quieter. ⊠ *20 Pease's Point Way* ⍋ *Box 1293, 02539* ☎ *508/627–4671, 800/439–4671 in eastern Massachusetts* 🖷 *508/627–4271* ⊕ *www.edgartowncommons.com* ⤙ *35 units* ♿ *Picnic area, some kitchens, pool, playground, laundry facilities; no room phones* ⊟ *AE, MC, V* ☯ *Closed mid-Oct.–Apr.*

¢–$ ⊡ **Edgartown Inn.** The inside of this former home of whaling captain Thomas Worth still evokes its late 18th century origins. In fact, its cozy parlor and antique-filled rooms look as if the captain still lives here. The inn was also the spot where Nathaniel Hawthorne wrote much of his "Twice Told Tales" during a stay here. In the paneled dining room or the back garden, many an Edgartonian, as well as inn guests, come for breakfast in summertime. ⊠ *56 N. Water St., 02539* ☎ *508/627–4794* 🖷 *508/627–9420* ⊕ *www.edgartowninn.com* ⤙ *20 rooms, 4 with shared bath* ⊟ *No credit cards.*

Nightlife & the Arts

NIGHTLIFE The downstairs bar at **Alchemy** (⊠ 71 Main St. ☎ 508/627–9999) is fun and friendly and the restaurant's excellent fare is available, too. Food and drink are a bit pricey but worth it. The upstairs bar is small, loud, and crowded, and you have to go through the restaurant to reach it; however, it does have a pool table to entertain the crowd of thirty- and fortysomethings.

The **Atria Bar** (⊠ 137 Main St. ☎ 508/627–5850) is off the beaten path but is a quiet, comfortable place to escape the summer crowds. Enjoy one of the clever drinks, including the Green Bamboo (gin and mint and fresh ginger), and the Espresso Martini (Ketel One vodka, Kahlúa, Tia Maria, and a shot of fresh espresso). You'll also find an extensive wine list. Play a game of bumper pool, curl up on one of the leather sofas, or sit at the bar and watch the tropical fish. The bar hosts live music, including jazz, Thursday through Saturday.

The **Boathouse Bar** (✉ 2 Main St. ☎ 508/627–4320) is the closest thing Edgartown has to a singles scene. Right on the harbor, it attracts mostly boat enthusiasts of all ages and is a large, noisy party bar with dancing and rock bands. If the noise becomes too much, you can take your drink out on the patio and watch the boats sail in and out of the harbor.

The **Clubhouse Bar** (✉ 131 N. Water St., in the Harbor View Hotel ☎ 508/627–3761) is a small bar that dispenses high-end liquors, fine cigars to be puffed outside, and a gorgeous view of the Edgartown lighthouse. The ambience is good old boys' club, with lots of dark wood in the decor. There's a porch where you can enjoy your drink and the view.

David Ryan's Restaurant and Cafe (✉ 11 N. Water St. ☎ 508/627–4100) is packed with an older, lively crowd in summer and is a hang-out for locals in the winter. It's crowded and there's only DJ music in the bar, though there's karaoke Thursdays in the dining room. You may have to wait in line to squeeze in.

Hideaway Lounge (✉ 44 N. Water ☎ 508/627–1387), a martini bar, is aptly named for its location behind the Shiretown Inn and for the intimacy of its bar. You can have a Caramel Apple Martini (apple liqueur, butterscotch liqueur, Triple Sec, lime juice, and Absolut vodka). Food from the Ciao Bella restaurant is also available. Share a crab cake or fried calamari appetizer with someone special.

Hot Tin Roof (✉ Martha's Vineyard Airport, Edgartown–West Tisbury Rd. ☎ 508/693–1137), opened by Carly Simon in 1976, is a venue for big-name acts such as Medeski, Martin and Wood, Soulive, Kate Taylor, and the Derek Trucks Band. Dance to reggae, salsa, rock, and jazz, surrounded by fanciful murals by Margot Datz.

The **Newes from America** (✉ Kelley House, Kelly St. ☎ 508/627–4397) is quieter than most of the island's pubs, and the exposed wooden beams, fireplace, and brick walls of the circa 1742 building create a cozy ambience. Order one of the 13 microbrewed beers on tap or a snack from the bar menu.

The **Wharf Pub** (✉ Lower Main St. ☎ 508/627–9966) is stuffed with young, friendly party people in the summer and crusty fishermen in the winter. In summer, the bar hosts live music Wednesday and DJ music weekends.

THE ARTS **Old Sculpin Gallery** (✉ Dock St. ☎ 508/627–4881) holds classes such as watercolor and life drawing for adults and various art classes for children throughout the summer. Call for a schedule.

The **Old Whaling Church** (✉ 89 Main St. ☎ 508/627–4442) hosts classical, pop, and other musical events in the summer and community activities in the off-season, in a beautiful, acoustically grand old church. Watch the papers, or check the kiosk out front for a listing of events.

Shopping

ART   The **Christina Gallery** (✉ 32 N. Water St. ☎ 508/627–8794) represents artists of regional, national, and international repute and displays a wide selection of oil paintings, watercolors, and nautical maps and charts.

The **Edgartown Art Gallery** (✉ 19 and 27 S. Summer St. ☎ 508/627–6227) largely exhibits Ray Ellis watercolors of the Vineyard. Other work includes Vineyard paintings by Timothy Thies and Marjorie Mason. The **Edgartown Scrimshaw Gallery** (✉ 43 Main St. ☎ 508/627–9439) showcases a large collection of scrimshaw, including some antique pieces, as well as Nantucket lightship baskets and 14-karat lightship-basket jewelry.

The **Gardner-Colby Gallery** (✉ 27 N. Water St. ☎ 508/627–6002) displays an eclectic mix of some Vineyard land- and seascapes and figurative and still-life paintings.

The **Old Sculpin Gallery** (✉ 58 Dock St., next to the On-Time ferry ☎ 508/627–4881) is the Martha's Vineyard Art Association's headquarters. Only original art by island artists is on display in this building, which dates back before 1800. Don't miss the fabulous seaweed collages by Rose Treat.

BOOKS   David Le Breton, the owner of **Edgartown Books** (✉ 44 Main St. ☎ 508/627–8463), is a true bibliophile and carries a large selection of current and island-related titles. He will be happy to make a recommendation for your summer reading.

CLOTHES   **Brickman's** (✉ 33 Main St. ☎ 508/697–4700) sells sportswear, surf-style clothing, and major-label footwear for the family.

Dream Weaver (✉ 1 S. Water St. ☎ 508/627–9683) purports to be "a gallery of art to wear," and that's pretty accurate. It sells clothing and accessories produced by the top 100 fiber artists in the world, and the stock is absolutely dazzling. Everything is handmade of the most luxurious fabrics, furs, and yarns. Prices are very steep, but if you're looking for something special to wear, bite the bullet and indulge. There's usually a sale rack upstairs.

In the Pink (✉ 17–13 Winter St. ☎ 508/627 1209) harks back to the 1960s when Edgartown had one of the signature stores for Lilly Pulitzer's perky pink and powder blue summer wear, which was de rigueur at the Edgartown Yacht Club. Lilly Pulitzer bathing suits, shorts, slacks, skirts, blouses and handbags are all on sale here.

Fodor'sChoice   **Murray's** (✉ 27 N. Water St. ☎ 508/627–4131), a sister shop of Nan-
★   tucket's Murray's Toggery, sells not only the Nantucket red pants that fade to pink on washing, but men's and women's sports clothes of all sorts for all seasons.

Sundog (✉ 41 Lower Main St. ☎ 508/627–5254) is Edgartown's stylish men's sportswear and casual wear store that had its beginnings in Cambridge and still has a very Harvard Yard feel.

Very Vineyard (✉ 20 S. Summer St. ☎ 508/627–8468) carries easygoing, colorful batik clothes, designed with flowers and tendrils and leaves by landscaper Carol Lattmann.

JEWELRY **Claudia** (✉ 35 Winter St. ☎ 508/627–8306) brings you back to another era with its clever windows, antique display cases, and fabulous French fragrances. You'll find designer, vintage-looking, and fine gold and silver jewelry in a variety of price ranges.

Edgartown Jewelers Studio (✉ 261 Upper Main St. ☎ 508/627–6820) sells work from four island jewelers: enamel designer Lucinda Sheldon, goldsmith Richard Hamilton, resin and glass artist Karen English-Malin, and appraiser Kathrine Kittredge.

Optional Art (✉ 7 Winter St. ☎ 508/627–5373) carries fine jewelry in 18-karat gold and platinum, handcrafted by more than 25 top American artisans. You'll pay a lot, but the inventory here isn't typical of other island shops.

ODDS & ENDS **Abby-Ems** (✉ 270 Upper Main St. ☎ 508/627–5181) sells those collectibles you might find in the attic of a Vineyard summer house—old oil lamps and milk bottles, locks and pulleys, canning jars, chenille bedspreads, and old Vineyard books.

The Golden Door (✉ 18 N. Summer St. ☎ 508/627–7740) opens into the exotic world of the Orient and is filled with gift items—from statuary and porcelain to paintings and jewelry—from China, Japan, Indonesia, New Guinea, and Thailand. An African collection is housed in the basement.

In the Woods (✉ 55 Main St. ☎ 508/627–8989) stocks nearly every type of wood in almost any guise. It's a great source for wooden salad bowls, birch-bark birdhouses, and wooden toys. Sharing space with it is an Edgartown branch of Bowl and Board.

Lamplighter Corner (✉ 89 Pease's Point Way S. ☎ 508/627–4656) has artisans making brass and copper lanterns, but also sells 18th- and 19th-century American furniture.

Once in a Blue Moon (✉ 22 Winter St. ☎ 508/627–9177) carries high-quality contemporary ceramics, textiles, turned wood, lamps and mirrors, small paintings, and furniture. The hand-painted silk wall hangings by Kathy Schorr are worth the visit. Be sure to visit their new showroom next door that sells an outstanding collection of contemporary jewelry made from nontraditional materials with unique designs.

Past & Presents (✉ 37 Main St. ☎ 508/627–6686) sells gift items and decorative accessories—including Staffordshire china, Majolica, silver, and reproduction English furniture—in two shops, one on each side of Main Street.

For those who like to keep busy, even on vacation, **Vineyard Stitches** (✉ 9 Winter St. ☎ 508/627–8212) is the perfect place to pick up an island-theme needlepoint kit. It stocks distinctive hand-painted canvases and other needlepoint supplies. Look for island lighthouse kits.

Sports & the Outdoors

BEACHES **Bend-in-the-Road Beach** (⊠ Beach Rd.), Edgartown's town beach, is a protected area marked by floats adjacent to Joseph A. Sylvia State Beach. Backed by low, grassy dunes and wild roses, the beach has calm, shallow waters; some parking; and lifeguards. It is on the shuttle-bus and bike routes.

Lighthouse Beach is accessible from North Water Street or by continuing toward downtown Edgartown from Little Beach. The beach wraps around the Edgartown Lighthouse, a classic backdrop for wedding pictures. Though you will have no privacy, as many strollers pass along here, it commands a great view of all of Edgartown Harbor.

Little Beach (⊠ end of Fuller St.) is a little-known beach that looks like a crooked pinkie that points into Eel Pond, a great place for bird-watching (be careful of the fenced-off piping plover breeding grounds in the dunes). From here you can look across and see the lighthouse at Cape Poge, at the northern tip of Chappaquiddick. This is a good beach for quiet sunbathing and shallow water wading. There's limited parking along Fuller Street. From Pease's Point Way, turn right onto Morse Street, then left onto Fuller.

South Beach (⊠ Katama Rd.), also called Katama Beach, is the island's largest and most popular. A 3-mi ribbon of sand on the Atlantic, it sustains strong surf and occasional dangerous riptides, so check with the lifeguards before swimming. Also check the weather conditions, as fog can quickly turn a glorious blue-sky morning here into what seems like an afternoon in London. There is limited parking.

BIKING Several bike paths lace through the Edgartown area, including a path to Oak Bluffs that has a spectacular view of Sengekontacket Pond on one side and Nantucket Sound on the other.

Edgartown Bicycles (⊠ Upper Main St. ☎ 508/627–9008) provides a full array of rentals and repairs.

R. W. Cutler Bike (⊠ 1 Main St. ☎ 508/627–4052) rents and repairs all types of bicycles.

Wheelhappy (⊠ 8 S. Water St. ☎ 508/627–5928) rents bicycles and will deliver them to you.

FISHING The annual **Martha's Vineyard Striped Bass & Bluefish Derby** (✉ Box 2101, Edgartown 02539 ☎ 508/693–0728), from mid-September to mid-October, presents daily, weekly, and derby prizes for striped bass, bluefish, bonito, and false albacore catches, from boat or shore. The derby is a real Vineyard tradition, cause for loyal devotion among locals who drop everything to cast their lines at all hours of day and night in search of that prizewinning whopper. Avid fisherfolk come from all over the rest of the country, too, to cast their fates to the fishing gods.

Big Eye Charters (☎ 508/627–3649) leads fishing charters that leave from Edgartown Harbor.

Coop's Bait and Tackle (⊠ 147 W. Tisbury Rd. ☎ 508/627–3909) sells accessories and bait, rents fishing gear, books fishing charters and keeps a current listing of fishing regulations.

Larry's Tackle Shop (⊠ 141 Main St. ☎ 508/627–5088) rents gear and sells accessories and bait, books fishing charters and has a copy of the fishing regulations.

HEALTH & **Triangle Fitness** (⊠ Post Office Square at the Triangle ☎ 508/627–
FITNESS CLUB 3393) has stair climbers, stationary bikes, elliptical cross-trainers, and Body Master weight-lifting equipment; personal trainers are available. There are also classes in aerobics, spinning, yoga, conditioning, step, karate, and kickboxing. Daily, weekly, monthly, and yearly memberships are available.

RECREATION **Edgartown Recreation Area** (⊠ Robinson Rd. ☎ 508/627–4154) has five
AREAS tennis courts, a basketball court, a softball field, a roller hockey court, a picnic area, and playground equipment. Activities (published in local papers) include tennis round-robins, softball and basketball games, arts and crafts, and rainy-day events.

Chappaquiddick Island

㉕ *6 mi southeast of Oak Bluffs, across the bay from Edgartown.*

A sparsely populated islet with a great number of nature preserves, Chappaquiddick Island makes for a pleasant day trip or bike ride on a sunny day. If you are interested in covering a lot of it, cycling is the best way to go. The island is actually connected to the Vineyard by a long sand spit from South Beach in Katama—a spectacular 2¾-mi walk if you have the energy. If not, the On-Time ferry (⇨ Martha's Vineyard A to Z) makes the short trip from Edgartown across from 7 AM to midnight in season. The ferry departs every five minutes or so but posts no schedule, thereby earning its name—technically, it cannot be late.

The Land Bank's 226-acre **Three Ponds Preserve** (⊠ off Chappaquiddick Rd.) is a popular, scenic picnicking spot. Mown grasses surround a serpentine pond with an island in its center and a woodland backdrop behind—a truly lovely setting. Across the road are fields and woods and another pond.

★ The Trustees of Reservations' 14-acre **Mytoi** preserve is a quiet, Japanese-inspired garden with a creek-fed pool, spanned by a bridge and rimmed with Japanese maples, azaleas, bamboo, and irises. The garden was created in 1958 by a private citizen. Restroom facilities are available. ⊠ *Dike Rd., ⅕ mi from intersection with Chappaquiddick Rd.* ☎ *508/693–7662* ☞ *Free* ☉ *Daily sunrise–sunset.*

At the end of Dike Road is **Dike Bridge,** infamous as the scene of the 1969 accident in which a young woman died in a car driven by Ted Kennedy. The rickety bridge has been replaced, after having been dismantled in 1991, but for ecological reasons, vehicle access over it is limited. There is a ranger station on the bridge that is manned June to September. The

HOOKED ON THE DERBY

F THERE'S A SPIRITUAL PILGRIMAGE for fishermen, it's probably the annual **Martha's Vineyard Striped Bass & Bluefish Derby**. Since its start in 1946, it has evoked near religious reaction among those to whom hooking a striper, bluefish, bonito, or false albacore ranks right up there with seeing a burning bush.

Why? "First, Martha's Vineyard is a beautiful place to fish," says Derby board member and Martha's Vineyard Times fishing columnist Nelson Sigelman. "Second, with so many categories, everyone has an opportunity to win. And it's one of the largest shore tournaments in the country."

The categories are for both boat and shore fishing, either all-tackle or fly-fishing, with daily and overall prizes for winners—men, women, senior citizens, and juniors. And this isn't just for the lifelong fanatics. There's even a free kid's miniderby, a Saturday morning contest held in September at the steamship wharf in Oak Bluffs.

But the real magic is not in connecting with a big one. It's connecting with a fellow fisher that brings the addicts back every year.

"There you are at 2 AM out on Cape Poge bar having a conversation with someone you never met before, and then meeting that same person year after year—same time, same place—until you become fast friends," says Sigelman.

No wonder the event, held from mid-September to mid-October, attracts some 2,000 entrants from around the world who compete for cash and other prizes, including the grand prize of a Boston Whaler. A portion of the proceeds from derby entry fees goes to support scholastic scholarships for island students.

And while no true fisherman will reveal his or her favorite spot, in true fishing fashion they will all gladly tell you about the "one that got away"—the one that would have won them the derby grand prize.

Cape Poge Wildlife Refuge, which includes the spectacular **East Beach** and the **Cape Poge Light,** is across the bridge. You can only go to the top of the light by joining a 1½-hour, $20 Trustees of Reservations tour. ✉ *End of Dike Rd.* ☎ *508/627–3599* 🏷 *Walk-on $3 June–Sept., free rest of year* ☉ *Daily sunrise–sunset.*

The **Poucha Pond Reservation,** near the southeast corner of the island, encompasses 99 acres of varied environments. Its trails wander among shady pitch pine and oak forests and around a marshy pond on one-time farmland. One trail end has a great view of the pond, Dike Bridge, and the East Beach dunes in the distance. Bring binoculars for the birds—terns, various herons, gulls, plovers—and repellent for the mosquitoes. ⊠ *4 mi from Chappaquiddick ferry landing* ☎ *508/627–7141* ▣ *Free* ☉ *Daily sunrise–sunset.*

A conglomeration of habitats where you can swim, walk, fish, or just sit and enjoy the surroundings, the **Cape Poge Wildlife Refuge** (⊠ east end of Dike Rd., 3 mi from the Chappaquiddick ferry landing), on the easternmost shore of Chappaquiddick Island, is more than 6 square mi of wilderness. Its dunes, woods, cedar thickets, moors, salt marshes, ponds, tidal flats, and barrier beach serve as an important migration stopover and nesting area for numerous sea and shore birds. The best way to get to the refuge is as part of a naturalist-led **Jeep drive** (☎ 508/627–3599). You can also get there from Wasque Reservation, on the south shore of the island. You'll need a four-wheel-drive vehicle to do that, and to get to much of the acreage. The Trustees of Reservations requires an annual permit ($90–$110) for a four-wheel drive, available on-site or through Coop's Bait and Tackle (⇨ Sports & the Outdoors *in* Edgartown).

★   The 200-acre **Wasque Reservation** (pronounced *wayce*-kwee), mostly a vast beach, connects Chappaquiddick "Island" with the mainland of the Vineyard in Katama, closing off the south end of Katama Bay. You can fish, sunbathe, take the trail by Swan Pond, walk to the island's southeasternmost tip at Wasque Point, or dip into the surf—with caution, due to strong currents. Wasque Beach is accessed by a flat boardwalk with benches overlooking the west end of Swan Pond. It's a pretty walk skirting the pond, with ocean views on one side and poles for osprey nests on the other. Atop a bluff is a pine-shaded picnic grove with a spectacular, practically 180-degree panorama. Below, Swan Pond teems with bird life, including the requisite swans, in the surrounding marsh and beach grasses. Beyond that lie beach, sky, and boat-dotted sea. From the grove, a long boardwalk leads down amid the grasses to Wasque Point, a prime surf-casting spot for bluefish and stripers. Restrooms and drinking water are available. ⊠ *At east end of Wasque Rd., 5 mi from Chappaquiddick ferry landing* ☎ *508/627–7260* ▣ *Cars $3, plus $3 per adult, late May–mid-Sept.; free rest of yr* ☉ *Property 24 hrs. Gatehouse late May–mid-Oct., daily 9–5.*

Sports & the Outdoors

BEACHES   **East Beach,** one of the area's best beaches, is accessible by car from Chappaquiddick Road to Dyke Road, or by boat or Jeep from the Wasque Reservation. It has heavy surf, good bird-watching, and relative isolation in a lovely setting. There is a $3 fee to enter the beach.

Wasque Beach, at the Wasque Reservation, is an uncrowded ½-mi sandy beach with sometimes strong surf and currents, a parking lot, and rest rooms.

UP-ISLAND

Much of what makes the Vineyard special is found in its rural reaches, in the agricultural heart of the island and the largely undeveloped lands south and west of the Vineyard Haven–to–Edgartown line known as Up-Island. Country roads meander through woods and tranquil farmland, and dirt side roads lead past crystalline ponds, abandoned cranberry bogs, and conservation lands. In Chilmark, West Tisbury, and Aquinnah, nature lovers, writers, artists, and others have established close, ongoing summer communities. In winter, the isolation and bitter winds generally send even year-round Vineyarders from their Up-Island homes to places in the cozier Down-Island towns.

West Tisbury

 6½ mi southwest of Vineyard Haven, 12 mi northeast of Aquinnah.

Founded in the 1670s by settlers from Edgartown, among them the son of Myles Standish and the son-in-law of the *Mayflower* Aldens, West Tisbury was known for its first 200 Westernized years simply as Tisbury. Most important among the settlement's advantages over Down-Island outposts was a strong-flowing stream that ran into a pond, creating a perfect mill site—a rarity on the Vineyard. Farming, especially sheep farming, became Tisbury's mainstay.

West Tisbury retains its rural appeal and maintains its agricultural tradition at several active horse and produce farms. The town center looks very much the small New England village, complete with a white, steepled church. Half the 5,146-acre Manuel F. Correllus State Forest lies within the town limits.

The **West Tisbury Farmers' Market**—Massachusetts' largest—is held Wednesday and Saturday in summer at the 1859 **Old Agricultural Hall**, near the town hall. The colorful stands overflow with fresh produce, most of it organic—a refreshing return to life before fluorescent-lit, impersonal supermarkets. ⊠ *South Rd.* ☎ *508/693–9549.*

Built in 1996, the **New Ag Hall,** about a mile from the Old Agricultural Hall, is the setting for various shows, lectures, dances, and potluck dinners. A yearly county fair—including a woodsman contest, dog show, games, baked goods and jams for sale, and, of course, livestock- and produce-judging—is held here in late August. ⊠ *35 Panhandle Rd.* ☎ *508/693–9549.*

A rich and expansive collection of flora and serene walking trails are the attractions of the **Polly Hill Arboretum.** A horticulturist and part-time Vineyard resident, Polly Hill, now in her 90s, has over the years tended some 2,000 species of plants and developed nearly 100 species herself on her old sheep farm in West Tisbury. On site are azaleas, tree peonies, dogwoods, hollies, lilacs, magnolias, and more. Hill raised them from seeds without the use of a greenhouse, and her patience is the inspiration of the arboretum. Now run as a nonprofit center, the arboretum also runs guided tours, a lecture series, and a visitor center and gift shop.

✉ *809 State Rd.* ☎ *508/693–9426* 💵 *$5* 🕑 *Late May–mid-Oct.,
Thurs.–Tues. 7–7; mid-Oct.–late May, Thurs.–Tues. sunrise–sunset.*

An unusual sight awaits at the **Field Gallery,** where the late Tom Maley's
ponderous white sculptures, such as a colonial horse and rider or a whimsical piper, are displayed on a wide lawn. Inside there are changing summer exhibitions of island artists' work, which is for sale. ✉ *State Rd.*
☎ *508/693–5595.*

Music Street, named for the numerous parlor pianos bought with the whaling money of successful sea captains, is lined with the oldest houses in
West Tisbury.

> need a
> break?

Step back in time with a visit to **Alley's General Store** (✉ State Rd.
☎ 508/693–0088), the heart of town since 1858. Alley's sells a truly
general variety of goods: everything from hammers and housewares
and dill pickles to sweet muffins and all those great things you find
only in a country store. There's even a post office inside. Behind the
parking lot, Back Alley's serves tasty sandwiches and pastries to go
year-round.

The **Mill Pond** is a lovely spot graced with swans—at the right time of
year you might see a cygnet with the swan couple. The small building
nearest the pond has been a grammar school, an icehouse, and a police
station. The mill stands across the road. Originally a gristmill, it opened
in 1847 to manufacture island wool for pea coats, which whalers wore.
The Martha's Vineyard Garden Club uses the building now. The pond
is just around the corner from the town center on the way toward
Edgartown. ✉ *Edgartown–West Tisbury Rd.*

㉗ Its limbs twisting into the sky and along the ground, the **Old Oak Tree**
stands near the intersection of State and North roads. This massive, much-
loved member of the *quercus* family is thought to be about 150 years
old, and it's a perennial subject for nature photographers.

The **Martha's Vineyard Glassworks** gives you a chance to watch glass being
blown—a fascinating process—by glassmakers who have pieces displayed
in Boston's Museum of Fine Arts. Their work is also for sale. ✉ *529
State Rd., North Tisbury* ☎ *508/693–6026.*

West Tisbury has a wealth of conservation areas, each of them unique.
A paradise for bird-watchers, **Sepiessa Point Reservation,** a Land Bank–Nature Conservancy property, consists of 164 acres on splendid Tisbury
Great Pond, with expansive pond and ocean views, walking trails around
coves and saltwater marshes, bird-watching, horse trails, swimming, and
a boat launch. On the pond beach, watch out for razor-sharp oyster shells.
Beaches across the pond along the ocean are privately owned. ✉ *New
La., which becomes Tiah's Cove Rd., off W. Tisbury Rd.* ☎ *508/627–
7141* 💵 *Free* 🕑 *Daily sunrise–sunset.*

Long Point, a 633-acre Trustees of Reservations preserve with an open
area of grassland and heath, provides a lovely walk with the promise
of a refreshing swim at its end. The area is bounded on the east by

freshwater Homer's Pond, on the west by saltwater West Tisbury Great Pond, and on the south by fantastic, mile-long South Beach on the Atlantic Ocean. Tisbury Great Pond and Long Cove Pond, a sandy freshwater swimming pond, are ideal spots for bird-watchers. Drinking water and a restroom facility are available. Arrive early on summer days if you're coming by car, since the lot fills quickly. The **Trustees of Reservations** (☎ 508/693–7392) organizes informative and fun two-hour canoe trips through the reserve. Call ahead to reserve a spot on one of the two trips per day (Friday–Tuesday). ⊹ *Mid-June–mid-Sept., turn left onto unmarked dirt road (Waldron's Bottom Rd., look for mailboxes)* 3⁄10 *mi west of airport on Edgartown–West Tisbury Rd.; at end, follow signs to Long Point parking lot. Mid-Sept.–mid-June, follow unpaved Deep Bottom Rd. (1 mi west of airport) 2 mi to lot* ☎ *508/693–7392* ✉ *Mid-June–mid-Sept., $7 per vehicle, $3 per adult; free rest of yr* ☉ *Daily 9–6.*

★ ㉘ A rather unique island undertaking, the **Winery at Chicama Vineyards** is the fruit of the Mathiesen family's labors. From 3 acres of trees and rocks, George—a broadcaster from San Francisco—his wife, Cathy, and their six children have built a fine vineyard. They started in 1971 with 18,000 vinifera vines, and today the winery produces nearly 100,000 bottles a year from chardonnay, cabernet, and other European grapes. Chenin blanc, merlot, and a cranberry dessert wine are among their 10 or more tasty varieties. A shop selling their wine, along with herbed vinegars, mustards, jellies, and other foods prepared on the premises, is open year-round. A Christmas shop with glassware, gift baskets, wreaths, and wine-related items is open mid-November through New Year's Eve. ✉ *Stoney Hill Rd.* ☎ *508/693–0309* ✉ *Free tours and tastings* ☉ *Late May–mid-Oct., Mon.–Sat. 11–5, Sun. 1–5; call for off-season hrs and tastings.*

In season you can pick your own strawberries, raspberries, and flowers at **Thimble Farm,** where you can also buy preboxed fruit if you're not feeling quite so agrarian. The farm also sells cut flowers, melons, pumpkins, hydroponic tomatoes, and other produce. ✉ *Stoney Hill Rd.* ☎ *508/693–6396* ☉ *June–early Oct., Tues.–Sun. 10–5.*

㉙ Just outside the center of Vineyard Haven, on the way to West Tisbury, the **Tashmoo Overlook** surveys a public meadow leading down to Lake Tashmoo and Vineyard Sound beyond. Across the lane from the meadow is the amphitheater where the Vineyard Playhouse holds summer productions. ✉ *State Rd. and Spring St.*

One of the rare meadows open for hiking on the island, the 83-acre **Tisbury Meadow Preserve** isn't being farmed but is mowed to keep it from reverting to woodland. An old farmstead sits on the property, and the back acres are wooded except for an 18th-century cart path. You can walk Tisbury Meadow in less than an hour or combine it with two other areas, the Wompesket and Ripley's Fields preserves across State Road, for a longer hike. ✉ *Trailhead on east side of State Rd., ½ mi south of Tashmoo Overlook.*

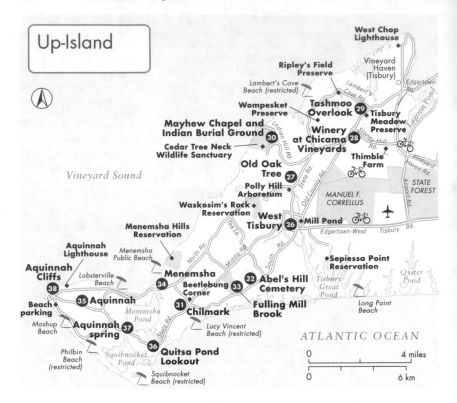

Up-Island

Ripley's Field Preserve gives an idea of what the island must have looked like 200 years ago. The 56-acre preserve spreads over undulating, glacier-formed meadows and woodland. A windmill and wildflowers are pleasant attractions. The preserve connects via old cart paths to Tisbury Meadow and Wompesket preserves in North Tisbury. A parking area and bike rack are on the left. ⊠ *John Hoft Rd., off north end of Lambert's Cove Rd., ⅔ mi from State Rd.*

Bordering part of Merry Farm, **Wompesket Preserve** includes an interesting wet meadow and ponds that are good for birding. The walk to the 18-acre area overlooks the farm and the Atlantic in the distance. To get here, follow marked dirt roads from Ripley's Field or Tisbury Meadow Preserve. ⊠ *Red Coat Hill Rd.*

③⓪ Deep in the woods off a dirt road, the **Mayhew Chapel and Indian Burial Ground** are suffused with history. The tiny chapel, built in 1829 to replace an earlier one, and a memorial plaque are dedicated to the pastor Thomas Mayhew, Jr., leader of the original colonists who landed at Edgartown in 1642. Mayhew was noted for his fair dealings with the local Wampanoags. Within a few years, he had converted a number of them to Christianity. Called Praying Indians, they established a community here called Christiantown.

An overgrown wildflower garden grows near the chapel. Beyond the boulder with the plaque are rough-hewn stones marking Native American grave mounds—the dead are not named, for fear of calling down evil spirits. Behind the chapel is the beginning of the Christiantown Woods loop trail, which leads to a lookout tower. You'll find a map at the head of the trail. ⊠ *Off Indian Hill Rd., off State Rd.*

Cedar Tree Neck Wildlife Sanctuary, 250 hilly acres of unspoiled West Tisbury woods managed by the Sheriff's Meadow Foundation, consists of varied environments, among them a sphagnum bog and a pond. The sanctuary has interesting flora, including bayberry and swamp azalea bushes, tupelo, sassafras, and pygmy beech trees. Wooded trails lead to a stony but secluded North Shore beach (swimming, picnicking, and fishing prohibited), and from the summit of a headland are views of Aquinnah and the Elizabeth Islands. To get here, follow Indian Hill Road off State Road for 2 mi, and then turn right 1 mi on Obed Daggett Road, an occasionally steep, rocky dirt road to the parking lot. ⊠ *Indian Hill Rd.* ☎ *508/693–5207* ⊕ *Free* ⊗ *Daily 8:30–5:30.*

★ At the center of the island, the **Manuel F. Correllus State Forest** is a 5,000-acre pine and scrub-oak forest crisscrossed with hiking trails and circled by a paved but rough bike trail (mopeds are prohibited). There's a 2-mi nature trail, a 2-mi par fitness course, and horse trails. The West Tisbury side of the state forest joins with an equally large Edgartown parcel to virtually surround the airport. ⊠ *Headquarters on Barnes Rd. by airport* ☎ *508/693–2540* ⊕ *Free* ⊗ *Daily sunrise–sunset.*

A memorial to Thomas Mayhew, Jr., called **Place on the Wayside,** stands along Edgartown–West Tisbury Road, just east of the airport entrance on the south side of the road. A plaque identifies the spot where Mayhew had his "last worship and interview with them the Wampanoags before embarking for England" in 1657, never to return: the ship was lost at sea. Wampanoags passing this spot would leave a stone in Mayhew's memory, and the stones were later cemented together to form the memorial.

Where to Stay & Eat

$$$–$$$$ ✕ **Bittersweet.** A pronounced Mediterranean flavor enhances the progressive American cuisine that chef Job Yacubian creates here. Rosemary, olives, and celery hearts are part of the braised lamb shank, and the pan-roasted skate wing is flavored with kumquats and almonds, cauliflower, and capers. Despite its exciting menu, this place can be a bit noisy. To escape the din, ask for a seat on the porch. ⊠ *State Rd.* ☎ *508/696–3966* ⚭ *Reservations essential* ⬤ *BYOB* ▭ *MC, V.*

$–$$ ✕⬚ **Lambert's Cove Country Inn.** A narrow road winds through pine woods and beside creeper-covered stone walls to this secluded inn surrounded by gardens and old stone walls. Rooms in the rambling 1790 farmhouse have light floral wallpapers and a sunny, country feel. Those in outbuildings have screened porches or decks. Except for a brief winter vacation, the inn is open year-round. The soft candlelight and excellent contemporary cuisine make the restaurant ($$$–$$$$; reservations essential; BYOB) a destination for a special occasion. The fare is classic

New England with an original spin. Especially good is the fresh cod with littleneck clams. ⊠ *Off Lambert's Cove Rd., West Tisbury* ⌖ *R.R. 1, Box 422, Vineyard Haven 02568* ☎ *508/693–2298* 🖷 *508/693–7890* ⊕ *www.lambertscoveinn.com* ↘ *15 rooms* ⚙ *Restaurant, tennis court; no room phones, no room TVs* ⊟ *AE, MC, V* ⦿ *BP.*

¢–$ ▦ **Bayberry Bed and Breakfast.** The farmhouse-style home in the bucolic Up-Island countryside sits on land once owned by Thomas Mayhew, the founder of the island. The rooms are decorated in a country Victorian style, with lots of blue highlights in the rugs, trim, and wallpapers. Two rooms on the first floor share a bath, and the three upstairs rooms have private or semiprivate (designated for the room, but in the hall) baths. The common sitting room has comfy chairs, a fireplace, and a piano, but the heart of the inn is the big kitchen, which has a hearth and glass doors opening to a cherry tree–shaded brick patio. Don't miss owner Rosalie Powell's famous breakfast Dreamboat, a boat-shape pastry filled with fresh fruit, yogurt, honey, and granola. ⊠ *49 Old Courthouse Rd.* ⌖ *Box 654, 02575* ☎ *508/693–1984 or 800/693–9960* ⊕ *www.vineyard.net/biz/bayberry* ↘ *5 rooms, 3 with bath* ⚙ *No kids under 12, no smoking* ⊟ *MC, V* ⦿ *BP.*

¢–$ ▦ **The Old Parsonage Bed & Breakfast.** Miles Standish's son, Josiah, built this house in 1668, and in 1760 it was purchased to become the Congregational Church parsonage. Later, the property became a farm, and sheep still feed on the sloping, pond-front acreage. Now a bed-and-breakfast, its spacious rooms are furnished with Victorian antiques, with floors brightened by braided rugs. ⌖ *P.O. Box 3114, 02575* ☎ *508/696–7745* 🖷 *508-696-6712* ↘ *4 rooms, 2 with bath* ⚙ *No kids under 12; no smoking* ⊟ *AE, MC, V* ⦿ *CP.*

¢ ▦ **Martha's Vineyard International Hostel.** The only budget, roof-over-your-head alternative in season, this hostel is one of the country's best. The large, common kitchen is outfitted with multiple refrigerators and stoves (barbecue grills are available, too), the common room has a fireplace and plenty of books, and you'll catch wind of local events on the bulletin board. Morning chores are required in summer. The hostel runs summer programs on island history, as well as nature tours. It is near a bike path and is 2 mi from the airport and about 3 mi from the nearest beach. Buses stop out front. ⊠ *Edgartown–West Tisbury Rd.* ⌖ *Box 158, 02575* ☎ *508/693–2665* ⊕ *www.usahostels.org* ↘ *78 dorm-style beds* ⚙ *Volleyball, laundry facilities* ⊟ *MC, V* ⊗ *Closed mid-Oct.–mid-April.*

Nightlife & the Arts

M.V. Wellness Center (⊠ 489 State Rd. ☎ 508/696–0644) holds classes year-round in dance, yoga, and healthy cooking.

West Tisbury Library (⊠ State Rd. at West Tisbury Center ☎ 508/693–3366) shows vintage, classic, and children's movies every Monday night, year-round in its Music Street Annex (with more family fare in the summer), at 7. Check the local papers or call for a schedule.

WIMP (⊠ Grange Hall, State Rd. ☎ 508/939–9368) is the island's not-to-be-missed premier comedy improvisation troupe. The group performs every Wednesday night at 8 PM. The teen troupe, IMPers, performs every Monday night at 8 PM.

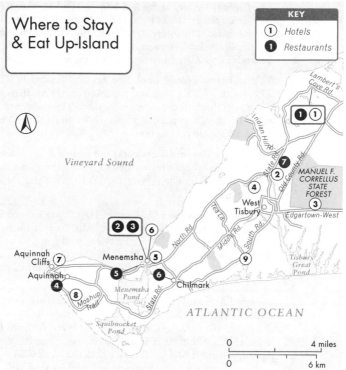

Where to Stay
& Eat Up-Island

Shopping

ANTIQUES **Forget-Me-Not Antiques** (✉ State Rd. ☎ 508/693–1788) sells European pine furniture, including Hungarian country hutches and cupboards and tables.

Hull Antiques (✉ Edgartown Rd. ☎ 508/693–5713) specializes in decoys, sterling, and folk art. What you won't find here are reproductions and fussy gifts. When trying to find it, look for sign and a ladder-back chair hanging from a tree.

ART **Chilmark Pottery** (✉ Fieldview La., off State Rd. ☎ 508/693–6476) is a workshop and gallery selling hand-formed stoneware, porcelain, and raku-ware made on the island.

Craven Gallery (✉ 459 State Rd. ☎ 508/693–3535) showcases contemporary paintings (including work by the late Thomas Hart Benton), drawings, photography, and sculpture.

Davis House (✉ State Rd. ☎ 508/693–4691) exhibits oil landscapes of the Vineyard by West Tisbury artist Allen Whiting.

The **Field Gallery and Sculpture Garden** (✉ State Rd. ☎ 508/693–5595) showcases local artists. Tom Maley's whimsical sculptures grace the garden, and Heather Goff's tile murals are a treat.

The **Granary Gallery at the Red Barn** (⊠ Old County Rd. ☎ 508/693–0455) exhibits artworks by island and international artists and displays Early American furniture. Don't miss the back room, where black-and-white photos by Margaret Bourke White, Norman Bergsma, Arthur Rickerby, and Alfred Eisenstaedt line the walls.

To find **Hermine Merel Smith Fine Art** (⊠ Edgartown Rd. ☎ 508/693–7719) watch for the sign and the mounds of impatiens at the entrance. Then step through the beautiful, arched glass doors to the cool, quiet interior, where fine paintings and works on paper by Vineyard and national artists are on display.

At **Martha's Vineyard Glassworks** (⊠ State Rd. ☎ 508/693–6026) you can pick out a beautiful art-glass gift and then watch the glassblowers at their craft. The service here is friendly and the staff is knowledgeable.

Vineyard Artisans Fairs (⊠ Grange Hall, State Rd. ☎ 508/693–8989) bring shoppers into direct contact with Vineyard artists and artisans whose work is jury-selected. Fairs are held from 10 to 2 on Sunday in June and September and Sunday and Thursday in July and August. Look for the island seascapes by Millie Briggs, and limited-edition prints by Janet Woodcock.

Vineyard Artisans Festivals (☎ 508/693–8989) are special juried shows held at either the Grange Hall (State Road) or the Agricultural Hall (35 Panhandle Road). They include the Vineyard Artisans Labor Day Festival, Holiday Festival at Thanksgiving time, and the Vineyard Artisans Spring Festival at Memorial Day. Check the local papers or call the phone number listed above for times, dates, and locations.

FOOD **Cronig's Market** (⊠ 489 State Rd. ☎ 508/693–2234) is a smaller version of the Down-Island store.

West Tisbury Farmers' Market (⊠ State Rd. ☎ 508/693–9549)—with booths selling fresh flowers, plants, fruits and vegetables, honey, and homemade baked goods and jams—is held at the Grange Hall mid-June to mid-October, Saturday 9–noon and Wednesday 2:30–5:30.

ODDS & ENDS **Alley's General Store** (⊠ State Rd. ☎ 508/693–0088), in business since 1858, deals in everything from fresh fruit and preserves to shoelaces, suntan lotions, and video rentals. There's even a post office.

North Tisbury (⊠ State Rd., West Tisbury) is a small shopping district that includes **Craven Gallery** (☎ 508/693–3535), a little shop that carries original artwork by local and nationally known artists; **Conroy Apothecary** (☎ 508/693–7070), with its harried but cheerful pharmacists and shelves full of suntan lotions, greeting cards, and other necessities; **Biga Bakery & Deli** (☎ 508/693–6924), a great place to pick up fresh bread, gooey pastries, and sandwiches (not to mention its breakfast sandwich of ham, sausage, spinach, onions and hot sauce); and **Humphrey's Vineyard Food Shop** (☎ 508/693–1879), known for its turkey gobbler bursting with fresh roasted turkey, cranberry sauce, and stuffing, as well fresh breads and pastries.

MARTHA'S VINEYARD TRIVIA

THE YEAR-ROUND POPULATION of the island is 14,901. On any given day in summer, the population increases fivefold, to an estimated 75,000.

Some four decades after the island was charted in 1602, Bay Colony businessman Thomas Mayhew struck a deal with the Crown and purchased Martha's Vineyard, as well as Nantucket and the Elizabeth Islands, for £40.

Carly Simon and partners established the island's premier music venue, Hot Tin Roof, in 1979.

Jeanne and Hugh Taylor, the latter the brother of recording star James Taylor, operate the Outermost Inn, by the lighthouse in Aquinnah.

Total shoreline: 126 mi. Total land area: 100 square mi.

Martha's Vineyard was formed more than 20,000 years ago as great sheets of ice, as thick as 2 mi, descended from the frigid northern climes into what is now New England, pushing great chunks of earth and rock before them. When the glaciers melted and receded, the island, as well as Nantucket and Cape Cod, remained in their wake.

When residents say they are going "Up-Island," they mean they're heading to the western areas of Aquinnah, Chilmark, Menemsha, and West Tisbury. The designation is based on nautical terminology, where heading west means going "up" in longitude. "Down-Island" refers to Vineyard Haven, Oak Bluffs, and Edgartown.

During the height of the 19th-century whaling era, it was considered good luck to have an Aquinnah Wampanoag on board. The Wampanoags were renowned as sailors and harpooners. Town residents voted to change the name of Gay Head to Aquinnah in 1997, and the official change was signed into law on May 7, 1998.

The North American continent's last heath hen, an eastern prairie chicken, died in a forest fire on Martha's Vineyard in 1932. A monument to it stands in the State Forest just off the West Tisbury-Edgartown Road.

West Tisbury resident, farmer, and sailor Joshua Slocum became the first man to sail solo around the world. He set out in 1895 in his 36-foot sloop and returned three years later. Ten years later he was lost at sea.

Despite the fact that Great Harbour was renamed Edgartown after the young son of the Duke of York, the unfortunate three-year-old Edgar died one month before the name became official.

Sports & the Outdoors

BEACHES To reach **Cedar Tree Neck Wildlife Sanctuary,** take Indian Hill Road to Obed Daggett Road, a dirt road that leads to the trailhead of this Sheriff's Meadow Foundation conservation area. From the ample parking area, the trailhead leads through an enchanted forest down a hill, across a tiny footbridge, and over dunes to a long beach with giant boulders. This is not a swimming beach, but it invites long, contemplative walks.

Lambert's Cove Beach (✉ Lambert's Cove Rd.), one of the island's prettiest, has fine sand and clear water. The Vineyard Sound–side beach has calm waters good for children and views of the Elizabeth Islands. In season it is restricted to residents and those staying in West Tisbury.

Long Point, a Trustees of Reservations preserve, has a beautiful beach on the Atlantic, as well as freshwater and saltwater ponds for swimming, including the brackish Tisbury Great Pond. Restrooms are available.

Sepiessa Point Reservation (✉ off Tiah's Cove Rd.) is a 164-acre area of the Land Bank Commission. A long walk along Tiah's Cove leads to a beach, at the southerly point, alongside Tisbury Great Pond. Across the pond you can see the ocean. The very narrow beach is delightful, though not for laying out a towel and sunbathing. Those with canoes or kayaks can put in at the trailhead and paddle across the pond to a barrier beach for picnicking and swimming. There's parking for only a few cars at the trailhead.

Uncle Seth's Pond is a warm freshwater pond on Lambert's Cove Road, with a small beach right off the road. Seth's is very popular with families—toddlers enjoy frolicking in the shallow waters along the shore—as well as with the lap swimmers crisscrossing the pond. Parking is very limited.

HORSEBACK
RIDING

Arrowhead Farm (✉ Indian Hill Rd. ☎ 508/693–8831) has riding lessons for adults and children year-round, as well as children's summer horsemanship programs. The farm has an indoor ring and leases horses and has trail rides.

Crow Hollow Farm (✉ Tiah's Cove Rd. ☎ 508/696–4554) has trail rides for experienced riders only, plus lessons and clinics.

Manuel F. Corellus State Forest (✉ access off Barnes Rd., Old County Rd., and Edgartown–West Tisbury Rd.) is laced with horse trails open to the public, but it has no stables.

Pond View Farm (✉ off New Lane ☎ 508/693–2949) holds a summer camp for children 6 and up and gives riding lessons.

Red Pony Farm (✉ off Edgartown–West Tisbury Rd. ☎ 508/693–3788) conducts trail rides for experienced riders only and gives dressage clinics. A bed-and-breakfast package includes a room above the barn plus a weekend of riding and lessons for all levels.

TENNIS

Stop by to reserve hard-surface courts at the grammar school on Old County Road in West Tisbury. There is a small fee for using the courts, which are open year-round.

On rainy days you can head to the **Vineyard Tennis Center** (✉ 22 Airport Rd. ☎ 508/696–8000) at the entrance to the airport. For a fee you can play at the indoor courts until 9 PM. A fitness club at the tennis center has Precor EFX and Cybex circuit equipment, as well as free weights.

Chilmark

③① *5½ mi southwest of West Tisbury, 12 mi southwest of Vineyard Haven.*

A rural, unspoiled village with scenic ocean-view roads, rustic woodlands, and no crowds, Chilmark draws chic summer visitors and, hard on their heels, stratospheric real-estate prices. Lucy Vincent Beach (residents only in summer) here is perhaps the island's most beautiful. Laced with ribbons of rough roads and winding stone fences that once separated fields and pastures, Chilmark reminds visitors what the Vineyard was like in an earlier time, before developers took over.

Waskosim's Rock Reservation, bought by the Land Bank in 1990 from a developer who had planned to build 40 houses on it, comprises diverse habitats—rolling green hills, wetlands, oak and black-gum woods, and 1,500 feet of frontage on Mill Brook—as well as the ruins of an 18th-century homestead. Waskosim's Rock itself was deposited by the retreating glacier 10,000 years ago and is said to resemble the head of a breaching whale. It is one of the highest points on the Vineyard, situated on a ridge above the valley, from which there is a panoramic view of more than 1,000 acres of protected land. At the trailhead off North Road, a map outlines a 3-mi hike throughout the 166 acres. ⊠ *Parking areas on North Rd.* ☎ *508/627–7141* ☜ *Free* ☉ *Daily sunrise–sunset.*

③② **Abel's Hill Cemetery** provides an interesting look into the island's past. Longtime summer resident and writer Lillian Hellman, one of many who continued the Vineyard's tradition of liberal politics, is buried here, as is John Belushi, in an unmarked grave. A boulder, engraved with the comedian's name, sits near the entrance. A few steps away is a headstone sporting a skull and crossbones, with the notation "Here Lies the Body of John Belushi. I May Be Gone but Rock and Roll Lives On"; common knowledge is that it's a decoy placed to deter overzealous fans from finding the actual burial site. Visitors often leave, as tokens of remembrance, empty champagne bottles, cigarette butts, flowers, and notes. ⊠ *South Rd.*

Beetlebung Corner, a crossroads named for the tupelo, or black gum, trees that grow here, which were used to make wooden mallets and plugs for casks (called "beetles" and "bungs"), marks Chilmark's town center. Here are the town's public buildings, including the firehouse and the post office, as well as the **Chilmark Community Center** (☎ 508/645–9484), where events such as town meetings, auctions, children's activities, and chamber music concerts take place. In summer, a general store, a clothing boutique, a restaurant and breakfast café, a gallery, and a bank turn the little crossroads into a minimetropolis. ⊠ *Middle, State, South, and Menemsha Cross Rds.*

need a break? The **Chilmark Store** (⊠ 7 State Rd. ☎ 508/645–3655) serves up pizza, burgers, salads, and deli sandwiches—a solid take-out lunch spot. If you've bicycled into town, the wooden rockers on the porch may be just the place to take a break—or find a picnic spot of your own nearby to enjoy a fish burger or a slice of the pizza of the day. It's open from May to mid-October.

③ Jointly owned by the Land Bank and the town, **Fulling Mill Brook** (⊠ Middle or South Rd.) is a 50-acre conservation area. Its easy walking trail slopes gently down toward the lowlands along the brook, where there are boulders to sit and sun on, and a bike rack at the property's edge at South Road.

Where to Stay & Eat

$$$–$$$$ ✕ **At the Cornerway.** Jamaican chef Deon Thomas brings cuisine rich in Jamaican flavors to this American-style bistro. Braised goat shoulder with prunes and pearl onions is on the menu for the adventurous; duck, lamb, venison or garlic-crusted snapper for those with less exotic tastes. Whichever pleases your palate, make sure to finish with either the coconut bread pudding or chocolate rum cake. If you want to hear what your dinner companions have to say, ask for a corner seat away from the atrium. The acoustics are terrible in this barnlike structure that once hosted square dances. ⊠ *Beetlebung Corner* ☎ *508/645–9300* ▭ *AE, MC, V* ⍣ *BYOB.*

$$ ✕▥ **Inn at Blueberry Hill.** Exclusive and secluded, this cedar-shingle retreat and its 56 acres of former farmland put you in the heart of the rural Vineyard. The restaurant, Theo's, is relaxed and elegant, and the fresh, health-conscious food is thoughtfully prepared. A cold breakfast is included in the room rate, and a box lunch is available for a picnic on the beach (the inn runs a guest shuttle to Lucy Vincent and Squibnocket beaches). Guest rooms are sparsely but tastefully decorated with simple island-made furniture. Most rooms have glass doors that open onto terraces or private decks. There is a large parlor-library with a fireplace. Rooms can be combined to create two- or three-bedroom suites. ⊠ *74 North Rd., Chilmark 02535* ☎ *508/645–3322 or 800/356–3322* ⊟ *508/645–3799* ⊕ *www.blueberryinn.com* ↩ *25 rooms* ⌂ *Restaurant, tennis court, pool, gym, hot tub, massage, meeting room, airport shuttle; no kids under 12, no smoking* ▭ *AE, MC, V* ☉ *Closed Nov.–Apr.* ⍣⍥ *CP.*

Nightlife & the Arts

The **Chilmark Community Center** (⊠ Beetlebung Corner ☎ 508/645–9484) holds square dances, concerts, and other events for families throughout the summer. Watch for announcements in the papers.

Find the writer in you at **Chilmark Writing Workshop** (☎ 508/645–9085), a series of four morning classes held weekly during the summer. Lead by Nancy Slonim Aronie—a teaching fellow at Harvard University, author of "Writing from the Heart," and a former NPR commentator—the workshop is held in the sculpture garden of her Chilmark home (or in her studio if it rains) and provides a safe and nurturing atmosphere for self-expression. This is a very popular course for year-round islanders as well as visitors. It's best to reserve a spot in the spring for summer classes.

Martha's Vineyard Chamber Music Society (☎ 508/696–8055) performs 12 concerts in Chilmark and Edgartown in July and August and two in winter.

The **Yard** (⊠ off Middle Rd. ☎ 508/645–9662)—a colony for dancers and choreographers formed in 1973—gives several performances throughout the summer at its 100-seat barn theater in a wooded setting. Artists are selected each year from auditions held in New York. Dance classes are available to visitors.

Shopping

A shop at **Allen Farm** (⊠ South Rd. ☎ 508/645–9064) sells handwoven blankets and knitted items made from the farm's wool. Prices range from $165 for a simple sweater to $600 for something a bit more complicated.

Chilmark Chocolates (⊠ State Rd. ☎ 508/645–3013) sells superior chocolates and the world's finest butter crunch, which you can sometimes watch being made in the back room. Don't forget to pick up a catalog—mail orders are available except during warm months.

Chilmark Flea Market (⊠ Middle Rd. ☎ 508/645–9216), known affectionately as The Flea in the Meadow, sells antiques and collectibles from all over the island from June to Labor Day, Wednesday and Saturday 8:30–2.

Fielder & Fielder (⊠North Rd. ☎508/645–9666), housed in an outbuilding at The Captain Flanders House, sells mostly colorful, traditional Turkish pottery from Kutahya, old and new rugs from Turkey and the Caucasus, and super-thick Turkish towels and bathrobes from Bursa.

Sports & the Outdoors

BEACHES **Chilmark Pond Preserve** (⊠ off South Rd.), on the south side of the road about 3 mi from West Tisbury Center, is an 8-acre Land Bank property at the foot of Abel's Hill (look for the white post with the Land Bank signage). From a landing at the bottom of the driveway, you reach the north side of magnificent Chilmark Lower Pond. You can either plant yourself right there or, if you bring your own canoe, kayak, small rowboat, or inflatable raft, you can paddle a short distance across the pond to 200 feet of Land Bank–owned Atlantic Ocean beach. If you're not a Chilmark resident or Chilmark summer renter with a beach pass, this is the only public Atlantic Ocean beach access in town. There is parking for about 10 cars.

Fodor'sChoice **Lucy Vincent Beach** (⊠ off South Rd.), on the south shore, is one of the
★ island's most beautiful. The wide strand of fine sand is backed by high clay bluffs facing the Atlantic surf. Keep walking to the left (east, or Down-Island) to reach the unofficial nude beach. Walking to the right, toward the private Windy Gates beach, is restricted to those who own beachfront property here. All others are prohibited. There's great bodysurfing for all ages in these waters. In season, Lucy Vincent is restricted to town residents and visitors with passes. Off-season a stroll here is the perfect getaway. Parking is available.

A narrow beach that is part smooth rocks and pebbles, part fine sand, **Squibnocket Beach** (⊠ off South Rd.), on the south shore, provides an appealing boulder-strewn coastline and gentle waves. Surfers know this area for its good waves. Tide-pool lovers can study marine life close up. During the season, this beach is restricted to residents and visitors with passes.

FISHING   **Flashy Lady Charters** (⊠ Menemsha Harbor ☎ 508/645–2462) leads inshore charters twice a day, for trolling bass and blues. The only charter boat with the guarantee: No fish—no charge.

Galatea Charters (⊠ Charter Dock, Basin Rd., Menemsha Harbor ☎ 508/645–9238) leads fly-fishing and light-tackle fishing jaunts for bass, bluefish, bonito, and false albacore.

Menemsha Blues Charters (⊠ Basin Rd., Menemsha Harbor ☎ 508/645–3778) runs bass, bluefish, and bonita charters out of Menemsha.

North Shore Charters (⊠ Menemsha Harbor ☎ 508/645–2993) leads full- or half-day inshore charters for bass and blues and offshore charters for tuna and shark.

Sortie Charters (⊠ Charter Dock, Basin Rd., Menemsha Harbor ☎ 508/645–3015) leads inshore trolling excursions and jigging for bass and blues twice daily. You can also take a scenic trip for lunch and leisurely stroll around fabled Cuttyhunk Island.

Menemsha

★ ㉞ *1½ mi northwest of Chilmark, 3½ mi east of Aquinnah.*

A fishing village unspoiled by the "progress" of the past few decades, Menemsha is a jumble of weathered fishing shacks, fishing and pleasure boats, drying nets and lobster pots, and parents and kids pole-fishing from the jetty. Though the picturesque scene is not lost on myriad photographers and artists, this is very much a working village. The catch of the day, taken off boats returning to port, is sold at markets along Dutcher's Dock. Romantics bring picnic suppers to the public Menemsha Beach to catch perfect sunsets over the water. If you feel you've seen this town before, you probably have: it was used for location shots in the film *Jaws.*

Very different from most other island conservation areas, **Menemsha Hills Reservation,** a 210-acre Trustees of Reservations property, includes a mile of rocky shoreline and high sand bluffs along Vineyard Sound. Its hilly walking trails through scrub oak and heathland have interpretive signs at viewing points, and the 309-foot Prospect Hill, the island's highest, affords excellent views of the Elizabeth Islands and beyond. Call ahead about naturalist-led tours. ⊠ *Off North Rd., 1 mi east of Menemsha Cross Rd.* ☎ *508/693–7662* 🎫 *Free* ☉ *Daily sunrise–sunset.*

Where to Stay & Eat

$$$–$$$$ ✕ **Home Port.** A classic seafood-in-the-rough experience since the 1930s, this breezy seasonal island institution serves absolutely the freshest lobster around, plus steamers, scallops, and local fish. The knotty-pine walls and the fishing nets and other nautical wall hangings bring you back to a bygone era. Sailors from all around southern New England savor the chance to pull into Menemsha for a meal at this stalwart, where commoners often rub shoulders with celebs. You can also get your meal to

A PERFECT DAY FOR ROMANCE

ONE DAY ISN'T LONG ENOUGH for all of the activities couples can enjoy on the island, but here are a few good suggestions.

Start with a romantic breakfast. Enjoy straight-from-the-oven cinnamon coffee cake in the garden at the Edgartown Inn, where you'll feel the aura of the old whaling days. Linda Jean's in Oak Bluffs is the place to hold hands and people-watch while noshing on fruit-filled pancakes.

If you're on-island on a summer Saturday, drop by the Farmer's Market in West Tisbury. Stroll from table to table and purchase a lunch of island-made jams or salsas, a loaf of bread, some fresh carrots and other snacking vegetables, and a muffin or two for dessert. Or try the Vineyard Foodshop (better known as Humphrey's Bakery) on State Road in West Tisbury, a favorite among the locals.

Once you've assembled your lunch, head for the beach. Since romance is your goal, opt for the quiet, less-populated Long Point Beach off Edgartown–West Tisbury Road. Turn on to Waldron's Bottom Road and follow the signs. In July and August, get there early; the parking lot fills up fast. Parking is $9 a day and each adult costs an additional $3. Spend your day relaxing in the sun and watching the osprey dive for fish or viewing little brown crabs scooting through the water near shore. The beach closes at 5 PM, which gives you just enough time to shower, pick up a bottle of wine, and head for Menemsha. Buy carry-out lobster dinners from the back door of the popular Home Port Restaurant. Take them to the beach in Menemsha and settle onto a big rock or throw out a blanket on the sand. There's nothing more romantic than one of Menemsha's famous sunsets to complete your day. But be warned, the parking lot fills fast there too.

go and enjoy it on the lawn or by the dock overlooking the harbor. ⊠ *At end of North Rd.* ☎ *508/645–2679* ⚠ *Reservations essential* ⊟ *MC, V* BYOB ⊘ *Closed mid-Oct.–mid-Apr. No lunch.*

¢–$ ✕ **The Bite.** Fried everything—clams, fish-and-chips, you name it—is on the menu at this simple, roadside shack, where two outdoor picnic tables are the only seating options. Small, medium, and large are the three options: all of them are perfect if you're craving that classic seaside fried lunch. But don't come on a rainy day, unless you want to get wet—the lines here can be long. To beat the crowds, try arriving between traditional mealtimes. The best advice, however, is be patient and don't arrive too hungry. The Bite is open 11 AM–3 PM in spring and fall and until 8:45 PM in summer. ⊠ *Basin Rd.* ☎ *509/645–9239* ⊟ *No credit cards* ⊘ *Closed Oct.–late May.*

¢–$ ✕ **Larsen's.** Basically a retail fish store, Larsen's also has a raw take-out **Fodor's**Choice counter and will boil lobsters for you as well. A plate of fresh littlenecks ★ or cherrystones goes for $9 a dozen. Oysters at $15 a dozen are not a bad alternative. There's also seafood chowder and a variety of smoked fish and dips. Bring your own bottle of wine or beer, buy your dinner here, and then set up on the rocks, on the docks, or at the beach: there's no finer alfresco rustic dining on the island. Larsen's closes at 6 PM weekdays, 7 PM weekends. ✉ *Dutcher's Dock* ☎ *508/645–2680* ▤ *MC, V* ⌷ *BYOB* ◌ *Closed mid-Oct.–mid-May.*

★ **$$–$$$** 🏨 **Beach Plum Inn.** This mansard-roof inn, surrounded by 7 acres of lavish formal gardens and lush woodland, sits on a bluff over Menemsha Harbor. The floral-theme rooms—five in the main house and four in cottages—have gorgeous furnishings; in the Daffodil room, bathed in shades of yellow and blue, you'll find a hand-painted queen bed and a romantic balcony. A vaulted, beamed ceiling rises over the bedroom of the secluded Morning Glory Cottage. You will receive complimentary passes to a health club and free use of chairs, towels, and umbrellas to be taken to the two private beaches nearby. From many rooms, and also from the first-rate restaurant, you're treated to stunning harbor and ocean views. ✉ *North Rd., 02552* ☎ *508/645–9454 or 877/645–7398* ⊕ *www. beachpluminn.com* ↪ *9 rooms* ♿ *Some in-room hot tubs, refrigerators, cable TV, tennis court, concierge; no smoking* ▤ *AE, D, MC, V* ◌ *Closed Dec.–Apr.* ❢⊘ *BP.*

$$ 🏨 **Menemsha Inn and Cottages.** For 40 years the late *Life* photographer Alfred Eisenstaedt returned to his cottage on the hill here for the panoramic view of Vineyard Sound and Cuttyhunk beyond the trees below. All with screened porches, fireplaces, and kitchens, the cottages tumble down a hillside behind the main house and vary in privacy and view. You can also stay in the 1989 inn building or in the pleasant Carriage House. All rooms have private decks, most with sunset views. Suites include sitting areas, desks, and big tiled baths. The Continental breakfast is served in a solarium-style breakfast room with a deck facing the ocean. Passes and shuttle transportation to both Squibnocket and Lucy Vincent Beaches are provided. ✉ *North Rd.* ⌂ *Box 38, 02552* ☎ *508/ 645–2521* ⊕ *www.menemshainn.com* ↪ *15 rooms, 11 cottages, one 2-bedroom house* ♿ *In-room data ports, some kitchens, some refrigerators, cable TV, in-room VCRs, tennis court, gym, Ping-Pong* ▤ *MC, V* ◌ *Closed Dec.–mid-Apr.* ❢⊘ *CP.*

Shopping

On your way to watching the sunset at the beach on Menemsha Bight, visit the clothing and crafts shops that line **Basin Road.** Don't expect much in the way of bargains at the Menemsha shops, however, as these stores are strictly seasonal.

Harbor Craft Shop (☎ 508/645–2929 or 508/645–2655) carries a not particularly distinctive line of gifts, soaps, and home goods, but it's nicely fragrant inside. **Menemsha Blues** (☎ 508/645–3800) sells casual clothes for men, women, and children, most adorned with the shop's trademark embroidered bluefish. **Over South** (☎ 508/645–3348) stocks antiques of every vintage, sterling silver, nautical items, furniture, books, and pictures. **Pandora's Box** (☎ 508/645–9696) stocks unique, expensive, quality fashions for women, as well as soaps and gifts. **Up on the Roof** (☎ 508/ 645–3735) gets its name from Daisy, the friendly dog that hangs out on the roof of the shop, which is home to humorous signs and sayings in faux antique and primitive frames.

Larsen's (✉ Dutcher's Dock ☎ 508/645–2680) is a retail fish store with reasonable prices and superb quality—they'll open oysters, stuff quahogs, and cook a lobster to order. The best deal is a dozen littlenecks or cherrystones for $9.

In **Chilmark Gallery** (⊠ 76 State Rd. ☎ 508/645–258) sculptor Heather Sussman displays and sells her fountains and garden sculptures, animal studies, and whimseys in July and August, Wednesday–Sunday.

Sports & the Outdoors

BEACHES **Great Rock Bight Preserve** (⊠ on North Rd., about 1 mi from Menemsha Hills Reservation) is a Land Bank–managed tract of 28 acres. Parking is at the end of a ½-mi dirt road; it's a ½-mi walk to the beach, a secluded sandy cove of about 1,300 feet. It's well worth the trek.

Menemsha Beach (⊠ adjacent to Dutcher's Dock) is a pebbly public beach with gentle surf on Vineyard Sound and, with views to the northwest, a great place to catch the sunset. This is an active harbor for both commercial and sport fishermen; you'll be able to catch an eyeful of the handsome yachts and smaller boats. There are always anglers working the tides on the jetty, too. On site are restrooms and lifeguards. Snack stands and restaurants are a short walk from the parking lot, which can get crowded in summer (there's room for about 60 cars).

Menemsha Hills Reservation (⊠ off North Rd., on the left about 1 mi Down-Island coming from Menemsha Cross Rd.) is administered by the Trustees of Reservation. From the parking lot, it's 1 mi to the second-highest point on the island, Prospect Hill (308 feet), with a spectacular view. Then it's another mile on the Upper Trail to Great Sand Cliffs and the rocky shoreline of Vineyard Sound.

Aquinnah

㉟ *4 mi west of Menemsha, 12 mi southwest of West Tisbury, 20 mi west of Edgartown.*

Aquinnah, formerly called Gay Head, is an official Native American township. In 1987, after more than a decade of struggle in the courts, the Wampanoag tribe won guardianship of 420 acres of land, which are held in trust by the federal government in perpetuity and constitute the Aquinnah Native American Reservation. In 1997, the town voted to change the town's name from Gay Head back to its original Native American name, Aquinnah (pronounced a-*kwih*-nah), Wampanoag for "Land Under the Hill." Although the name has changed, it will take some time for the state and Martha's Vineyard authorities to convert road signs, maps, and other documents to the new name—so you can expect minor confusion. Some private businesses that use the name Gay Head might elect to retain it, so keep in mind that Gay Head and Aquinnah refer to the same place.

The "center" of Aquinnah consists of a combination fire and police station, the town hall, a Tribal Council office, and a public library, formerly the little red schoolhouse. Because the town's year-round population hovers around 650, Aquinnah children attend schools in other towns.

㊱ **Quitsa Pond Lookout** has a good view of the adjoining Menemsha and Nashaquitsa ponds, the woods, and the ocean beyond. ⊠ *State Rd.*

㊲ Aquinnah spring is channeled through a roadside iron pipe, gushing water cold enough to slake a cyclist's thirst on the hottest day. Feel free to fill a canteen. Locals come from all over the island to fill jugs. The spring is on the left, clearly visible from the road, ¹⁄₁₀ mi past the Aquinnah town line sign. ⊠ *State Rd.*

★ ㊳ The spectacular, dramatically striated walls of red clay at **Aquinnah Cliffs,** a National Historic Landmark and part of the Wampanoag reservation land, are the island's major tourist attraction, as evidenced by the tour bus–filled parking lot. Native American crafts and food shops line the short approach to the overlook, from which you can see the Elizabeth Islands to the northeast across Vineyard Sound and Noman's Land Island, part wildlife preserve, part military-bombing practice site, 3 mi off the Vineyard's southern coast.

If you've reached a state of quiet, vacationland bliss, keep in mind that this *is* a heavily touristed spot, and it might turn out to be a shock to your peace of mind. When you come, consider going to Aquinnah Lighthouse first, then down and around to the beach and cliffs.

There is no immediate access to the beach from the light—nothing like an easy staircase down the cliffs to the sand below. To reach the cliffs, park in the Moshup Beach (⇨ Sports and the Outdoors) lot by the lighthouse loop, walk 5-plus minutes south on the boardwalk, then continue another 20 or more minutes on the sand to get back around to the lighthouse. The cliffs themselves are pretty marvelous, and you should plan ahead if you want to see them. It takes a while to get to Aquinnah from elsewhere on the island, and in summer the parking lot and beach fill up, so start early to get a jump on the throngs. Although the lot costs $15 a day, you'll get $10 of your deposit back if you stay only an hour and $5 if you stay two, which is plenty of time to see the cliffs, have a meal, or do a little shopping. ⊠ *State Rd.*

Aquinnah Lighthouse, adjacent to the Aquinnah Cliffs overlook, is the largest of the Vineyard's five, precariously stationed atop the rapidly eroding cliffs. In 1799 a wooden lighthouse was built here—the island's first—to warn ships of Devil's Bridge, an area of shoals ¼ mi offshore. The current incarnation, built in 1856 of red brick, carries on with its alternating pattern of red and white flashes. Despite the light, the Vineyard's worst wreck occurred here in January 1884, when the *City of Columbus* sank, taking with it into the icy waters more than 100 passengers and crew. The original Fresnel lens was removed when the lighthouse was automated in 1952, and it is preserved at the Vineyard Museum in Edgartown. The lighthouse is open to the public for sunsets Friday, Saturday, and Sunday in summer, weather permitting; private tours can also be arranged. ⊠ *Lighthouse Rd.* ☎ *508/627–4441* ✆ *$3.*

A scenic route worth the trip is West Basin Road, which takes you along the Vineyard Sound shore of Menemsha Light and through the **Cranberry Lands,** an area of cranberry bogs gone wild that is a popular nesting site for birds. No humans can nest here, but you can drive by and look. At the end of the road, with marshland on the right and low dunes, grasses, and the long blue arc of the bight on the left, you get a terrific view of the quiet fishing village of Menemsha, across the water. **Lobsterville Road Beach** here is public, but public parking is limited to three spots, so get here early if you want one of them.

Where to Stay & Eat

$$$–$$$$ ✕ **The Aquinnah Shop.** At the far end of the row of fast-food take-out spots and souvenir shops at the Gay Head Cliffs is this restaurant owned and operated by members of the Vanderhoop and Madison families, native Wampanoags. The family took back the lease in 2000 after a four-year hiatus and has regained its reputation as a homey place to eat. For breakfast try the Tomahawk Special, two homemade fish cakes covered with salsa on top of poached eggs with melted cheddar cheese. The lunch menu includes sandwiches, burgers, and healthy-sounding salads. Dinner entrées include sautéed shrimp, scallops, and lobster with rotini in a chardonnay sauce and striped bass in a mussel-and-saffron sauce. The home-baked pies (banana cream, pecan, or fruit) come wrapped in a moist and flaky crust. ⊠ *State Rd.* ☎ *508/645–3867* ▭ *MC, V* ☉ *Closed mid-Oct.–mid-Apr.*

★ **$$–$$$** ✕▣ **Outermost Inn.** Hugh (brother of singer James) and Jeanne Taylor's B&B by the Aquinnah Cliffs stands alone on acres of moorland. The house is wrapped in windows revealing views of sea and sky in three directions. From the wide porch and patio are great views of the Aquinnah Lighthouse. In the restaurant, open to the public, dinner is served nightly in summer and is all prix-fixe at $72 (reservations are essential, and it's BYOB). The inn is clean and contemporary, with white walls and polished light-wood floors. Each room has a phone, and one has a whirlpool tub. The beach is a 10-minute walk away. Hugh has sailed area waters since childhood and captains his 50-foot catamaran on excursions to Cuttyhunk Island. ⊠ *Lighthouse Rd.* ☎ *R.R. 1, Box 171, 02535* ☎ *508/645–3511* ▤ *508/645–3514* ⊕ *www.outermostinn.com* ➹ *7 rooms* ♿ *Restaurant, some in-room hot tubs; no a/c, no kids under 12, no smoking* ▭ *AE, D, MC, V* ☉ *Closed mid-Oct.–May* ❖ *BP.*

★ **¢–$** ▣ **Duck Inn.** The Duck Inn, originally an 18th-century home built by Native American seafarer George Belain, sits on a bucolic 5-acre bluff overlooking the ocean, with the Aquinnah Lighthouse standing sentinel to the north. The eclectic, fun interior blends peach stucco walls, Native American rugs and wall hangings, and ducks. Three upstairs rooms come with balconies; a suite in the stone-wall lower level (cool in summer, warm in winter) has views of the rolling fields; and a small attached cabin (closed in winter) with separate bath is the least expensive room. The first floor's common room, with a working 1928 Glenwood stove, piano, and fireplace, is the heart of the inn. Massage and facial therapies are available, and the healthful breakfast fare includes waffles with strawberries and omelets or chocolate crepes. This inn is very informal—kids and pets are welcome, and one night is free with a week's stay. ⊠ *10 Duck Pond Way, off State Rd.* ☎ *Box 160, 02535* ☎ *508/645–9018* ▤ *508/645–2790* ➹ *4 rooms, 1 suite* ♿ *Outdoor hot tub, massage, meeting room, some pets allowed* ▭ *MC, V* ❖ *BP.*

Shopping

A small group of souvenir and crafts shops cater to the day-trippers who unload off the buses at Aquinnah Circle for a view of the Aquinnah Cliffs. You'll have no trouble finding the T-shirt or refrigerator magnet of your dreams in one of the several visitor-oriented shops, but you can also find Native American (specifically Wampanoag) crafts.

Stony Creek Gifts (☎ 508/645–3595) carries handmade Native American crafts, including wampum and dream catchers, mostly from the Vineyard and the Southwest.

Sports & the Outdoors

BEACHES **Lobsterville Beach** encompasses 2 mi of beautiful sand and dune beach directly off Lobsterville Road on the Vineyard Sound. It's a seagull nesting area and a favorite fishing spot. Though the water tends to be cold, and the pebbles along the shore make getting in and out difficult, the beach is protected and suitable for children. The view looking east— of Menemsha Harbor, the rest of the Vineyard, and the Elizabeth Islands across the sound—makes you feel like you're surrounded by the Greek islands. Given the limited parking (for about eight cars), this is an ideal stop-off for cyclists exploring this area of the island.

Moshup Beach (✉ at intersection of State Rd. and Moshup Trail) is, according to the Land Bank, "probably the most glamorous" of its holdings, because the beach provides access to the awesome Aquinnah Cliffs. The best views of the cliffs and up to the lighthouse are from a 25-plus-minute walk via boardwalk and beach. On clear days Noman's Land looms like a giant mirage. There is a drop-off area close to the beach, but you still must park in the lot and walk to the sand. The island shuttle bus stops here, too, and there are bike racks on the beach. Come early in the day to ensure both a quieter experience and an available parking spot. Keep in mind that climbing the cliffs is against the law—they're eroding much too quickly on their own. It's also illegal to take any of the clay with you. There's a parking fee of $15 from Memorial Day to Labor Day.

Philbin Beach, off Moshup Trail, is restricted to town residents or renters with a lease. It's a nice, wide beach with a wild Atlantic Ocean challenging you to master it. Beach passes can be obtained from the **Aquinnah town hall** (✉ 65 State Rd. ☎ 508/645–2300).

FISHING **Conomo Charters** (✉ 10 Old South Rd. ☎ 508/645–9278), under Captain Brian Vanderhoop, leads striped-bass and bluefish trips.

Menemsha Creek Charters (☎ 508/645–3511), run by Captain Hugh Taylor, leads two trips a day aboard the catamaran *Arabella* for swimming and picnicking for up to 40 people at a time. Day trips to Cuttyhunk depart at 10:30 AM and return at 3:30 PM; daily sunset cruises are also available.

Tomahawk Charters (☎ 508/645–3201), with Captain Buddy Vanderhoop at the helm, specializes in striped-bass fishing trips as well as bluefish, tuna, bonita, and sharks. Captain Lisa Vanderhoop also leads fishing charters especially for kids.

MARTHA'S VINEYARD A TO Z

BIKE TRAVEL

Martha's Vineyard is superb terrain for biking—you can pick up a map that lists safety tips and shows the island's many dedicated bike paths from the chamber of commerce (⇨ Visitor Information). Several shops throughout the island rent bicycles, many of them close to the ferry terminals. Martha's Vineyard Strictly Bikes rents bike racks for your car. ☷ **Bike Rentals DeBettencourt's** ✉ Circuit Ave. Exit, Oak Bluffs ☎ 508/693-0011. **Martha's Vineyard Strictly Bikes** ✉ 24 Union St., Vineyard Haven ☎ 508/693-0782. **Wheel Happy** ✉ 8 S. Water St., Edgartown ☎ 508/627-5928.

BOAT & FERRY TRAVEL

Car-and-passenger ferries travel to Vineyard Haven from Woods Hole on Cape Cod year-round. In season, passenger ferries from Falmouth and Hyannis on Cape Cod, and from New Bedford, serve Vineyard Haven and Oak Bluffs. All provide parking lots where you can leave your car overnight ($8–$15 per night). Service below is often limited during the fall through spring.

FROM FALMOUTH The Falmouth–Edgartown ferry makes the one-hour trip to Edgartown late May through early October. During high season, the passenger ferry runs daily, weekends in the slower months. Reservations are recommended. The *Island Queen* makes the 35-minute trip to Oak Bluffs from late May through early October. No passenger reservations are necessary.

Patriot Party Boats, which also charters party cruises, allows passengers on its Oak Bluffs mail runs starting with 3:30 AM departures from Falmouth Harbor. Last run is about 4:30 PM. Patriot usually runs on weekdays (and some Saturdays), and also operates a year-round 24-hour water taxi. Times of the earliest departures of the day aren't guaranteed—these are the newspaper runs, and departure depends on when the papers arrive from Boston. Keep in mind that parking is some distance away and although there is a shuttle, you may have to wait for it, so it is best to be dropped off at the boat. ☷ **Falmouth Ferries Falmouth-Edgartown Ferry** ✉ Falmouth Marine ☎ 508/548-9400 ⊕ www.falmouthferry.com ⛴ Round-trip $30, bicycles $8 additional; one-way $15, bicycles $4 additional. *Island Queen* ✉ Falmouth Harbor ☎ 508/548-4800 ⛴ Round-trip $12, bicycles $6 additional; one-way $7, bicycles $3 additional. **Patriot Party Boats** ✉ 227 Clinton Ave., Falmouth Harbor ☎ 508/548-2626 ⊕ www. patriotpartyboats.com ⛴ One-way $7.

FROM HYANNIS Hy-Line makes the 1¾-hour run to Oak Bluffs May to October. From June to mid-September, Hy-Line also carries passengers between Oak Bluffs and Nantucket. ☷ **Hyannis Ferry Hy-Line** ✉ Ocean St. dock ☎ 508/778-2600, 508/693-0112 in Oak Bluffs ⊕ www.hy-linecruises.com ⛴ One-way $15, bicycles $5 additional.

FROM NANTUCKET Hy-Line carries passengers between Oak Bluffs and Nantucket, from June to mid-September. The parking lot fills up in summer, so call to reserve a space in high season. Note: this is not a car ferry; to get a car from Nantucket to the Vineyard, you must return to the mainland and drive from Hyannis to Woods Hole.

🚢 **Nantucket Ferry Hy-Line** ⊠ Ocean St. dock ☎ 508/778-2600, 508/693-0112 in Oak Bluffs ⊕ www.hy-linecruises.com 🎫 One-way $14, bicycles $5 additional.

FROM NEW BEDFORD

The *Portuguese Princess* travels between 49 State Pier and Oak Bluffs from mid-May to mid-October. The 150-passenger ferry makes the 2-hour trip at least once a day, several times in high season, allowing you to avoid Cape traffic. A New England Fast Ferry, making the trip in about one hour, also leaves from the State Pier.

🚢 **New Bedford Ferries** *Portuguese Princess* ⊠ Steamship Authority Dock, Oak Bluffs ☎ 617/748-1428 ⊕ www.nbtraditionalferry.com 🎫 Round-trip $12.50, bicycles $5 additional. **New England Fast Ferry** ⊠ Steamship Authority Dock, Oak Bluffs ☎ 866/453-6800 ⊕ www.mvfastferry.com 🎫 $20.50 one-way, bicycles $5 additional.

FROM WOODS HOLE

The Steamship Authority runs the only car ferries, which make the 45-minute trip to Vineyard Haven daily year-round and to Oak Bluffs from late May through September.

If you plan to take a car to the island in summer, you *must* have a reservation (specifically Memorial Day weekend, Friday through Monday from the end of June to mid-September, and every day for the first two weeks of July); it's also a good idea to make advance reservations for any weekend the rest of the year. Standby reservations are otherwise available, but make it easy on yourself and get an advance reservation, whenever you travel during the summer. You should book your car reservation as far ahead as possible; in season, call weekdays from 5 AM to 9:55 PM for faster service. Those with confirmed car reservations must be at the terminal 30 minutes (45 minutes in season) before sailing time. Passenger reservations are never necessary.

A number of parking lots in Falmouth hold the overflow of cars when the Woods Hole lot is filled, and free shuttle buses take passengers to the ferry, about 15 minutes away. Signs along Route 28 heading south from the Bourne Bridge direct you to open parking lots, as does AM radio station 1610, which can be picked up within 5 mi of Falmouth.

A free Martha's Vineyard Chamber of Commerce reservations phone at the ticket office in Woods Hole connects you with many lodgings and car- and moped-rental firms on the island.

🚢 **Woods Hole Ferries** **Steamship Authority** ☎ 508/477-8600 information and car reservations, 508/693-9130 on the Vineyard ⊕ www.islandferry.com 🎫 Passengers one-way year-round $6, bicycles $3 additional; car one-way mid-May–mid-Oct. $57; call for off-season rates.

TO CHAPPAQUIDDICK

The three-car On-Time ferry—so named because it has no printed schedules and therefore can never be late—makes the five-minute run to Chappaquiddick Island year-round; late May to mid-October it runs about every five minutes daily 7 AM to midnight, less frequently off-season.

🚢 **Chappaquiddick Ferry** *On-Time* ⊠ Dock St., Edgartown ☎ 508/627-9427 🎫 Round-trip passenger $2, car and driver $8, bicycle and rider $5, moped and rider $6, motorcycle and rider $6.

BY PRIVATE BOAT Town harbor facilities are available at Vineyard Haven, Oak Bluffs, Edgartown, and Menemsha. Private marine companies include The Black Dog Company and Tisbury Wharf in Vineyard Haven, Dockside Marina in Oak Bluffs, and Mad Max Marina in Edgartown.

🔌 **Black Dog Wharf** ☎ 508/693-3854. **Dockside Marina** ☎ 508/693-3392. **Edgartown** ☎ 508/627-4746. **Mad Max Marina** ☎ 508/627-7400. **Menemsha** ☎ 508/645-2846. **Oak Bluffs** ☎ 508/693-4355. **Tisbury Wharf** ☎ 508/693-9300. **Vineyard Haven** ☎ 508/696-4249.

BUS TRAVEL ON MARTHA'S VINEYARD

The big buses of the Martha's Vineyard Transit Authority (VTA) run year-round with less frequent service between mid-October and April; VTA provides both in-town services and selected routes among different towns, such as Edgartown to Vineyard Haven, West Tisbury to Chilmark and Aquinnah, and Edgartown to South Beach. The fare is $1 per town, including the town of departure. One day ($6), three-day ($15) and one-week ($25) passes are available at the Edgartown Visitors Center. Seniors 70 or older are half price, if requested. Times vary, but in peak season, some buses run as early as 5:30 AM and as late, on Friday and Saturday, as 1 AM. Buses are equipped with bike racks and are wheelchair-accessible.

The VTA also has two free in-town shuttle-bus routes, one in Edgartown and one in Vineyard Haven. From mid-May to mid-September, white-and-purple shuttle buses make a continuous circuit through downtown Edgartown, beginning at the free parking lot at the Triangle off Upper Main Street and going to Mayhew Lane near the harbor. It's well worth taking it to avoid parking headaches in town. The shuttle buses run every 15 minutes from 6:50 AM to 12:30 AM daily. Service is also available between the Park 'n' Ride free parking lot beside the minigolf range on the State Road in Vineyard Haven and the steamship terminal. Minibuses run every 15 minutes from the first ferry in the morning to the last ferry at night.

Shuttle-bus service to South Beach via Herring Creek and Katama roads is available late May–mid-September for $1 one-way. Pickup is at the corner of Main and Church streets. In good weather frequent pickups occur daily between 10 and 6:30, every half hour in inclement weather, or you can flag a shuttle bus whenever you see one. In July and August, evening service to and from South Beach runs to 10:30 PM.

🔌 **Bus Information Martha's Vineyard Transit Authority (VTA)** ☎ 508/693-9940 ⊕ www.vineyardtransit.com.

CAR RENTAL

You can book rentals through the Woods Hole ferry terminal free phone. The agencies listed below have rental desks at the airport; be aware, though, that cars rented from the airport incur a small surcharge. Adventure Rentals rents cars (through Thrifty), as well as mopeds, Jeeps, and buggies, and has half-day rates. Cost is $80–$150 per day for a basic car. Renting a four-wheel-drive vehicle costs $150 per day (seasonal prices fluctuate widely).

🔌 **Local Agencies AAA Island** ☎ 508/627-6800. **Adventure Rentals** ✉ Beach Rd., Vineyard Haven ☎ 508/693-1959. **Consumer Car & Truck Rental** ☎ 508/627-3000.

CAR TRAVEL

In season, the Vineyard is overrun with cars, and many innkeepers will advise you to leave your car at home, saying you won't need it. This is true if you are coming over for just a few days and plan to spend most of your time in the three main towns—Oak Bluffs, Vineyard Haven, and Edgartown—which are connected in summer by a shuttle bus. If you're planning to explore the more remote, Up-Island parts of the island, a car is handy. In summer, you're often better off renting one on the island than trying to bring one over on the ferry; the cost, depending on the length of the rental, is comparable, plus you avoid the hassle of bringing your car on the ferry. Driving on the island is fairly simple. There are few main roads, and they are all well marked. Local bookstores sell a number of excellent maps of the island.

BY FOUR-WHEEL-DRIVE Four-wheel-drive vehicles are allowed from Katama Beach to Wasque Reservation with $60 annual permits ($100 for vehicles not registered on the island), which are sold on the beach in summer or weekdays 8:30–4:30 at the Dukes County Administration Office at the Martha's Vineyard Airport. Wasque Reservation has a separate mandatory permit available at Wasque Reservation entrances. It requires vehicles to carry certain equipment, such as a shovel, tow chains, and rope; call the rangers before setting out for the dunes. Be aware that due to the protected status of the piping plover, which uses the shore for nesting, some sections are occasionally closed off to vehicular traffic.

Jeeps are a good idea for exploring areas approachable only by dirt roads, but the going can be difficult in over-sand travel, and even Jeeps can get stuck. Stay on existing tracks whenever possible, since wet sand by the water line can suck you in. Most rental companies don't allow their Jeeps to be driven over sand for insurance reasons.

🚹 **Permit Information Dukes County Administration Building** ✉ 9 Airport Rd., inside the Martha's Vineyard Airport, Edgartown 02539 ☎ 508/696-3610.

PARKING Parking is tight in the main Vineyard towns of Edgartown, Oak Bluffs, and Vineyard Haven. Public parking is found on streets and in some public lots (off Cromwell Street in Vineyard Haven, across from Kelly Street and Dock Street in Edgartown). Cars illegally parked will be ticketed and, in cases, towed, and laws are strictly enforced during the busy summer months.

CHILDREN ON MARTHA'S VINEYARD

Martha's Vineyard is very family-oriented and provides every imaginable diversion for kids, including lodgings and restaurants that cater to them and that are affordable for families on a budget. Cottages and condominiums are popular with families, providing privacy, room, kitchens, and sometimes laundry facilities. Often cottage or condo communities have play yards and pools, sometimes even full children's programs.

Edgartown, Oak Bluffs, Vineyard Haven, and West Tisbury all have recreational programs. All the island's libraries have storytelling hours. Call towns about days and times.

🚹 **Children's Activities Edgartown** ☎ 508/627-6145. **Oak Bluffs** ☎ 508/693-2303. **Vineyard Haven** ☎ 508/696-4200. **West Tisbury** ☎ 508/696-0147.

🏛 **Libraries Chilmark** ✉ State Rd., Chilmark Center ☎ 508/645-3360. **Edgartown** ✉ 58 N. Water St. ☎ 508/627-4221. **Oak Bluffs** ✉ Circuit and Pennacook Aves. ☎ 508/693-9433. **Vineyard Haven** ✉ 200 Main St. ☎ 508/696-4210. **West Tisbury** ✉ State Rd. ☎ 508/693-3366.

MONEY MATTERS

ATMS ATM machines are plentiful in Edgartown, Vineyard Haven, and Oak Bluffs. Call Cirrus or Plus for for locations in the United States and Canada, or visit your local bank.

🏛 **ATM Locations Cirrus** ☎ 800/424-7787. **Plus** ☎ 800/843-7587.

TAXIS & LIMOUSINES

Taxis meet all scheduled ferries and flights, and there are taxi stands by the Flying Horses Carousel in Oak Bluffs, at the foot of Main Street in Edgartown, and by the steamship office in Vineyard Haven. Fares range from $5 within a town to $35–$40 one-way from Vineyard Haven to Aquinnah.

Rates double between 1 AM and 7 AM. Note that limousine companies often provide service both on- and off-island.

🏛 **Taxi Companies AdamCab** ☎ 508/627-4462 or 800/281-4462 ⊕ www.adamcab. com. **All Island Taxi** ☎ 508/693-2929 or 800/693-8294. **Mario's** ☎ 508/693-8399. **Martha's Vineyard Taxi** ☎ 508/693-8660 or 877/454-5900.

🏛 **By Limousine Muzik's Limousine Service** ✉ 10 Kennebec Ave., Oak Bluffs ☎ 508/693-2212 ⊕ www.mvy.com/muzik.

TOURS

BUS TOURS You can see the African-American Heritage Trail on tours organized by Elaine Weintraub, a high school history teacher who created the trail. The trail, which covers the entire island, highlights 14 spots that are important to the history of people of color of Martha's Vineyard. About half the sites are marked with plaques and include the homes of prominent African-American islanders such as the former wife of Adam Clayton Powell, the Shearer Cottage of Oak Bluffs, and outdoor areas where African-Americans gathered to worship. The half-day bus tour doesn't leave at specific times, so call for details. If you want to jump in your car and see it yourself, Weintraub's guide to the trail, "African-American Heritage Trail of Martha's Vineyard," is available at bookstores.

🏛 **Tour Operator African-American Heritage Trail** ✉ West Tisbury ☎ 508/693-4361 ⊕ www.mvheritagetrail.freeservers.com.

CRUISES The 50-foot sailing catamaran *Arabella* makes day and sunset sails out of Menemsha to Cuttyhunk and the Elizabeth Islands with Captain Hugh Taylor, co-owner of the Outermost Inn. The teakwood sailing yacht *Ayuthia* runs half-day, full-day, and overnight sails to Nantucket or the Elizabeth Islands out of the Black Dog Wharf in Vineyard Haven. *Mad Max,* a 60-foot high-tech catamaran, makes day sails and charters out of Edgartown. The *Shenandoah,* a 108-foot square topsail schooner, runs six-day cruises including meals for kids 9–16 to the Elizabeth Islands and New Bedford. The 90-foot gaff-rigged schooner *Alabama* makes kids' cruises to Nantucket, Block Island, and Newport. Cruises depart from the Black Dog Wharf in Vineyard Haven.

🚍 Tour Operators *Arabella* ☎ 508/645-3511 ⊕ www.outermostinn.com/htboat.htm. *Ayuthia* ☎ 508/693-7245 ⊕ www.mvy.com/ayuthia. *Mad Max* ☎ 508/627-7500 ⊕ www. mvy.com/madmax. *Shenandoah* ☎ 508/693-1699 ⊕ www.theblackdogtallships.com.

FLIGHTSEEING   Warbird Flight gives 35-minute or one-hour island tours, including buzzes over Nantucket and Woods Hole on Cape Cod, in a vintage 1948 L-17 warplane.

🚍 Tour Operator Warbird Flight ⊠ Martha's Vineyard Airport, Edgartown–West Tisbury Rd., West Tisbury ☎ 1508/221-0741 ⊕ www.warbirdflight.com.

WALKING TOURS   Liz Villard's Vineyard History Tours leads walking tours of Edgartown's "history, architecture, ghosts, and gossip" that include visits to the historic Dr. Daniel Fisher House, the Vincent House, and the Old Whaling Church. Tours are run from April through December; call for times. Liz and her guides also lead similar tours of Oak Bluffs and Vineyard Haven. Walks last a little over an hour.

🚍 Tour Operator Vineyard History Tours ☎ 508/627-2529.

VISITOR INFORMATION

Martha's Vineyard Chamber of Commerce is two blocks from the Vineyard Haven ferry. The chamber information booth by the Vineyard Haven steamship terminal is open late May to the last weekend in June, Friday–Sunday 8–8; July–early September, daily 8–8; and early September–mid-October, Friday–Sunday 8:30–5:30. The chamber itself is open year-round, weekdays 9–5, with some weekend hours in July and August. There are also town information kiosks on Circuit Avenue in Oak Bluffs and on Church Street in Edgartown.

🚍 Visitor Information Martha's Vineyard Chamber of Commerce ⊠ Beach Rd. ⬠ Box 1698, Vineyard Haven 02568 ☎ 508/693-4486 ⊕ www.mvy.com.

NANTUCKET

2

By Sandy
MacDonald

FOR THE FIRST TIME SINCE ITS GOLDEN AGE as a world-renowned whaling capital in the early 1800s, the tiny island of Nantucket is decidedly on a roll. Modest shingled cottages that might have gone begging for a buyer a few decades ago now fetch an easy million. The 800-plus pre-1840 structures that compose the core of town—a National Landmark Historic District—only rarely change hands, and then at exalted prices. As for the trophy houses—mega-mansions built in the hinterlands for rich arrivistes—they're consistently off the charts, setting new records only to break them.

And yet its ascending chic has very little to do with what attracts most people to Nantucket in the first place, or keeps them coming back. The allure has more to do with how, at the height of summer, a cooling fog will drift in across the multihued moors or the way rambling wild roses, the gaudy pink Rosa rugosa, perfume a hidden path to the beach.

Essentially Nantucket is *all* beach—a boomerang-shape sand spit consisting of detritus left by a glacier that receded millennia ago. Off Cape Cod, some 26 mi out to sea, the island measures 3½ by 14 mi at its widest points, while encompassing—such are the miracles of inlet and bay—about 80 mi of sandy shoreline, all of it open, as a matter of local pride, to absolutely everyone.

Whereas elsewhere along the New England coast private interests have carved prime beachfront into exclusive enclaves, Nantucketers are resolved that the beaches should remain accessible to the general public. A half dozen or so town-supervised beaches have amenities such as snack bars and lifeguard stations. The rest are the purview of solitary strollers—or, unfortunately, ever-growing convoys of dune-destroying SUVs. Nantucket's laissez-faire approach to beach management poses a delicate and perhaps ultimately untenable balancing act. So far islanders seem shockingly sanguine about the escalating presence of cars on their pristine beaches, even as they carp about congestion in town.

This is but one of the issues that percolate to the surface every April, during a weeklong town meeting that draws a good portion of the island's 12,000 year-round residents (the summer population expands to five times that figure). Far more immediate are concerns about overbuilding. The level of concern is such that, in 2000, Nantucket made the National Trust for Historic Preservation's list of Most Endangered Historic Places, a dubious honor at best. At present the island is too prosperous for its own good—a paradise in crisis. But residents are actively addressing these and other concerns and are building consensus for a Comprehensive Plan that will include affordable housing and sustainable businesses.

The small commercial area of Nantucket Town is the center of island activity, just as it has been since the early 1700s. It's only a few square blocks of mostly historical buildings, lovingly restored inns, and boutiques and galleries leading up from the pretty harbor and waterfront, where the ferries dock. Beyond it, quiet residential roads fan out to points around the island; Siasconset (known locally as Sconset) lies 8 mi to the east, Surfside 3 mi to the south, and Madaket 6 mi west of town. Thus

The island is small enough to cover in about four days, three if you hustle. In a weekend you can reasonably explore Nantucket Town and one other area such as Sconset, Sanford Farm, or one of the beaches. (For a good walking tour in town, see the Nantucket Town section.) Each of the outings below covers one aspect of the island's best activities. Since they're all different, you can pick one that matches your inner beachcomber when you're feeling lazy or something more rigorous when you've closed the cover on that fat summer novel.

2

a perfect day on the water

Before a long journey at sea, you've got to rise early and fuel up. Provisions on Harbor Square is a great source for morning munchies and picnic stuff for the voyage out. After breakfast, mosey along the slips at **Straight Wharf** to see which boat most appeals.

If you're not already a boat owner, you can board a beauty like the **Endeavor,** a replica Friendship sloop. Group sails on this and other craft leave the wharf at set times, or you might arrange for a private picnic-and-champagne charter to a cove along **Coatue.** Those sticking to a beer budget can always paddle out and have a picnic on the beach. Sea Nantucket rents kayaks and small sailboats at the vest-pocket Francis Street Beach, about ¼ mi southeast along Washington Street. The water here is usually calm enough for amateurs, but if you really want to learn the ropes and are here for several weeks, check out the courses offered by Nantucket Island Community Sailing. Another good place to try out water toys—kayaks, sailboards, and small sailboats—is broad and gentle **Jetties Beach.**

To prolong your communion with the water into the evening, consider having dinner at RopeWalk or Straight Wharf. Both are right on the harbor. Or go for the America's Cup of dining experiences and take a dinner cruise to the Wauwinet. The **Wauwinet Lady** will spirit you smoothly from Straight Wharf through the moorings—keeping the cocktails served en route steady—and 6 mi further to the island's most luxurious resort for a superlative meal. On the way back you can count on an equally spectacular sunset.

a naturalist's perfect day

Any self-respecting naturalist will want to head out at dawn to see what the birds are up to. The Downyfluke, a homey mid-island breakfast joint, starts serving at 5:30 AM—a laggardly 6 AM on Sunday. Pick up a couple of homemade doughnuts for carbo-loading on the road.

The best way to bird is on bike. (Rent one from one of the high-quality island shops.) A couple of miles west of Downyflake, the Nantucket Conservation Foundation maintains a 900-acre preserve comprising **Sanford Farm, the Woods,** and **Ram Pasture.** To get to here, follow Sparks Avenue to the high school; then it's a scenic zigzag past the **Old Mill** (consult a bike map available from the tourism office) to reach the start of the **Madaket Bike Path.** A few miles farther on the path, just before the intersection with Cliff Road, you'll see a rough-hewn parking lot. From here (you'll have to ditch your bike—there's a place to lock it up), 6½ mi of **hiking trails** cross forest and meadow to reach pond and sea, wetlands, and rare sandplain grassland—all of Nantucket's distinctive habitats in succession. Figure on at least two hours of walking and gawking, more if you're an avid stalker.

After emerging from the preserve, the strong of leg may bike another 3 mi west along the bike path to **Madaket Beach,** pausing to pick up a picnic lunch at the Westender, and plod onward along **Smith's Point,** where the endangered piping plovers dwell. (You will, of course, tread carefully and in no way harass them.) Then, head back into town and poke around the **Maria Mitchell Association,** a natural history museum and library, where you can read up on the environs you've just explored. For dinner, retire to Even Keel Cafe in the center of town, where you can dine amid the surprising peace of the patio out back before swooping home on your bike through the cool, starry night.

a perfect day for biking

It could easily be argued that every day is a perfect day for biking on Nantucket. Winter, summer, rain or sun, Nantucket terrain seems custom-made for biking—never too steep and always scenic. Start with a hearty breakfast at the Rotary, at the outset of Milestone Road about 1 mi southeast of the center of town. From here it's another 7 absolutely straight mi to **Sconset,** but plan to take your second left to get onto the **Polpis Bike Path,** the prettiest in Nantucket's network.

On your right, about 3½ mi out, look for Altar Rock Road, a dirt track that will take you to **Altar Rock,** the island's highest point (just past the weird '50s-futuristic weather station), which is also the nexus of the best mountain-biking trails. This area was common sheep pasturage during the 19th century. In other words, it's rocky and choppy. The crimson fields to the southeast are actually cranberry bogs. You can eventually regain Milestone Road in that direction, but it's more rewarding to return to the Polpis Bike Path, which makes a leisurely loop past **Sesachacha Pond** and the iconic striped **Sankaty Lighthouse.** Clamber up to its base to see how precariously it's perched on the eroding bluff before you pull into the cluster of sea-beaten cottages that is Sconset. Pause at the Sconset Market for rarefied refreshments before heading back into town—straight along Milestone Road or back the way you came.

You probably still have a good half day ahead of you, which is time enough and more to bike the other half of the island, out Madaket Road. Or you could rest your weary muscles, and save the westerly route for its spectacular sunset.

---

far, the outlying areas appear relatively rural; however, increasing "infill" threatens the idyll.

Still, on a day when sun scintillates on sand and the thrumming waves hint at an eternal rhythm, it's hard to imagine that anything could ever go too terribly wrong here. As summer succeeds summer, children will continue to construct their fanciful if foredoomed sand castles and marvel over the odd treasures the tides drag in. Adults will gladly play along, if allowed, remembering their own seemingly endless days of summer and imagining more of the same for their children's children and so on and on. Perfection can be surprisingly simple, after all, and even if Nantucket's current cachet should fade, the island's timeless pleasures will endure.

About the Restaurants

For such a tiny island, Nantucket is rife with great restaurants—"world class" would be no exaggeration. Of course, with New York–level sophistication come New York–level prices. And whereas the titans of industry who flock here for a bit of high-rent R&R might not blink at the prospect of a $40 or even $50 entrée, the rest of us must sometimes suppress a nervous gulp. Is it worth it? Again and again, in venues that vie for the title of most recherché, the answer is yes.

New American fever hit Nantucket about two decades ago and shows no signs of abating. Often, the chefs brought in to dazzle at established front-runners decide to stay on and open places of their own. Thus, the restaurant scene is constantly expanding and improving.

Even though the island itself isn't agriculturally equipped to furnish much more than a bit of produce and some homegrown herbs and greens (lovely as they can be), New England's top greengrocers are on tap to provide regional delicacies. The seafood, naturally, is nonpareil, especially local scallops in season. So don't let the prices deter you. The general excellence of Nantucket's restaurants seems to have a trickle-down effect: even many of the more modest eateries pack unexpected panache.

In any month other than July or August, call ahead to check hours of operation, which tend to shrink. Dining off-season used to be a dicey proposition, but in the past few years, enough talented resident chef-owners have set up shop so that the options even in the dead of winter can be mighty inviting. For restaurants, we list months closed; otherwise, it's safe to assume that places are open year-round. And, by the way, smoking is prohibited in all Nantucket restaurants.

Reservations can be hard to come by in high season, as well as popular weekends such as December's Christmas Stroll and the Daffodil Festival in April, so plan and make dinner reservations well ahead. The better restaurants can get booked up weeks in advance. (We mention only when reservations are absolutely essential.) Or consider alternative time slots: the odds will be in your favor if you're willing to eat unfashionably early or decadently late.

WHAT IT COSTS				
$$$$	$$$	$$	$	¢
AT DINNER over $28	$20–$28	$12–$20	$8–$12	under $8

Prices are for per person for a main course at dinner.

About the Hotels

From small bed-and-breakfasts to the island's few surviving grand hotels, Nantucket knows the value of hospitality. A unique "product" plus good service—as busy as this little island gets—are the deciding factors that keep visitors coming back year after year.

The majority of lodgings are in town, convenient to the shops and restaurants; the downside is that you may be subjected to street noise on summer evenings. Those seeking quiet might prefer the inns on the periphery of town, a 5- to 10-minute walk from Main Street. The most remote inns, in Sconset and Wauwinet, also tend to be among the most expensive. Families with children will probably want to consider the larger, less formal hotels, since many of the small, historic B&Bs are furnished with antiques—not an ideal match for rambunctious little ones. Or for smokers, for that matter: an ever-increasing number of inns are smoke-free.

Nantucket is notoriously expensive, so don't expect to find many bargains in terms of lodging, especially in summer. The best rates can be found in the off-season; however, the spring and fall shoulder seasons are also growing in popularity, and such special-event weekends as the Daffodil Festival in late April and Christmas Stroll in early December command peak-season rates. Most inns charge upwards of $150 a night in summer, and many go higher—way higher in the case of the Wauwinet and White Elephant, whose cottages can fetch in a night what others charge per week.

Although many islanders remain nonplussed by such lofty prices, both venues tend to be booked solid and actually offer good value for the type of clientele they attract. The only truly "budget" facility you'll find is the youth hostel, which is also the only option for roughing it, since camping is prohibited anywhere on-island. In any case, this is not a place to pinch pennies: Nantucket is all about charm and comfort, at an admittedly steep price. If you plan to stay, come prepared to splurge.

If you're stranded for some reason or want to make your day trip a last-minute overnight, check with Nantucket Visitor Services at 25 Federal Street (☎ 508/228–0925, ⊕ www.nantucket.net/town/departments/visitor.html): they track cancellations daily and might be able to refer you an inn with newly available rooms. For more lodging information, including rental properties and B&Bs, *see* Lodging *in* Smart Travel Tips.

WHAT IT COSTS				
$$$$	$$$	$$	$	¢
HOTELS over $450	$325–$450	$225–$325	$150–$225	under $150

Prices are for a standard double room in high season, excluding 4% Nantucket and 5.7% state taxes.

Exploring Nantucket

More than a few visitors debark from the ferries only to find themselves mildly disoriented. While it's true that the journey from Hyannis to Nantucket is pretty much southward, by the time the boat rounds Brandt Point to enter the Nantucket Town harbor, it's facing due west. Nantucket Town's Main Street, at the core of the historic district, has an east–west orientation, stemming from Straight Wharf out to Madaket Road, which

Architecture

In addition to Nantucket's cranberry bogs and roadside daffodils, there are dozens of lovely and interesting man-made sights to see, from a working windmill to a trio of lighthouses; from the Quaker Friends Meeting House to centuries-old Greek Revival town houses. In fact, in 1972, the entire island was declared a historic district—800 buildings predate the Civil War—and it's one of the country's finest. Look for the 2½-story typical Nantucket house, immediately identifiable by its gabled roof, roof walks, and wind-proofing white cedar shingles, which in no time weather to their familiar mottled lead gray. During your stay, sign up for a guided walking tours on architecture and the island's history, or set off on your own using the Nantucket Town walk *in* Exploring Nantucket.

2

Cultural Activities & Events

Intellectual curiosity is as alive today on Nantucket as it was in the mid-18th century, when citizens flocked to the Atheneum's Great Hall to hear such speakers as Melville, Emerson, and Thoreau. Today the roster runs to Paul Theroux, Anna Quindlen, and other nationally known names. Nantucket supports several homegrown theater companies—"amateur" in the best sense—which can be counted on for gripping performances. While plans percolate for a permanent performing arts center, plays often go up in a handful of church halls, which may also host concerts. On Friday evenings in summer, a scattering of art galleries hold their openings, and you can wander from one to the next, feasting on the art and complimentary canapés. As for cinema, Nantucket has three distinctive venues covering Hollywood's latest blockbusters as well as independents—and a popular, annual Film Festival. "Christmas Stroll," held the first weekend of December, is the centerpiece of the festive holiday season that is fast becoming as busy as summer. Many businesses and restaurants stay open right up until New Year.

Outdoor Activities

When the phrase "the great outdoors" was coined, its author must have had Nantucket in mind. Walking alongside the dunes you might be surprised by a heron soaring out of the grass or detect the flukes of a humpback surging up from the sea. Gardening is practically the official island sport, as are biking, sailing, and hiking. Here even an unremarkable game of Frisbee or a ball toss on one of the many beautiful beaches becomes a memorable experience thanks to the stunning setting. Whether on land, shore, or sea, let Nantucket inspire your inner naturalist, adventure seeker, or athlete.

Shopping

Ever since sea captains initiated the China Trade in the early 1800s, Nantucket has enjoyed pride of place as a market for luxury goods from around the world. Today the town supports an active—one might even say hyperactive—retail scene. Chain stores have for the most part been kept at bay. The 19th-century storefronts are packed with recherché boutiques proffering *très cher* goods, from fashion to furnishings and everything in between. Even the smattering of T-shirt shops tend to be tasteful (and their stock surprisingly costly). There's no Nantucket "uniform," though preppie style still rules the day and the ladies do love their summer hats.

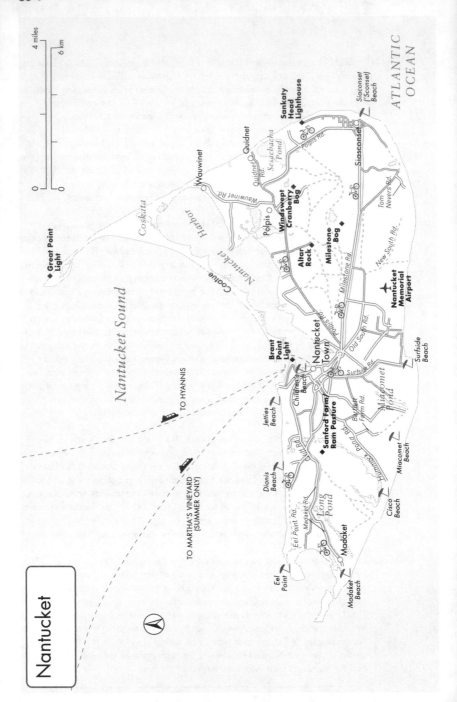

Nantucket

KEEPING WILDLIFE WILD

NANTUCKET AND THE NEARBY ISLANDS of Tuckernuck and Muskeget host a unique community of plants and animals. The largely treeless expanse of sandplain grassland and coastal heath (also called moors) along Nantucket's southern half is the largest ecosystem of its kind in the world—now endangered. This setting of stark beauty supports a number of species in the rhododendron or heath family as well as blueberry, huckleberry, and bearberry. The islands also comprise forests, swamps, salt marshes, and barrier beaches.

When the tourism boom began in the 1960s, it quickly became clear that something had to be done to preserve the miles of heath-covered moors and clean, white-sand beaches. Led by the Nantucket Conservation Foundation (NCF), established in 1963, organizations such as the Trustees of Reservations, the Land Bank, and the Massachusetts Audubon Society have acquired through purchase or gift more than 9,000 acres, including working cranberry bogs and great tracts of moorland for conservation. Now about 40% of Nantucket is protected from development, and open to the public for hikes, nature study, and scientific research.

Take your binoculars and camera and walk the trails of Sanford Farm or the moors around Altar Rock. If you're observant you might spot a Northern harrier gliding low over the hummocks in search of a meal, and if you're extremely lucky, you might catch a glimpse of the endangered short-eared owl. The absence of typical ground-dwelling predators such as weasels and coyotes makes Nantucket a haven for ground-nesting birds such as these, as well as several species of gulls and terns. Around your feet you might also see the American burying beetle, the Northeastern beach tiger beetle, bushy rock roses, and wood lilies. In spring and early summer some beaches are closed to vehicles and have restricted pedestrian access in order to protect the nests and chicks of least terns and piping plovers.

---

proceeds 6 mi west to Madaket Beach. Milestone Road, accessed from a rotary at the end of Orange Street off Main Street, is a straight, 8-mi shot to the easternmost town of Sconset (formally, Siasconset).

To find your way to the south-shore beaches or among the hillocks of Polpis—Altar Rock is the island's highest point, at a mere 100 feet—

you'll want to use a map. The bike shops along the piers and the Nantucket Visitor Services and Information Bureau, at 25 Federal Street in the center of town, provide a useful assortment of maps for free.

NANTUCKET TOWN

With so many landmarks packed into a small area, Nantucket Town is perfect for an afternoon stroll or a serious self-guided tour. Either way, you'll pass several dozen historical sights while taking in the lovely gardens, imposing Greek Revival buildings, cobblestone streets, and salty sea air. If you're staying all summer, you might want to buy a pass from the Nantucket Historical Association and the Maria (pronounced mah-*rye*-ah) Mitchell Association for discounted admission to several sites.

Numbers in the text correspond to numbers in the margin and on the Nantucket Town map.

A Good Walk

Begin your walk at the **African Meeting House** ❶, at Pleasant and York streets. In the 1880s it was a cultural center for emancipated slaves. Head up West York Street to see the island's only remaining windmill, **Old Mill** ❷. Returning to Pleasant Street via South Mill Street, you'll pass **Moors' End** ❸, an 1834 Federal-style house. Turning left at Mill Street, you'll find quite a different kind of structure, the simple **1800 House** ❹. It's a good example of a typical Nantucket home—one not enriched by whaling money. Follow New Dollar Lane past the remains of the **Starbuck refinery and candle works** ❺, toward Vestal Street and the Maria Mitchell Association's **Hinchman House Natural Science Museum** ❻, **Maria Mitchell Association Science Library** ❼, and **Mitchell House** ❽, as well as the 1805 **Old Gaol** ❾. Backtrack a bit, take a left onto Bloom Street, and a right on Main Street to reach Howard Street; No. 8 is **Greater Light** ❿, a good example of an early artist's house. Then, round the corner onto Gardner Street to see the **Fire Hose Cart House** ⓫.

Walking from Gardner Street along Main toward the harbor, you'll find the **"Three Bricks"** ⓬ on Upper Main Street and the **Hadwen House** ⓭ at No. 96. In 1846 a fire destroyed all of the simple Quaker buildings in the downtown area, and many were rebuilt in brick, in the Federal and Greek Revival styles that were prevalent on the mainland at the time. Peek down Winter Street for a look at the **Coffin School** ⓮ as you head toward the **Coffin houses** ⓯ at 75 and 78 Main Street and the **John Wendell Barrett House** ⓰ at No. 72. Around the corner from the **Pacific National Bank** ⓱ at 62, with its landmark meridian stone outside, is the colonnaded Greek Revival **United Methodist Church** ⓲, overlooking Center Street (also know as Petticoat Row, a historical shopping district). South of Main Street are several houses of worship: the **Quaker Meeting House** ⓳, **St. Paul's Episcopal Church** ⓴, and the **Unitarian Universalist Church** ㉑. Heading down Main, check the wall on the left on Washington Street: behind the Ralph Lauren shop, a sign lists distances from Nantucket to various points of the globe (for example, it's 14,650 mi to Tahiti).

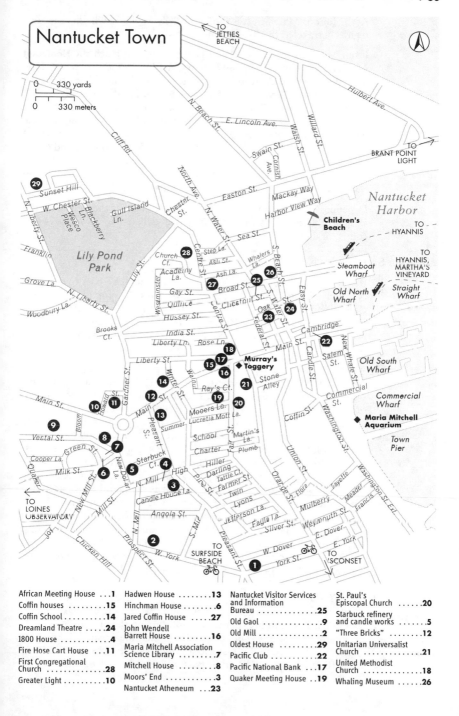

Nantucket Town

At the foot of Main Street is the **Pacific Club** ㉒, whose whaling captains regularly traveled the Pacific route.

From Main Street take a left on Federal Street to reach the **Nantucket Atheneum** ㉓, Nantucket's 1847 library, at 1 Lower India Street, and the **Dreamland Theatre** ㉔. Stop in for some brochures and advice from the **Nantucket Visitor Services and Information Bureau** ㉕ before jogging toward the Easy Street Boat Basin, where you can grab a bench and watch the ferries come and go. After your respite, drop by the **Whaling Museum and Peter Foulger Museum** ㉖ on Broad Street—try to time your arrival to catch a lecture. Then head west on Broad Street to the **Jared Coffin House** ㉗. Take a right onto Centre Street to climb the spire of the elegant **First Congregational Church** ㉘. Just beyond it is the 1686 **Oldest House** ㉙, a point of interest for architecture buffs.

TIMING   Depending on how how long you choose to linger in the museums and shops you'll pass, this walk might take anywhere from two hours to a couple of days.

What to See

If you plan to do a lot of sightseeing, an all-inclusive pass to the eight Nantucket Historical Association (NHA) sites ($15 for adults, $10 for children ages 5 to 14, $35 family rate) or the to Maria Mitchell Association (MMA) sites ($10 for adults, $7 for children ages 6 to 14) gets you unlimited annual visits and other money-saving membership perks.

❶ **African Meeting House.** Nantucket's only public building constructed and occupied by African-Americans in the 19th century is one of nine sights associated with the island's African-American heritage. (All are on the self-guided Black Heritage Trail tour, a free pamphlet available at Nantucket Visitor Services and NHA sites.) As far back as the early 1700s, there was a small African-American population on Nantucket; the earliest blacks were slaves of the island's first settlers. When the island abolished slavery in 1773, Nantucket became a destination for free blacks and escaping slaves. The African Meeting House was built in the 1820s as a schoolhouse, and it functioned as such until 1846, when the island's schools were integrated. The building was later used as a church and social center. A complete restoration has returned the site to its authentic 1880s appearance. Rooms for lectures, concerts, and readings help to preserve the contributions and experiences of African-Americans on Nantucket. ✉ *29 York St.* ☎ *508/228–9833* ⊕ *www.afroammuseum. org* 🎟 *Free* ☉ *July–Aug., Tues.–Sat. 11–3, Sun. 1–3.*

off the beaten path

Fodor'sChoice

★

BRANT POINT LIGHT – The 26-foot-tall, white-painted beauty has views of the harbor and town. The point was the site of the second-oldest lighthouse in the country (1746), though the present, much-photographed light was built in 1902. In fact, the existing lighthouse is the 10th to occupy this historic spot; its reassuring beacon is visible from 10 mi offshore. ✉ *End of Easton St., across a footbridge.*

WHAT MELVILLE KNEW: NANTUCKET'S WHALING TRADITION

SURPRISINGLY, HERMAN MELVILLE had no firsthand knowledge of Nantucket when he set out to write Moby-Dick. In fact, he didn't visit the island until 1855, a year after the book was published. By that time, Captain George Pollard Jr., who had experienced the whale attack that inspired Melville's tale, was an old man who roamed the quiet streets as a night watchman. What Melville did know, having himself shipped out on a whaler from New Bedford (he called it "my Harvard and my Yale"), was just how grueling these voyages could be.

Nantucket's preeminence as the world's whaling capital (at least until the early 1800s, when New Bedford's deeper harbor took the lead) resulted from a fluke, when, in 1712, Captain Christopher Hussey's crew speared a sperm whale. The whale's waxy spermaceti, it was found, could be used for candles in place of lantern oil, produced by the messy, endless task of cooking down whale blubber. Hence, the chase was on: Nantucket's whaling fleet spread all the way to the Far East in search of "greasy luck."

Barring pirate and military attacks, shipwrecks and other acts of God, and the certainty of vermin and scurvy on the interminably long voyages, the captains made out like bandits; their grand houses still stand as proof. The crews had a harder time of it, but whaling had its advantages. It was virtually the only trade open to all races (hands were tough to sign on, with good reason), as well as one of the few offering a chance of upward mobility. Survive enough outings, and a diligent cabin boy might work his way up to captain.

The trade went into a downward spiral with the discovery of petroleum in 1836 and the commercial introduction of kerosene in 1959. Nantucket's fleet limped on a while longer, but the glory days were over—and so, too, was the seemingly limitless supply of stock. Today, there are thought to be fewer than 300 right whales in the Atlantic, and they're vulnerable to ever-increasing marine traffic. We may not have them around much longer—another thing Melville couldn't have known.

---

15 **Coffin houses.** The two attractive brick homes, the Henry Coffin House and the Charles G. Coffin House, face each other and were built for brothers. The Coffins were wealthy shipping agents and whale-oil merchants who used the same mason for these 1830s houses and the later Three Bricks. The houses are privately owned and not open to the public. ⊠ 75 and 78 Main St.

⑭ Coffin School. The impressive Greek Revival building was built in 1854 to house a school founded three decades earlier by Admiral Sir Isaac Coffin to train the youth of Nantucket (at the time, half the inhabitants were Coffin descendants) in the ways of the sea. It is now home to the Egan Institute of Maritime Studies, whose mission is to "advance the study and appreciation of the history, literature, art, and maritime traditions of Nantucket" through changing art exhibits, publications, and nautical instruction. At the evening lecture series in summer, you can hear the fascinating tales of such ships as the *Essex,* which inspired Herman Melville's writing as well as founding director's Nathaniel Philbrick's 2000 best seller, *In the Heart of the Sea.* ✉ *4 Winter St.* ☎ *508/228–2505* ⊕ *www.eganinstitute.org* ✒ *Free* ☉ *Late May–mid-Oct., daily 1–5.*

㉔ Dreamland Theatre. Currently a summer cinema, the handsome wooden theater was built as a Quaker meetinghouse in 1829 and then became a straw factory and, later, an entertainment hall. It was moved to Brant Point as part of the grand Nantucket Hotel in the late 19th century and was floated across the harbor by barge in about 1905 to its present location—a good illustration of early Nantucketers' penchant for the multiple use of dwellings, as well as the relocation of houses. Trees (and therefore lumber) were so scarce that Herman Melville wrote in *Moby-Dick* that "pieces of wood in Nantucket are carried about like bits of the true cross in Rome." ✉ *17 S. Water St.* ☎ *508/228–5356.*

④ 1800 House. Once the residence of the high sheriff, not a rich whaling family, the typical Nantucket home remains an example of how the other half lived at the time of its construction. The house has a six-flue chimney (with beehive oven), which you'll have to admire from the outside for now, as the NHA is retrofitting it as a learning center. ✉ *10 Mill St.*

☾ ⑪ Fire Hose Cart House. Built in 1886 as one of several neighborhood fire stations—Nantucketers had learned their lesson after the 1846 conflagration—the minimuseum displays a small collection of fire-fighting equipment used in the 18th century, including dousing buckets and a hand-pumped fire cart. ✉ *8 Gardner St.* ☎ *508/228–1894* ⊕ *www.nha.org* ✒ *NHA History ticket only* ☉ *Late May–early Sept., daily 10–5.*

★ ㉘ First Congregational Church. Nantucket's largest and most elegant church is also known as the Old North Church. Its tower—whose steeple is capped with a weather vane depicting a whale catch—rises 120 feet, providing the best island view. On a clear day the reward for climbing the 92 steps (with many landings as rest stops) is a panorama encompassing Great Point, Sankaty Head Lighthouse, Muskeget and Tuckernuck islands, moors, ponds, beaches, and the winding streets and rooftops of town. A peek at the church's interior reveals its old box pews, a turn-of-the-20th-century organ, and a trompe-l'oeil ceiling done by an unknown Italian painter in 1850 and since restored. The Old North Vestry in the rear, the oldest house of worship on the island, was built circa 1725 about a mile north of its present site. The main church was built in 1834. ✉ *62 Centre St.* ☎ *508/228–0950* ⊕ *www.nantucketfcc.org*

✉ *Tower tour $2.50 donation* ☉ *Mid-June–mid-Oct., Mon.–Sat. 10–4.
Services Sun. 9 and 10 AM.*

🔟 **Greater Light.** With its whimsical blend of necessity and creativity, Greater
Light is an example of the summer homes of the artists who flocked to
Nantucket in its early resort days. In the 1930s two unusual Quaker
sisters from Philadelphia—actress Hanna and artist Gertrude Mon-
aghan—converted a barn into what now looks like the lavish set for an
old movie. The exotic decor includes Italian furniture, Native American artifacts and textiles, a wrought-iron balcony, bas-reliefs, and a coat
of arms. The sisters also remodeled the private house next door, called
Lesser Light, for their parents. ✉ *8 Howard St.* ☏ *No phone.*

⒀ **Hadwen House.** The pair of magnificent white porticoed Greek Revival
mansions on upper Main Street—commonly referred to as the Two
Greeks—were built in 1845 and 1846 by wealthy factory owner William
Hadwen, a Newport native who made his money in whale oil and candles. No. 94, built as a wedding gift for his adopted niece, was mod-
eled on the Athenian Tower of the Winds, with Corinthian capitals on
the entry columns, a domed-stair hall with statuary niches, and an ocu-
lus. The Hadwens' own domicile, at No. 96, is now a museum, and its
contents reflect how the wealthy of the period lived. The house has been
restored to its mid-19th-century origins, with classic Victorian gas chandeliers and furnishings, as well as reproduction wallpapers and window
treatments. Inside, on a guided tour, you'll see such architectural details
as the grand circular staircase, fine plasterwork, and carved Italian-mar-
ble mantels. A second-floor gallery hosts changing exhibits. ✉ *96 Main
St.* ☏ *508/228–1894* ⊕ *www.nha.org* ✉ *NHA History Ticket only*
☉ *Late May–early Sept., daily 10–5.*

🖑 ⑥ **Hinchman House Natural Science Museum.** If you're interested in the natural history of Nantucket, browse through the displays here, which exhibit specimens of local birds, insects, and plants and their local habitats.
The museum offers children's nature classes and sponsors naturalist-led
walks in summer for $10. Bird walks are Tuesday and Thursday at 6:30
AM and Saturday at 8 AM; nature walks are Monday and Friday at 9 AM
and Wednesday at 6 PM. The building houses the Maria Mitchell Association's gift shop as well. ✉ *7 Milk St.* ☏ *508/228–0898* ⊕ *www.
mmo.org* ✉ *$4 or MMA pass* ☉ *Mid-June–Aug., Tues.–Sat. 10–4; Sept.,
Fri.-Sat., 10-4.*

㉗ **Jared Coffin House.** Operated as an inn since the mid-19th century, the
handsome landmark also houses a restaurant and pub. Coffin, a wealthy
merchant, built this brick house with Ionic portico, parapet, hip roof,
and cupola—the only three-story structure on the island at the time—
for his wife, who wanted to live closer to town. They moved here in
1845 from Moors End on Pleasant Street, but (so the story goes) nothing
would please Mrs. Coffin, and within two years they left the island al-
together for Boston. ✉ *29 Broad St.* ☏ *508/228–2400 or 800/248–2405*
⊕ *www.jaredcoffinhouse.com.*

⒃ **John Wendell Barrett House.** One of Nantucket's grand Main Street
homes, the Barrett House was built in 1820 in early Greek Revival style.

Legend has it that Lydia Mitchell Barrett stood on the steps and refused to budge when men tried to evacuate her so they could blow up the house to stop the spread of the Great Fire. Luckily, a shift in the wind settled the showdown. ⊠ *72 Main St.*

Lily Pond Park. This 5-acre conservation area on the edge of town is a prime bird-watching spot. Its lawn and wetlands—there is a trail, but it can be muddy—foster abundant wildlife, including birds, ducks, and deer. You can pick blackberries, raspberries, and grapes in season wherever you find them. ⊠ *N. Liberty St.*

off the
beaten
path

LOINES OBSERVATORY – On a clear night in 1847, a young woman peered through a telescope mounted on the roof of the Pacific Bank on Main Street. Although she had no formal training in astronomy, she had learned enough from her father, an amateur astronomer, to realize she was looking at a heretofore undiscovered comet. The young lady was Maria (pronounced Mah-*rye*-ah) Mitchell, a native of Nantucket, who was later to become a fellow in the American Academy of Arts and Sciences, the first woman Professor of Astronomy at Vassar College, and President of the American Association for Advancement of Women. In 1970, the Maria Mitchell Association built the Loines Observatory to honor this island luminary. The observatory has a full-time, year-round astronomer on staff who gives lectures; several graduate students in residence conduct tours and will cheerfully assist you, during "open nights," in adjusting the telescopes for a peek at the "Final Frontier." Who knows—maybe you'll discover a comet of your own. ⊠ *59 Milk St. Ext.* ☎ *508/228–9273* ⊕ *www.mmo.org* ▩ *$10* ☉ *Mid-June–mid-Sept., Mon., Wed., and Fri. at 9 PM; mid-Sept.–mid-Oct., Fri. at 9 PM; mid-Oct.–Apr., Fri. at 8 PM; May–mid-June, Fri. at 9 PM. Weather permitting.*

Main Street. The only broad avenue in town, Main Street was widened after the Great Fire of 1846 leveled all its wooden buildings, to safeguard against flames hopping across the street in the event of another fire. The cobblestone thoroughfare has a harmonious symmetry: the Pacific Club anchors its foot, and the Pacific National Bank, another red-brick building, squares off the head. The cobblestones were brought to the island as ballast in returning ships and laid to prevent the wheels of carts heavily laden with whale oil from sinking into the dirt on their passage from the waterfront to the factories. You might want to stop by the **Chamber of Commerce** (⊠ 48 Main St., upstairs ☎ 508/228–1700, ⊕ www.nantucketchamber.org) to get maps and island information, available weekdays 9–5, year-round.

At the center of Lower Main is an old horse trough, today overflowing with flowers. From here the street gently rises. At the bank it narrows to its prefire width and leaves the commercial district for an area of mansions that escaped the blaze. The simple shop buildings that replaced those lost are a pleasing hodgepodge of sizes, colors, and styles. Elm trees—thousands of which were planted in the 1850s by Henry and Charles Coffin—once formed a canopy over Main Street, but Dutch elm disease took most of them. The few remaining are tended like the treasures they are.

need a break? You can breakfast or lunch inexpensively at several lunch counters, including **Congdon's Pharmacy** (⊠ 47 Main St. ☎ 508/228–0020), and the **Nantucket Pharmacy** (⊠ 45 Main St. ☎ 508/228–0180). **"The Strip,"** a hodgepodge of fun fast-food eateries on Broad Street near Steamboat Wharf, is another good option. Besides fresh-squeezed juices, the **Juice Bar** (⊠ 12 Broad St. ☎ 508/228–5799), open April–mid-October, serves homemade ice cream and frozen yogurt with waffle cones and toppings. Long lines signal that good things come to those who wait.

off the beaten path **MARIA MITCHELL AQUARIUM** – The fresh- and saltwater tanks here are filled with local marine life, including flukes, skates, and lobsters, and children can pick up live crabs and starfish from the hands-on tank. Guided marine walks ($10) are held Friday and Saturday in summer at 10 AM. ⊠ *28 Washington St., near Commercial Wharf* ☎ *508/228–5387* ⊕ *www.mmo.org* ⊠ *$4 or MMA pass* ☉ *Mid-June–early Sept., Mon.–Sat. 10–4.*

Maria Mitchell Association (MMA). Established in 1902 by Vassar students and astronomer Maria Mitchell's family, the association administers the Mitchell House, the Maria Mitchell Science Library, the Hinchman House, the Maria Mitchell Aquarium, the Vestal Street Observatory, and the Loines Observatory. The MMA Museum Pass is a combination admission ticket to the Mitchell House, the Hinchman House, the Vestal Street Observatory, and the aquarium; it's $10 for adults and $7 for senior citizens and children ages 6 to 14. In summer, the association conducts inexpensive classes for adults and children on astronomy, natural science, and Nantucket history. ⊠ *4 Vestal St.* ☎ *508/228–9198* ⊕ *www. mmo.org.*

❼ **Maria Mitchell Association (MMA) Science Library.** The library has an extensive collection of science books and periodicals, including field guides and gardening books, as well as books on Nantucket history. ⊠ *2 Vestal St.* ☎ *508/228–9219* ⊕ *www.mmo.org* ⊠ *Free* ☉ *Mid-June–mid-Sept., Tues.–Sat. 10–4; mid-Sept.–mid-June, Wed.–Fri. 2–5, Sat. 9–noon.*

❽ **Mitchell House.** This 1790 house was the birthplace of astronomer and Vassar professor Maria Mitchell, who in 1847, at age 29, discovered a comet while surveying the sky from the top of the Pacific National Bank. Mitchell was the first woman astronomy professor in the United States, and the first woman to discover a comet. Her Quaker family—Maria was one of 10 children—had moved to quarters over the bank, where her father, also an amateur astronomer, served as banker. The house contains family possessions and Maria Mitchell memorabilia, including the telescope with which she spotted the comet. The kitchen, of authentic wide-board construction, retains the antique utensils, iron pump, and

CloseUp

PETTICOAT ROW

DURING THE WHALING ERA—*a time, remember, when women were generally considered better seen than heard—a circumstance developed in Nantucket Town that was perhaps unique in the country: a large portion of Centre Street shops near Main Street were almost completely run by women merchants. It eventually became known as Petticoat Row, and it still exists today.*

Women have always played a strong role in Nantucket's history, partly because of the

Quaker philosophy of sexual equality and partly because on whaling expeditions men could be gone for years at a time—and it was up to women to keep the town going. They became leaders in every arena, from religion to business. Mary Coffin Starbuck helped establish Quakerism on the island and was a celebrated preacher. Lucretia Coffin Mott became a powerful advocate for abolition and women's suffrage.

sink of the time. Tours of the house are included in the admission price. The adjacent observatory is used by researchers and is not open to the public. ⊠ *1 Vestal St.* ☎ *508/228–2896* ⊕ *www.mmo.org* 🎫 *$4 or MMA pass* ☉ *Mid-June–early Sept., Tues.–Sat. 10–4.*

❸ Moors' End. Built between 1829 and 1834, this handsome Federal brick house is where merchant Jared Coffin lived before moving to what is now the Jared Coffin House—the proximity to the fumes from the Starbuck refinery was one of Mrs. Coffin's complaints. It is a private home, so you won't be able to see Stanley Rowland's vast murals of the whaling era on the walls or the scrawled notes about shipwreck sightings in the cupola, but keep an eye out for pictures in any number of coffee-table books about Nantucket. Beside the home is the largest walled garden on Nantucket; like the house, it is not open to the public. ⊠ *19 Pleasant St.*

㉓ Nantucket Atheneum. Nantucket's town library is a great white Greek Revival building, with a windowless facade and fluted Ionic columns. Completed in 1847 to replace a structure lost to the 1846 fire, it's one of the oldest libraries in continuous service in the United States. The astronomer Maria Mitchell was its first librarian. Opening ceremonies included a dedication by Ralph Waldo Emerson, who—along with Daniel Webster, Henry David Thoreau, Frederick Douglass, Lucretia Mott, and John James Audubon—later delivered lectures in the library's second-floor Great Hall. During the 19th century the hall was the center of island culture—a role it fulfills to this day. The adjoining Atheneum Park is a great place to relax for a while, and the spacious Weezie Library for Children hosts readings and activities—a welcome respite for a rainy day. ⊠ *1 India St.* ☎ *508/228–1110* ⊕ *www.nantucketatheneum. org* ☉ *Late May–early Sept., Mon., Wed., and Fri.–Sat. 9:30–5, Tues. and Thurs. 9:30–8; early Sept.–late May, Tues. and Thurs. 9:30–8, Wed. and Fri.–Sat. 9:30–5.*

Nantucket Historical Association (NHA). The NHA, founded in 1894, currently operates seven museums, while looking after several other significant properties. At any one of the museums you can purchase a well-worth-it NHA History Ticket ($15 adults, $10 children 6–17, $35 family) which entitles you to entry at all of the properties as well as a historical walking tour of Nantucket Town. The Whaling Museum is open year-round; most other sites are open daily from late May to mid-October, with limited hours in the shoulder seasons.

㉕ Nantucket Visitor Services and Information Bureau. You'll find public phones, restrooms, maps, and a bulletin board posting special events here. This is the best resource if you're tempted to extend your stay and need accommodations—but it's also excellent for orientation or a bit of advice anytime. The helpful staff gives candid recommendations and can assist with reservations. Call ahead for off-season hours. ✉ *25 Federal St.* ☎ *508/228–0925* ☉ *Mid-Apr.–Dec., daily 9–6; Dec.–mid-Apr., Mon.–Sat. 9–5:30.*

❾ Old Gaol. It's tough to escape the law when you live on an island. Scofflaws ended up here, in an 1806 jailhouse in use until 1933. Shingles mask the building's construction of massive square timbers, plainly visible inside. Walls, ceilings, and floors are bolted with iron. The furnishings consist of rough plank bunks and open privies, but toward the end of the jail's useful existence things got a bit lax: prisoners were allowed out at night to sleep in their own beds. ✉ *15R Vestal St.* ☎ *508/228–1894* ⊕ *www.nha.org* ✇ *NHA History Ticket only* ☉ *Late May–early Sept., daily 10–5.*

✋ ❷ Old Mill. Several windmills sat on Nantucket hills in the 1700s, but only this 1746 Dutch-style octagonal one, built with lumber from shipwrecks, remains. The Douglas fir pivot pole used to turn the cap and sails into the wind is a replacement of the original pole, a ship's foremast. The mill's wooden gears work on wind power, and when the wind is strong enough, corn is ground into meal that is sold here. An NHA interpreter is on hand to lead tours and answer questions. ✉ *50 Prospect St., at S. Mill St.* ☎ *508/228–1894* ⊕ *www.nha.org* ✇ *NHA History Ticket only* ☉ *Late May–early Sept., daily 10–5.*

㉙ Oldest House. History and architecture buffs should be sure to get a look at this hilltop house, also called the Jethro Coffin House, built in 1686 as a wedding gift for Jethro and Mary Gardner Coffin. The most striking feature of the saltbox is the massive central brick chimney with brick horseshoe adornment said to ward away witches. Other highlights are the enormous hearths and diamond-pane leaded-glass windows. Cutaway panels show 17th-century construction techniques. An NHA interpreter will tell you about the home's history and the interior's sparse furnishings, including an antique loom. ✉ *Sunset Hill (a 10- to 15-min walk along Centre St. from Main St.)* ☎ *508/228–1894* ⊕ *www.nha. org* ✇ *NHA History Ticket only* ☉ *Late May–early Sept., daily 10–5.*

㉒ Pacific Club. The building still houses the elite club of Pacific whaling masters for which it's named. However, since the last whaling ship was seen here in 1870, the club now admits whalers' descendants, who gather to enjoy the odd cribbage game or to swap tales. The building first served in 1772 as the counting house of William Rotch, owner of the *Dartmouth* and the *Beaver,* two of the three ships that hosted a famous tea party in Boston. The club is not open to the public, but a gallery occupies the main floor. ⊠ *Main and S. Water Sts.*

⑰ Pacific National Bank. Like the Pacific Club it faces, the bank, dating to 1818 and still in use today, is a monument to the far-flung voyages of the Nantucket whaling ships it financed. Inside, above old-style teller cages, are 1954 murals of scenes from the whaling days. Note the **Meridian Stone** on the south side of the building and to the left—it's about 3 feet high and pointed on top. Placed here in the 1830s by astronomers Maria Mitchell and her father, William, it marks the town's precise meridian—an important point to early navigators. ⊠ *61 Main St.*

⑲ Quaker Meeting House. Built around 1838 as a Friends school, the Meeting House is now a year-round place of worship. A small room of quiet simplicity, with antique-glass 12-over-12 windows and unadorned wood benches, it is in keeping with the Quaker tenets that the divine spirit is within each person and that no one requires an intermediary (or elaborate church) to worship God. The adjoining **Fair Street Museum** was built in 1904 of poured concrete. Though it may seem a bit plain-Jane now, at the time its cost of $8,300 was high and its structure technically advanced. With the memory of Nantucket's Great Fire still fresh, planners wanted to safeguard their historical artifacts from that fate. Today the museum presents rotating NHA exhibits. ⊠ *1 Fair St.* ☎ *508/ 228–1655 or 508/228–1894* ⊕ *www.nha.org* ▨ *$10 or NHA History Ticket* ☉ *Services Sun. at 10 AM. Museum, late May–early Sept., daily 10–5; early Sept.–late May, Mon.–Sat. 10–5, Sun. noon–5.*

⑳ St. Paul's Episcopal Church. On a hot day, peek into the massive granite structure dating to 1901 and adorned at the front and back by beautiful Tiffany windows. The interior is cool and white, with dark exposed beams, and offers a quiet sanctuary from the summer crowds and the heat. ⊠ *20 Fair St.* ☎ *508/228–0916* ⊕ *www.stpaulsnantucket.org* ☉ *Services Sun. at 8 AM and 10 AM.*

⑤ Starbuck refinery and candle works. Nantucket is packed with places that speak of its history. Off New Dollar Lane by Milk Street, and down a long driveway, the remains of the refinery and works named for the Nantucket whaling family are now used as apartments and garages.

★ ⑫ "Three Bricks." Many of the mansions of the golden age of whaling were built on Upper Main Street. These well-known identical redbrick homes, with columned Greek Revival porches at their front entrances, were built between 1836 and 1838 by whaling merchant Joseph Starbuck for his three sons. One house still belongs to a Starbuck descendant. The Three Bricks are similar in design to the Jared Coffin House but have only two stories. They are not open to the public. ⊠ *93–97 Main St.*

㉑ Unitarian Universalist Church. The 1809 church, also known as South Church, has a gold-dome spire that soars above town, just as the First Congregational Church's slender white steeple does. Also like First

Congregational, South Church has a trompe-l'oeil ceiling painting, this one simulating an intricately detailed dome and painted by Swiss artist Carl Wendte in 1844. Here, however, illusion is taken to greater lengths: the curved chancel and paneled walls you see are also creations in paint. The 1831 mahogany-cased Goodrich organ in the loft is played at services and concerts. In the octagonal belfry of the tower, which houses the town clock, is a bell cast in Portugal that has been ringing out the noon hour ever since it was hung in 1830. ⊠ *11 Orange St.* ☎ *508/228–5466* ☉ *Services Sun. at 10:45* AM.

⑱ United Methodist Church. Another miraculous survivor of the Great Fire of 1846, this 1823 building was treated to a grand Doric-columned facade in 1840. Badly deteriorating by 1999, it was declared an endangered historic treasure and paid a visit by then-First Lady Hillary Clinton. Now undergoing a major restoration effort, it houses a small congregation, as well as two small theater spaces. Organ aficionados may want to have a look at the 1831 Appleton—one of only four extant. ⊠ *2 Centre St.* ☎ *508/228–0810* ☉ *Services Sun. at 10* AM.

Vestal Street Observatory. Daytime tours at the tiny brick observatory built in 1908 concentrate on the history and development of the telescope, and sunspot observations can be arranged. The museum also has an outdoor solar system model and an intricate sundial that is accurate almost to the minute. ⊠ *3 Vestal St.* ☎ *508/228–9273* ⊕ *www.mmo. org* ≤ *$4 or MMA pass* ☉ *Mid-June–mid-Sept., Tues.–Sat. tour at 11* AM; *mid-Sept.–mid-June, Sat. tour at 11* AM.

★ ☾ ㉖ Whaling Museum and Peter Foulger Museum. Immersing you in Nantucket's whaling past with exhibits that include a fully rigged whaleboat and a skeleton of a 43-foot finback whale, the museum, in an 1846 factory built for refining spermaceti and making candles, is a must-see. Also exhibited are harpoons and other whale-hunting implements; portraits of sea captains; a large collection of exquisitely carved scrimshaw; a full-size tryworks once used to process whale oil aboard ship; replicas of cooper, blacksmith, and other ship-fitting shops; and the original 16-foot-high lens from Sankaty Head Lighthouse. To help you contextualize all this paraphernalia, the knowledgeable and enthusiastic staff gives a 20- to 30-minute introductory talk peppered with compelling tales of a whaler's life at sea (call for times). The adjoining Foulger Museum, an exact replica of the Coffin School built in the 1970s, hosts engaging changing exhibits from the NHA's permanent collection, including portraits, historical documents, and furniture. Don't miss the gift shop, packed with tasteful souvenirs, from books to toys and home accessories. ⊠ *13–15 Broad St.* ☎ *508/228–1894* ≤ *$10 or NHA pass* ☉ *Late May–mid-Oct., daily 10–5; call for off-season hours.*

Where to Eat

Nantucket Town

$$$$ ✕ **Company of the Cauldron.** The tiny dining room, a sconce-lit haven of architectural salvage, is served by an even smaller kitchen, whence chef–owner All Kovalencik issues only one menu per evening. Adepts

gladly forego multiple-choice when the chef's choice is invariably so dead-on. (Rundowns of the weekly roster are available over the phone or online.) Given the close quarters, expect to come away not only sated but better acquainted with your near neighbors: the Cauldron is like a select dinner party where the guests are self-invited. ⊠ *7 India St.* ☎ *508/228–4016* ⚑ *Reservations essential* ▭ MC, V ⊘ *Closed Dec.–May. No lunch.*

★ $$$$ ✕ **the pearl.** This ultracool space—a sophisticated upstairs cousin to the Boarding House—is seriously chic, with a white onyx bar lit a Curaçao blue and, behind an aquarium divider, cushy leather banquettes. These— plus the garden porch, where tasting dinners can be prearranged—are the power seats. However, everyone is well served by Seth Raynor's en- thusiasm for clarion flavors, usually delivered with an Asian twist—for example, wok-fried quail with green-pea pancakes. For truly exciting cuisine, at somewhat dizzying prices, this is the place to patronize—pro- vided you can score a reservation. ⊠ *12 Federal St.* ☎ *508/228–9701* ▭ *AE, D, MC, V* ⊘ *Closed mid-Oct.–Mar. No lunch.*

$$$$ ✕ **Straight Wharf.** This loft–like restaurant with harborside deck has enjoyed legendary status for two decades. At the helm since 1995, ex- ecutive chef Steve Cavagnaro immediately inspires confidence with an intense lobster bisque with an undertone of caramel. The promise is upheld in subsequent dishes: everything from cuisine to service is just right, if a bit on the pricey side. If you'd like a preview, try the less costly café menu at the adjoining bar—that is, if you can get in. It be- comes quite the social scene as the evening progresses. ⊠ *6 Harbor Sq., Straight Wharf* ☎ *508/228–4499* ▭ *AE, MC, V* ⊘ *Closed late Sept.–mid-May. No lunch.*

★ $$$$ ✕ **21 Federal.** An avatar of the new American revolution since 1985, 21 Federal retains its creative edge, thanks to the ever-avant menus of chef Russell Jaehnig. Nothing is too outré, mind you, in this handsome 1847 Greek Revival house with sconce-lit, dove-gray interiors. But the food has a spark to match the spirited clientele (some of the celebrated bar's bonhomie invariably spills over): vide the slow-roasted porto- bello pudding or the lobster/short ribs combo with white truffle po- lenta. ⊠ *21 Federal St.* ☎ *508/228–2121* ▭ *AE, MC, V* ⊘ *Closed Jan.–Mar.*

$$$–$$$$ ✕ **The Boarding House.** Beyond the throngs of madly mingling twen- tysomethings—the bar is extremely popular—you'll encounter a culi- nary oasis, a semi-subterranean space lined with vaguely Mediterranean murals, where chef–owner Seth Raynor showcases his skill with the cui- sine of that region. The lively dishes here are every bit as good as those at the pearl and generally more affordable. The menu for the sidewalk café menu, open in summer, isn't all that steep, but good luck getting a table; everyone with any taste has already had the same bright idea. ⊠ *12 Federal St.* ☎ *508/228–9622* ▭ *AE, MC, V.*

$$$–$$$$ ✕ **Brant Point Grill.** With its beautiful broad lawn set harborside, the Brant Point Grill—in-house restaurant for the elegant White Elephant hotel— proffers a straightforward haute-steak house menu; the meats are as- suredly prime. You may also be tempted by the miso-marinated roast cod, or the salmon smoked in plain sight, on cedar planks poised down-

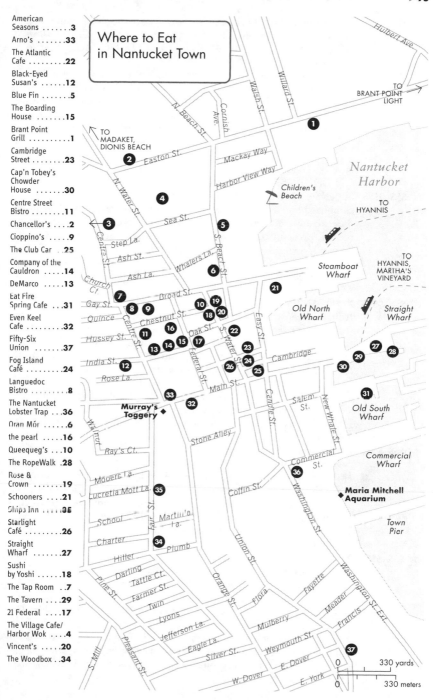

Where to Eat in Nantucket Town

wind from a blazing brazier. The desserts are fabulous (more so than the main event), and even breakfast becomes a feast. ✉ *50 Easton St.* ☎ *508/325–1320 or 800/445–6574* ▭ *AE, D, DC, MC, V* ☉ *Closed mid-Dec.–Apr.*

$$$–$$$$ ✕ **The Club Car.** A longtime favorite among the moneyed set, this boxy dining room—its adjoining piano bar is an actual railroad car from the dismantled Sconset narrow-gauge—has never quite shaken its Continental origins (read occasionally salty sauces). Richness, however, has its own rewards, as in a plump double-cut slab of swordfish rolled in moisture-retaining crushed almonds and walnuts, topped with pecan butter. As for the Opera Cake—a kind of stand-up tiramisu—tradition never tasted so good. ✉ *1 Main St.* ☎ *508/228–1101* ▭ *AE, MC, V* ☉ *Closed mid-Dec.–mid-May. No lunch.*

$$$–$$$$ ✕ **DeMarco.** Northern Italian cuisine debuted on-island at this cored-out clapboard house in 1980, slightly ahead of the wave. The delights endure: "badly cut" homemade pasta, for instance, in a sauce of wild mushrooms, prosciutto, and fresh sage or roasted-beet ravioli. Of late, however, owner Don DeMarco has begun tweaking the menu to cater to today's playful, global leanings. The result? The best of both worlds. ✉ *9 India St.* ☎ *508/228–1836* ▭ *AE, MC, V* ☉ *Closed Mid-Oct.–late May. No lunch.*

Ⓒ $$$–$$$$ ✕ **Fifty-Six Union.** You can tell there's a playful spirit at work here, just from the overdressed mannequin usually propped up at a café table out front. That party-time spirit extends to the rear patio, where kids actually have their own play corner. Peter Jannelle's cuisine, however, is as adult and "serious" as can be: his mussels in a mild Thai curry broth, for instance, are as good as they come, and his Javanese spice fried rice packs a wallop. You can tell he has been around, and happy patrons get to go along—the lucky ones—with a personalized tasting menu served at the chef's table in the garden. The restaurant also puts on a festive Sunday brunch. ✉ *56 Union St.* ☎ *508/228–6135* ▭ *AE, MC, V* ☉ *No lunch.*

$$$–$$$$ ✕ **Languedoc Bistro.** The name notwithstanding, this multifaceted restaurant, founded in 1975, long ago cast off Gallic convention to embrace new American eclecticism. A light menu is served noon to 5 PM in the garden, in the cheery cellar café bistro; dinner—an elegant, elaborate affair—unfurls in the formal dining rooms (one of which is a crimson-painted knockout). Every level satisfies. ✉ *24 Broad St.* ☎ *508/228–2552* ⚲ *Reservations essential* ▭ *AE, MC, V* ☉ *Closed Jan.–mid-Apr.*

★ $$$–$$$$ ✕ **Oran Mór.** Talk about locally sourced: Chef–owner Peter Wallace, who opened this tastefully decorated second-story hideaway in 1995 after putting Topper's at the Wauwinet on the culinary map, gets his fluke—presented as a *crépinette* enrobing lobster—exclusively from the "cord of the bay" extending from Great Point to Jetties. The samphire (sea beans) accompanying the crab cake with foamy cucumber vinaigrette and tomato-lemon jam, he picks himself, in Polpis Harbor. This is obviously someone who cares deeply about what he serves, and you can taste the artistry in every bite. ✉ *2 S. Beach St.* ☎ *508/228–8655* ▭ *AE, MC, V* ☉ *No lunch.*

$$$–$$$$ ✕ **The Ropewalk.** It's time to revise that tired old axiom of coastal living, that you can never find good food right on the water. Here at the very end of Straight Wharf (go any farther and you'll be boarding someone's yacht), the setting and cooking keep pace. Preparations are fairly straightforward—e.g., crispy lacquered salmon—but fish is often best unmessed with. ✉ *1 Straight Wharf* ☎ *508/228–8886* ▭ *AE, MC, V* ☉ *Closed Nov.–Apr.*

$$–$$$$ ✕ **Cioppino's.** Tracy and Susie Root's elegant house-restaurant has been popular since day one (in 1990). Beyond the signature dish—a San Franciscan seafood stew—the menu is ambitious, marrying classic technique and contemporary taste—for instance, a colorful beet, avocado, and goat cheese pyramid that's as tasty as it is pretty. Desserts have their own following: it's especially pleasant to stop in at the patio late in the evening for a light and convivial, if caloric, bite. ✉ *20 Broad St.* ☎ *508/228–4622* ▭ *D, DC, MC, V* ☉ *Closed Nov.–Apr.*

$$–$$$$ ✕ **Ships Inn.** Tucked into the *rez-de-chaussée* (demi-basement) of Captain Obed Starbuck's handsome 1831 mansion, this peach-tint, candlelit restaurant is a light and lovely haven wherein French cuisine meets a California sensibility and both cultures are the richer for it. If you want to eat healthy, you can—but why not sin a little and sup on foie gras with blackberry sauce or paillard of duck with fresh plums? Compound the transgression with the soufflé du jour. ✉ *13 Fair St.* ☎ *508/228–0040* ▭ *AE, D, MC, V* ☉ *Closed Nov.–Apr. No lunch.*

★ $$–$$$$ ✕ **The Woodbox.** Antiquity meets a modernist culinary sensibility in this 1709 house complete with its original "keeping room," or kitchen—the prize among three very lovely wattle-and-daub dining rooms. A parade of gifted chefs has passed through these portals over the decades. The current chef, Matthew Zadorozny, who transferred from the Company of the Cauldron, lives up to the tradition, creating such sophisticated concoctions as salmon roulade with edamame-lobster cassoulet. Regulars would rebel if the signature beef Wellington were ever to be dropped, or indeed the summer weekend breakfasts, with their signature popovers. ✉ *29 Fair St.* ☎ *508/228–0587* ⚑ *Reservations essential* ▭ *No credit cards* ☉ *Closed Mon. and Jan.–Apr. No lunch.*

¢–$$$$ ✕ **Sushi by Yoshi.** This little jewel box of a restaurant purveys the output of Yoshihisa Mabuchi, a welcome "washashore" originally from Japan. The sushi and sashimi, available in dozens of guises, are nonpareil: try a special concoction such as the Caterpillar, a veggie roll wrapped in avocado. Also available are classic dishes ranging from gyoza to udon, soba, and teriyaki and, for dessert, green-tea ice cream and banana tempura. ✉ *2 E. Chestnut St.* ☎ *508/228–1801* 🖷 *508/228–5827* ▭ *No credit cards* ⚐ *BYOB* ☉ *Closed Nov.–May.*

★ $$$ ✕ **American Seasons.** At once playful and tasteful, this intimate space arrayed with folk art—you'll be dining on a lacquered game table—is commensurately romantic. It's not just the subdued lighting and smooth service. Chef Michael LaScola started out here tending the garde-manger in 1991, at the tender age of sixteen. Now that he owns the place, he's exercising his full chefly genius in festively presented dishes that roam the continental United States, from the Pacific Coast to New England, by way of the Wild West and Down South. From his signature foie gras crème brûlée to orange-and-basil-marinated lobster in a salified vanilla puree, expect spectacular pan-regional pyrotechnics. ✉ *80 Centre St.* ☎ *508/228–7111* ☰ *AE, MC, V* ◷ *Closed Jan.–mid-Apr. No lunch.*

$$$ ✗ **Blue Fin.** It's only 6:30, it's a weekday, it's *off-season,* and still, every single seat in this intimate bistro (40, give or take, including the moon glow–lit bar) is occupied: the joint, done up in nautical navy and white, is indisputably jumping. The draw: good, affordable food that's attitude-free. The guy behind the sushi bar, filling orders with flying fingers, is young chef–owner Jonas Baker, who trained in New York chez Peter Kump. Simplicity triumphs, as in a straightforward but sensational dish of cornmeal-crusted whole red snapper with white bean ragout and fried leeks. No wonder locals are loyal fans. ✉ *15 S. Beach St.* ☎ *508/ 228–2033* ☰ *MC, V.*

$$–$$$ ✗ **The Atlantic Cafe.** Long popular with visitors and locals alike, the "AC" has a gifted chef in Dante Benatti, who graces the crowd-pleasers with a bit of culinary finesse. The nautical flotsam that represents the bulk of the decor is not some decorator's scheme but vestiges of the real thing. ✉ *15 S. Water St.* ☎ *508/228–0570* ☰ *AE, D, DC, MC, V.*

$$–$$$ ✗ **Black-Eyed Susan's.** From a passing glance, you'd never peg this
Fodor'sChoice seemingly humble storefront as one of Nantucket's chic eateries—but
★ as the invariable lines attest, it is. The luncheonette setup is offset by improbably fancy glass chandeliers, and foodies lay claim to the stools to observe chef Jeff Worster's often pyromaniacal "open kitchen." The dinner menu, which changes every three weeks, ventures boldly around the world and never lacks for novelty. The breakfasts (served until 1 PM) are just as stellar, including such eye-openers as sourdough French toast with orange, Jack Daniels butter and pecans. ✉ *10 India St.* ☎ *508/325–0308* ☰ *No credit cards* ⌂ *BYOB* ◷ *Closed Nov.–Mar. No dinner Sun., no lunch.*

$$–$$$ ✗ **Cambridge Street.** This in-town storefront started out primarily as a bar—and the original room, painted midnight-blue and decorated with bizarre artifacts (such as a Medusa chandelier), is still a primo spot for spirited mixing. Chef–owner Brand Gould's open-grill international fusion cuisine proved so popular, though, that a quieter nook had to be added on. Even the most jaded of palates will thrill to this pan-Asian–barbecue–Middle Eastern mélange. All ages and strata come here to be shaken *and* stirred and never, ever gouged. ✉ *12 Cambridge St.* ☎ *508/228–ₗ 7109* ☰ *AE, D, DC, MC, V* ◷ *Closed mid-Jan.–Mar. No lunch.*

$$–$$$ ✗ **Cap'n Tobey's Chowder House.** In 2002, Kate and John O'Connor (who also own the Atlantic Cafe) overhauled this retro-1950s dive: it's seaside-moderne now, awash in halogen-lit aqua tones. Late at night, it morphs into the closest thing on island to a disco. Before the dancers get going, you can dine on such well-priced preparations as pistachio-crusted pan-seared tuna with caramelized shallots or more typical fried seafood. ✉ *20 Straight Wharf* ☎ *508/228–0836* ☰ *AE, D, DC, MC, V* ◷ *Closed Nov.–Apr.*

$$–$$$ ✗ **Centre Street Bistro.** Tiny—there are only 20 seats indoors, and as many out—and perfect, this gem of a bistro is a find that devoted locals almost wish they could keep to themselves. Having honed their chops at the celebrated Summer House in Sconset, chef–owners Tim and Ruth Pitts provide an astounding three meals a day and stay open year-round (cutting back a bit in the slow season). The menu evolves throughout the year; desserts depend on inspiration and invariably receive it. ⊠ *29 Centre St.* ☎ *508/228–8470* ⊟ *MC, V.*

$$–$$$ ✕ **Chancellor's.** A once grand hotel, built in 1892, the Point Breeze has started to revive of late at the hands of attentive local owners. Its dining hall (a former basketball court), though fresh and airy, is not exactly intimate, and the food, alas, fails to transport. Stick with standards like filet mignon. ⊠ *71 Easton St.* ☎ *508/228–8674* ⊟ *AE, MC, V* ⊘ *Closed Mon. and early Sept.–mid-June. No lunch.*

$$–$$$ ✕ **Eat Fire Spring Cafe.** Tim Madden, who runs this festive awning-covered café with this three daughters (the youngest is the official dessert-taster), named it for the water source near his Wauwinet home. Like a spring, it bubbles—with fun, whether in the form of creative cocktails (the "Nanhattan" involves cranberries, of course), light and zesty cuisine, or the live jazz playing nightly. ⊠ *14 Old South Wharf* ☎ *508/ 228–7774* ⊟ *MC, V* ⊘ *Closed Sun. and Nov.–Apr.*

$$–$$$ ✕ **Even Keel Cafe.** This former ice-cream parlor, with its tin ceilings and pretty backyard patio, is no mere restaurant but the very heart of town—especially off-season, when patrons are treated to two-for-one entrées. Any time of year, it's the first place to head for a fancy coffee, pastry binge, or creative meal. ⊠ *40 Main St.* ☎ *508/228–1979* ⊟ *AE, MC, V.*

$$–$$$ ✕ **The Nantucket Lobster Trap.** You might not care much for the atmosphere at this fairly standard fish house with conventional offerings (bacon-wrapped scallops, stuffed quahogs, etc.). The ubiquity of TV screens gives it a sports-bar ambience—although no one seems to mind. Fussy types can always cart their feast to the beach: inquire about "Meals on Keels." ⊠ *25 Washington St.* ☎ *508/228–4200* ⊟ *AE, MC, V* ⊘ *Closed mid-Oct.–early May. No lunch.*

$$ $$$ ✕ **Queequeg's.** More casual in mood than some of its neighbors but nonetheless dedicated to quality, this indoor-outdoor bistro straddles classical cuisine (bay scallops with citrus beurre blanc) and fusiony experimentation (deep-fried calamari with Asian dipping sauce)—worth a shot when you're part of a disparate party. ⊠ *6 Oak St.* ☎ *508/325–0992* ⊟ *MC, V.*

$$–$$$ ✕ **Schooners.** The theme is definitely nautical, but smartly so: flags strung from the rafters and navy awnings over the sidewalk café seem right at home on Steamboat Wharf. The menu is fairly pro forma (rings, wings, steamers, shore dinners), but the pricing is nice, considering what they could get away with. ⊠ *31 Easy St.* ☎ *508/228–5824* ⊟ *AE, MC, V* ⊘ *Closed mid-Oct.–Mar.*

$$–$$$ ✕ **Starlight Café.** The tiny movie-theater anteroom and patio have been reconfigured and spiffed up with cinematic artifacts. The casual menu—mac 'n cheese with lobster!—is perfect for a pre- or post-flick feed. ⊠ *1 N. Union St.* ☎ *508/228–4479* ⊟ *AE, MC, V* ⊘ *Closed Nov.–Apr.*

☾ **$–$$$** ✕ **Rose & Crown.** Crayon-friendly paper tablecloths and a children's menu cater to a family audience early in the evening; later, DJs and signature drinks stoke the post-collegiate crowd. There's nothing very special about the menu (who could foresee the day when ahi tuna atop Szechuan noodles would seem ordinary?), but you can amuse yourself, while waiting, by studying the old signs hung about this former carriage livery. ⊠ *23 S. Water St.* ☎ *508/228–2595* ▭ *AE, MC, V* ☻ *Closed Jan.–Mar.*

$–$$$ ✕ **The Tap Room.** Dark and clubby, this basement eatery in the Jared Coffin House looks lifted from John Cheever territory: you'll see people huddled at the bar at all times of day. In summer the restaurant spills onto a flowery patio—a rather more cheerful place to partake of such staples as broiled cod and prime rib. ⊠ *29 Broad St.* ☎ *508/228–2400* ▭ *AE, D, DC, MC, V.*

☾ **$–$$$** ✕ **Vincent's.** One might be tempted to bypass Vincent's because, in this fiercely competitive field, it doesn't look like a real contender. That's precisely its strength. This relaxed Italian restaurant, little changed since 1954, is where islanders go to enjoy a really good meal, freshly prepared, generously portioned, and refreshingly free of pretense. The dishes may not be uniformly cutting-edge, but they're proven winners. The variety is phenomenal: the menu has upwards of three dozen entrées, and not one disappoints. ⊠ *21 S. Water St.* ☎ *508/228–0189* ▭ *D, MC, V* ☻ *Closed Jan.–Mar.*

☾ **$$** ✕ **Fog Island Café.** Cherished year-round for its stellar breakfasts, Fog Island is just as fine a spot for lunch or, in season, a most charitably priced dinner. The storefront space is cheerily decked out in a fresh country style (echoed in the friendly service), and chef–owners Mark and Anne Dawson—both Culinary Institute of America grads—seem determined to provide the best possible value to transients and natives alike. Consider starting the day with, say, pesto scrambled eggs and ending it with Caribbean-spiced smoked salmon with cucumber "noodles." Finally, fine food for the proletariat! ⊠ *7 S. Water St.* ☎ *508/228–1818* ▭ *MC, V* ☻ *Closed Jan.–Mar.*

$$ ✕ **The Tavern.** This is the two-tiered restaurant with deck you can't help noticing just off Straight Wharf. Its bar has colonized the bandstand in the middle of the cobblestone square, and the whole place is almost always mobbed—partly thanks to a middle-of-the-road menu that stresses seafood (mostly fried or broiled). ⊠ *1 Harbor Sq., Straight Wharf* ☎ *508/228–1266* ▭ *AE, MC, V* ☻ *Closed mid-Oct.–mid-May.*

☾ **$$** ✕ **The Village Cafe/Harbor Wok.** A mild-mannered sit-down/take-out breakfast spot called the Village Cafe by day reinvents itself at night as a classic Chinese restaurant. The family-oriented member of the Nantucket Island Resorts consortium, this 1886 grand hotel has found the perfect way to cater to its target demographic—as well as to locals who had resorted to flying their feasts in. It also comes as a great relief that the tradition of eclectic, all-you-can-eat Sunday buffet brunches is herein upheld. ⊠ *Harbor House Village, S. Beach St.* ☎ *508/325–1300 or 866/ 325–9300* ▭ *AE, MC, V* ☻ *Closed early Sept.–June.*

$–$$ ✕ **Arno's.** Arno's makes optimal use of its prime location right on Main Street to present lush breakfasts (some featuring lobster), hearty lunches, and surprisingly ambitious dinners, all generously apportioned and modestly priced. (Warning: the wonderful warm spinach salad, Greekified with feta and kalamatas, is a meal in itself.) Molly

Dee's nostalgic canvases adorn the brick walls. Expect some envious looks—from within and without—if you get to sit near the storefront windows. ⊠ *41 Main St.* ☎ *508/228–7001* ⊟ *AE, D, MC, V* ☻ *Closed Jan.–Mar.*

Nantucket Town Outskirts

A handful of restaurants are just outside Nantucket Town, and a few minutes away by bike or car. For these restaurants, *see* the Where to Stay & Eat Outside of Nantucket Town map. For restaurants in Siasconset and elsewhere, *see* Siasconset, the South Shore, and Madaket.

$$$$ ✕ **The Galley.** A beloved institution since 1958, this modest cottage plunked right on the Cliffside Beach Club's swath of sand has managed to stay fresh and luxe thanks to three generations of restaurateurs who know how to spot and foster talent in the kitchen. These days, that's Steven Polowy, who trained at the New England Culinary Institute and absorbed their philosophy regarding simplicity of preparation and clarity of taste. Everything dazzles here, from the crab cake (best ever) in a sunny lemongrass beurre blanc to the butter-laced lobster with fresh creamed corn. The deck, with its gay blue-and-white awning ringed with red geraniums, takes in a 180-degree beach view; it's perfectly oriented to capture what photographers call "the golden moment." ⊠ *54 Jefferson Ave.* ☎ *508/228–9641* ⊟ *AE, MC, V* ☻ *Closed Oct.–mid-May.*

$$$–$$$$ ✕ **West Creek Café.** A rehabbed ranch house in the mid-island commercial district would seem to be the last place to seek out cosmopolitan panache, but this hideaway—owned by Pat Tyler of the lamented Second Story restaurant, a trendsetter in the '80s—is full of surprises. Purple satin pillows and faux-zebra banquettes snazz up the cool gray barroom; the other two rooms are crackle-painted in a sunny palate, and one has a working fireplace. The menu shifts with the season, and fans gladly follow along. ⊠ *11 W. Creek Rd.* ☎ *508/228–4943* ⊟ *MC, V* ☻ *Closed Tues. No lunch.*

$$$ ✕ **Seagrille.** Though it may lack the flashy profile of other top island restaurants, this mid-island eatery deserves its popularity. The lobster bisque alone, even without the bonus of a dilled *en croute bonnet*, would warrant a following, as does the free-form seafood ravioli. Off-season, the dining room, with its murals of wharf and street scenes, is a peaceful haven. Come summer, and the crowds do, too. ⊡ *15 Sparks Ave.* ☎ *508/325–5700* ⊟ *AE, MC, V.*

$$–$$$ ✕ **The Hen House.** Another mid-island destination for the non-trust-funded, this unassuming restaurant started out as a breakfast joint catering to the island's large Irish summer workforce—you can still get rashers with your eggs—and soon turned into a source of three square meals, mostly of the stick-to-your-ribs school (baby-back ribs, grilled sirloin, etc.). In season, you can get take-out till all hours—well, till 2 AM, which is way late, island time. ⊠ *1 Chin's Way* ☎ *508/228–2639* ⍓ *BYOB* ⊟ *MC, V.*

$$–$$$ ✕ **Sfoglia.** Ron and Colleen Suhanosky enjoy a marriage made post–culinary school (both attended the Culinary Institute of America). Their celery-tinted trattoria is appointed with mismatched tables (including some enamel-top honeys from the '40s), chairs, crockery, even silverware, and the menu lists such home-style Italian dishes as fluffy gnocchi with pesto and lamb chops with figs, black olives, and rosemary. Desserts—Colleen's province—include an ultrasilky panna cotta. ⊠ *130 Pleasant St.* ☎ *508/325–4500* ▭ *No credit cards.*

$–$$$ **Kitty Murtaugh's.** A 2003 addition to mid-island, this pub does its best to replicate its Irish forebears, with cottage pie, bangers and mash, bacon and cabbage, and more. Steaks are a specialty (they rate their own menu heading, "The Butcher Shop"), and of course the fish-and-chips gets a Guinness batter. Much of the seasonal workforce hails from the Auld Sod, and now they need never feel homesick. ⊠ *4 West Creek Rd.* ☎ *508/325–0781* ▭ *MC, V.*

¢–$ ✕ **The Downyflake.** Locals flock here for bountiful breakfasts—featuring the much sought-after homemade doughnuts—and well-priced lunches, from codfish cakes to burgers. ⊠ *18 Sparks Ave.* ☎ *508/228–4533* ▭ *No credit cards* ◎ *No dinner.*

Where to Stay

Nantucket Town

$$$$ 🏨 **White Elephant.** A sister property to the Wauwinet since 1999, the White Elephant—a misnomered 1920s behemoth right on Nantucket Harbor—seems determined to keep raising the bar in terms of service and style. The complex, consisting of a main hotel plus several annexes treated to a breezy country-chic decor, hugs the harbor, leaving just enough room for an emerald lawn and the veranda of its in-house restaurant, the Brant Point Grill. Prices are up there but, for the echelon it attracts, not all that extreme. ⊠ *Easton St.* ⚓ *Box 1139, 02554* ☎ *508/228–2500 or 800/445–6574* 🖶 *508/325–1195* ⊕ *www.whiteelephanthotel.com* ⬎ *21 rooms, 31 suites, 11 cottages* ⚫ *Restaurant, room service, in-room data ports, refrigerators, cable TV, exercise equipment, dock, lounge, library, laundry service, concierge, business services, Internet, meeting rooms* ▭ *AE, D, DC, MC, V* ◎ *Closed Nov.–Mar.* ⦿*BP.*

$$$–$$$$ 🏨 **VNH (Vanessa Noel Hotel).** Minimalist chic has waltzed in the door—and in a sweet pair of kitty heels. Opened in 2002 by native New Yorker and island shoe designer Vanessa Noel, VNH, Nantucket's first boutique hotel, is decked out by the best: each room has Armani Casa bedside tables, Philippe Starck bathroom fixtures, and Bulgari toiletries. Though the concept is at odds with the island aesthetic, you'd be hard pressed to name a hotel with these touches—plus flat-screen plasma TVs and direct phone lines—in New York, London, or Paris. Mind you, some of the rooms are shoe boxes. ⊠ *5 Chestnut St, at Centre St., 02554* ☎ *508/ 228–5300* ⊕ *www.vanessanoel.com* ⬎ *8 rooms* ⚫ *Minibars, cable TV, bar; no kids* ▭ *AE, D, MC, V.*

$$–$$$$ 🏨 **The Cottages at the Boat Basin.** These weathered-shingle cottages sit on South Wharf, amid the yachts—in fact, you could reserve a mooring and bring your own boat. Cottages range from studios to three bedrooms, and each has attractive modern decor with a nautical flavor: white walls, navy blue rugs, and light-wood floors and furniture. All have water views, though they're not always equal—some cottages have picture windows—plus a little garden terrace. All of the amenities available at the Harbor House Village extend here, including the children's programs. ✉ *New Whale St.* 🕿 *Box 1139, 02554* ☎ *508/325–1499 or 866/838–9253* 🖷 *508/228–7639* ⊕ *www.thecottagesnantucket. com* 🔁 *33 cottages* ⚲ *Kitchenettes, in-room VCRs, dock, marina, Internet, some pets allowed* ⊟ *AE, D, DC, MC, V* ⊙ *Closed mid-Oct.–late Apr.* ⫢ *BP.*

★ **$$–$$$** ⚏ **Jared Coffin House.** The largest house in town when it was built in 1845, this three-story brick manse is still plenty impressive—and is guaranteed to remain so, having been added to the Island Resorts fold (White Elephant, Wauwinet, etc.) in 2004. The antiques-filled parlors and formal dining room are a study in timeless good taste. The inn's umbrella extends to three other nearby buildings, the handsomest of which is the 1842 Greek Revival Harrison Gray House. Rooms vary greatly in terms of size and grandeur (the inn even has some very affordable singles), but one thing is assured: stay—or just breakfast or dine—here, and you'll have a better sense of what Nantucket's all about. ✉ *29 Broad St.* 🕿 *Box 1580, 02554* ☎ *508/228–2405 or 800/248–2405* ⊕ *www. jaredcoffinhouse.com* 🔁 *60 rooms* ⚲ *Restaurant, café, cable TV, bar, concierge* ⊟ *AE, D, DC, MC, V* ⫢ *BP.*

★ **$$–$$$** ⚏ **Nantucket Whaler.** Let's not mince words: the suites carved out of this 1850 Greek Revival house are gorgeous. Neither Calliope Ligeles nor Randi Ott, the New Yorkers who rescued the place in 1999, had any design experience, but they approached the project as if preparing to welcome friends. Each suite has a private entrance and the wherewithal to whip up a meal. The spacious bedrooms are lavished with flowers, well-chosen antiques, and fine linens, including plush robes. Couples who have come to explore not so much the island as one another will scarcely have to come up for air. ✉ *8 N. Water St.* 🕿 *Box 1337, 02554* ☎ *508/228–6597 or 800/462–6882* 🖷 *508/228–6291* ⊕ *www.nantucketwhaler. com* 🔁 *10 suites* ⚲ *Kitchenettes, cable TV, in-room VCRs, boccie, croquet; no kids under 12, no smoking* ⊟ *AE, MC, V* ⊙ *Closed mid-Dec.–mid-Apr.*

★ **$$–$$$** ⚏ **Union Street Inn.** Ken Withrow worked in the hotel business, Debra Withrow in high-end retail display, and guests get the best of both worlds. This 1770 house, a stone's throw from the bustle of Main Street, has been respectfully yet lavishly restored. Guests are treated to Frette linens, plump duvets, and lush robes (the better to lounge around in, my dear), as well as a full gourmet breakfast served on the tree-shaded garden patio. ✉ *7 Union St., 02554* ☎ *508/228–9222 or 800/225 5116* 🖷 *508/325–0848* ⊕ *www.unioninn.com* 🔁 *12 rooms* ⚲ *Cable TV; no kids under 12, no smoking* ⊟ *AE, MC, V* ⫢ *BP.*

$–$$$ ⚏ **Manor House.** The porches of this 1846 house are ideal for people-watching, and the garden is one of the loveliest spots in town. Rooms are spacious, with reproduction rice-carved beds. If not dazzling, they're definitely romantic; half have working fireplaces. ✉ *31 Centre St., at India St.* 🕿 *Box 1436, 02554* ☎ *508/228–0600 or 800/872–6830* 🖷 *508/228–3052* ⊕ *www.themanorhouseinn.com* 🔁 *15 rooms, 1 cottage* ⚲ *Some refrigerators, cable TV* ⊟ *D, MC, V* ⫢ *CP.*

$–$$$ ⚏ **The Veranda House.** The old Overlook, whose tiers of balconies take in a sweeping harbor vista, has been treated to a trendy overhaul. The

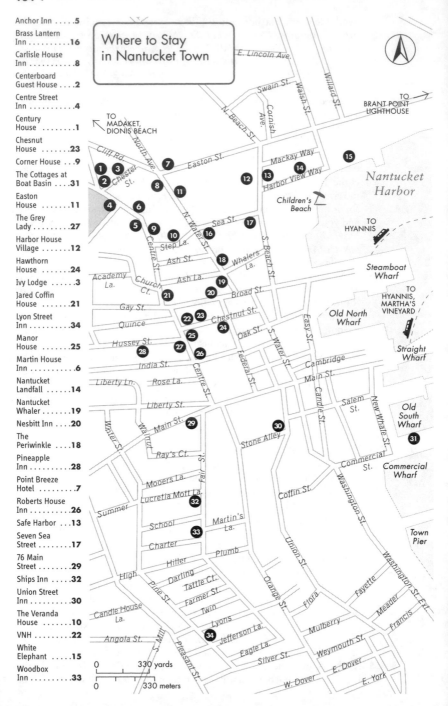

Where to Stay
in Nantucket Town

exterior may look unchanged, but in 2003 third-generation innkeeper Ethan Divine redid the rooms with Frette linens, Simon Pearce lamps, and the like, thereby restoring the 1884 institution to its original glory— and name. The breakfasts are unstinting as well, featuring frittatas or quiche, and artisanal cheeses. ⊠ *3 Step Lane* ⌂ *Box 1112, 02554* 📞 *508/228–0695* ⊕ *www.theverandahouse.com* ↝ *20 rooms* ⌖ *Internet, concierge; no kids under 10, no TV in some rooms, no room phones* ⊟ *MC, V* ☾ *Closed mid-Oct. to late May* ❑ *CP.*

☽ **$$** ▣ **Harbor House Village.** An 1886 grand hotel forms the core of this family-oriented complex, where nicely landscaped brick walkways lead to a half-dozen town houses and an outdoor heated pool. Rooms are decorated in a sunny pale-pine-and-wicker motif, and many come with private balconies. Parents longing for a little alone time can entrust their children to babysitters (in season) or the "Village Kids" program, where friendships quickly form. ⊠ *S. Beach St.* ⌂ *Box 1139, 02554* 📞 *508/228–1500 or 866/325–9300* 📠 *508/228–7639* ⊕ *www.harborhousevillage.com* ↝ *104 rooms* ⌖ *Restaurant, cable TV, pool, lounge, children's programs (ages 3–13), concierge, business services, meeting rooms* ⊟ *AE, D, DC, MC, V* ☾ *Closed mid-Dec.–mid-Apr.* ❑ *CP.*

★ **$–$$** ▣ **Brass Lantern Inn.** Behind the striking Greek Revival facade of the circa 1850 main inn is a Garden Wing of rather more recent provenance (the late 1970s), which harbors slightly more spacious examples of contemporary Nantucket decor. Whichever route you go, you'll have access to a home-baked Continental breakfast, as well as the Saturday evening wine-and-cheese garden parties—a fun way to meet your temporary neighbors and trade tips. ⊠ *11 N. Water St., 02554* 📞 *508/228–4064 or 800/377–6609* 📠 *508/325–0928* ⊕ *www.brasslanternnantucket.com* ↝ *17 rooms* ⌖ *Cable TV, some pets allowed* ⊟ *AE, MC, V* ❑ *CP.*

★ **$–$$** ▣ **Centerboard Guest House.** Victoriana, surprisingly, is in short supply on Nantucket: when the whaling boom fizzled, so did the island's disposable income. There's no dearth here, however. Stained-glass lamps and antique quilts adorn rooms ornate with original woodwork. Standouts include a first-floor suite with 11-foot ceilings and its own living room–library with parquet floors, fireplace, and bar; its green marble bath has a whirlpool tub. Also appealing is the "houseboat" room, which can sleep five; it even has a galley kitchen. ⊠ *8 Chester St., Box 456, 02554* 📞 *508/228–9696* ⊕ *www.centerboardguesthouse.com* ↝ *6 rooms, 1 suite* ⌖ *Refrigerators, cable TV; no smoking* ⊟ *MC, V* ❑ *CP.*

$–$$ ▣ **Hawthorn House.** Innkeepers since 1984, Mitchell and Diane Carl have filled their 1849 house with hooked rugs, stained glass, and works by island artists. Breakfast vouchers (worth $9 apiece) will help introduce you to a couple of nearby restaurants. ⊠ *2 Chestnut St., 02554* 📞📠 *508/228–1468* ⊕ *www.hawthornhouse.com* ↝ *9 rooms, 7 with bath* ⌖ *Some refrigerators; no a/c in some rooms, no room phones, no room TVs, no smoking* ⊟ *MC, V* ❑ *CP.*

$–$$ ▣ **Lyon Street Inn.** Ann Marie and Barry Foster's guesthouse, in a charming residential area a five-minute walk from the center of town, is packed with appealing period details, from salvaged Colonial mantles to antique soaking tubs. White walls create a clean stage for richly colored antique Oriental rugs and some lovely furnishings, such as English pine sleigh beds. Guests appreciate such subtle touches as hand-ironed sheets topped with quilts and down comforters, as well as the home-baked breakfast goodies. ⊠ *10 Lyon St., 02554* ☎ *508/228–5040* ⊕ *www.lyonstreetinn.com* ⇆ *7 rooms* ⚲ *No room phones, no room TVs* ⊟ *MC, V* ⊘ *Closed mid-Dec.–mid-Apr.* ⦿| *CP.*

$–$$ ⛉ **Martin House Inn.** At once elegant and festive, this 1804 house offers a range of rooms, from singles to suites, all bedecked in pretty linens and fresh flowers. Canopied four-posters abound, and four spacious rooms have fireplaces. The third-floor quarters under the eaves share baths and a certain quirky charm. A handsome living room with fireplace and a broad porch foster socializing, as does the generous Continental buffet breakfast. ⊠ *61 Centre St.* ⌂ *Box 743, 02554* ☎ *508/228–0678* ⊕ *www.martinhouseinn.net* ⇆ *13 rooms, 7 with bath; 2 suites* ⊟ *AE, MC, V* ⦿| *CP.*

$–$$ ⛉ **Nantucket Landfall.** Light dances off the harbor to suffuse this classic porch-front summer house overlooking Children's Beach. Most of the airy rooms have balconies with water views, and the innkeepers rustle up home-baked goodies for breakfast. ⊠ *4 Harbor View Way* ☎ *508/228–0500* ⊕ *www.nantucketlandfall.com* ⇆ *8 rooms* ⚲ *No kids under 12* ⊟ *No credit cards* ⊘ *Closed mid-Oct.–late May* ⦿| *CP.*

★ **$–$$** ⛉ **Pineapple Inn.** Now part of the Summer House's in-town holdings, this 1838 Greek Revival captain's house, decorated with impeccable taste, makes an ideal retreat. Down quilts, marble-finished baths—no expense was spared in retrofitting this gem for its new role as pamperer. Breakfast is served in a formal dining room or beside the garden fountain. Whaling captains used to display a pineapple on their stoops upon completion of a successful journey, to signal the neighbors and invite them to come celebrate; here, that spirit prevails daily. ⊠ *10 Hussey St., 02554* ☎ *508/228–9992* 🖷 *508/325–6051* ⊕ *www.pineappleinn.com* ⇆ *12 rooms* ⚲ *In-room data ports, cable TV* ⊟ *AE, MC, V* ⊘ *Closed mid-Dec.–late Apr.* ⦿| *CP.*

☙ **$–$$** ⛉ **Point Breeze Hotel.** The Point Breeze is what you might call broken in, if not down; this once-grand hotel debuted, after all, in 1892. Under the ministrations of creative local owners, it has lately recouped much of its former glory. The reception area and rooms are cheery and bright, the gardens lush, the wraparound veranda inviting—especially at cocktail time, when a jazz band entertains. ⊠ *71 Easton St., 02554* ☎ *508/228–0313 or 800/365–4371* 🖷 *508/325–6044* ⊕ *www.pointbreeze.com* ⇆ *8 rooms, 14 suites, 7 cottages* ⚲ *Restaurant, room service, in-room data ports, some kitchenettes, cable TV, massage, bar, concierge* ⊟ *AE, MC, V* ⊘ *Closed mid-Oct.–mid- May* ⦿| *BP.*

$–$$ ⛉ **Roberts House Inn.** A sister property to the neighboring Manor House (Sara and Michael O'Reilly own a a total of five Greek Revival B&Bs in town), this inn has a similar feel. The quarters, decorated with a mix of antique and reproduction furniture, have a comfy charm, and some have high ceilings, fireplaces, and hot tubs. ⊠ *11 India St.* ⌂ *Box 1436, 02554* ☎ *508/228–0600 or 800/872–6830* ⊕ *www.robertshouse.*

com 🖙 *24 rooms* ⚴ *Some refrigerators, some in-room hot tubs* ▭ *D, MC, V* ❚⊙❘ *CP.*

☝ **$–$$** ▦ **Safe Harbor.** The name is apt: children *and* pets are welcome at this homey B&B with an enviable location mere steps from Children's Beach. The rooms, harboring some American and Oriental antiques, all have water views, and the smaller ones have private decks. Everyone's welcome to sit on the wide front porch and enjoy the ocean breezes. ✉ *2 Harborview Way, 02554* ☎ *508/228–3222 or 800/651–9262* ⊕ *www. beesknees.net/safeharbor* 🖙 *5 rooms* ⚴ *Some pets allowed; no a/c* ▭ *AE, MC, V* ❚⊙❘ *CP.*

$–$$ ▦ **Seven Sea Street.** If this red oak post-and-beam B&B looks awfully
Fodor's Choice well preserved, that's because it was custom-built in 1987. Decked out
★ in Early American style (fishnet-canopy beds, braided rugs), it offers the ambience of antiquity without the creaky drawbacks; instead, you can count on all the modern comforts and then some. The Honeymoon Suite, with its cathedral ceiling, full kitchen, gas fireplace, and harbor view, warrants a leisurely stay. ✉ *7 Sea St., 02554* ☎ *508/228–3577* ☎ *508/ 228–3578* ⊕ *www.sevenseastreetinn.com* 🖙 *9 rooms, 2 suites* ⚴ *Refrigerators, cable TV, in-room VCRs, hot tub, steam room, library, Internet; no kids under 5, no smoking* ▭ *AE, D, MC, V* ❚⊙❘ *CP.*

¢–$$ ▦ **Carlisle House Inn.** A sister property to Marblehead's handsome Harbor Light Inn, this 1765 beauty shares the same traditionalist taste and dedication to comfort. Many rooms have four-posters and charming flocked wallpaper; one, overlooking the garden, is wood-paneled. The location couldn't be more convenient or the breakfast room cheerier. ✉ *26 N. Water St., 02554* ☎ *508/228–0720* ⊕ *www.carlislehouse. com* 🖙 *14 rooms* ⚴ *No a/c in some rooms, no room phones, no TV in some rooms, no smoking* ▭ *AE, MC, V* ☺ *Closed Jan.–Mar.* ❚⊙❘ *CP.*

¢–$$ ▦ **Centre Street Inn.** This 1742 house started out Quaker-plain, became a boardinghouse in the cash-poor late-19th century, and today holds its own with other cosseting B&Bs. Flouncy romanticism prevails in the pretty rooms, all named for holidays; the ones tucked under stenciled eaves are especially appealing. ✉ *78 Centre St., 02554* ☎ *508/ 228–0199* ⊕ *www.centrestreetinn.com* 🖙 *13 rooms* ⚴ *No a/c, no room phones, no room TVs, no smoking* ▭ *AE, D, MC, V* ☺ *Closed Nov.–mid-Apr.* ❚⊙❘ *CP.*

¢–$$ ▦ **Century House.** This 1840 sea captain's home became a rooming house in the early 1870s and has welcomed the public ever since, setting an island record. Rooms are furnished with a mix of reproductions and antiques—the feel favors comfort over style—and the book-filled common room invites lounging, as does the wraparound porch. A lavish buffet breakfast is served in the pine-paneled kitchen, and further snacks are set out on the patio at cocktail time. The innkeepers also help to manage two cottages, one set on Nantucket Harbor, the other in Sconset. ✉ *10 Cliff Rd., 02554* ☎ *508/228–0530* ☎ *508/228– 6811* ⊕ *www.centuryhouse.com* 🖙 *14 rooms* ▭ *MC, V* ☺ *Closed mid-Oct.–mid-May* ❚⊙❘ *CP.*

¢–$$ ▦ **Corner House.** Sandy and John Knox-Johnston have been puttering productively with their circa 1790 house since 1980. She's involved with the town's historic preservation and he, being an actor and British to boot, makes a wonderful host for afternoon tea featuring sandwiches, scones, cakes, and fruit breads; you'll find much the same bounty at breakfast. Rooms are individually decorated in a mélange of English and American antiques, and the original floors, paneling, and fireplaces blend history and romance. ✉ *49 Centre St., 02554* ☎ *508/228–1530* ⊕ *www. cornerhousenantucket.com* ⇨ *15 rooms, 2 suites* ♿ *Some refrigerators, Internet; no smoking* ▭ *AE, MC, V* ⦿*I CP.*

¢–$$ ▦ **Ivy Lodge.** Built in 1790, this center-chimney Colonial—which retains its beehive oven—operated as a guesthouse and museum in the 1800s. As updated by innkeeper Tuge Koseatac (a cosmopolitan MBA), the rooms are elegant, with canopy or brass beds, rich fabrics, and Oriental rugs. ✉ *2 Chester St., 02554* ☎ *508/228–7755* 🖷 *508/228– 0305* ⊕ *wwwtheivylodge.com* ⇨ *6 rooms, 1 suite* ♿ *No a/c, no room phones, no room TVs, no kids, no smoking* ▭ *MC, V* ⊘ *Closed Dec.–Apr.* ⦿*I CP.*

★ ¢–$$ ▦ **The Periwinkle.** A cousin to the Manor House Inn and the Roberts House Inn, and run by the O'Reillys' daughter Sara Shlosser-O'Reilly, this B&B has spark—and a variety of rooms ranging from affordable singles to nice-size quarters with canopied king-size beds and harbor views. In one especially pretty setting, the blue-ribbon pattern of the wallpaper matches the cushions and canopy: it's like living in a nicely wrapped gift. ✉ *7–9 N. Water St.* ⓓ *Box 1436, 02554* ☎ *508/228–9267 or 800/ 588–0074* 🖷 *508/325–4046* ⊕ *www.theperiwinkle.com* ⇨ *16 rooms, 1 cottage.* ♿ *Some in-room hot tubs, cable TV; no smoking* ▭ *D, MC, V* ⦿*I CP.*

🕲 ¢–$$ ▦ **76 Main Street.** Set among the grand houses of Upper Main Street, this 1883 Victorian has an ornate carved cherrywood entrance hall and a woodstove-warmed parlor. The dozen rooms within the house are fairly formal; families might prefer the nicely updated 1955 annex in the garden out back. ✉ *76 Main St., 02554* ☎ *508/228–2533 or 800/876–6858* ⊕ *www.76main.com* ⇨ *18 rooms* ♿ *Refrigerators, cable TV; no smoking* ▭ *AE, MC, V* ⦿*I CP.*

★ ¢–$$ ▦ **Ships Inn.** This 1831 home exudes history: Built for whaling captain Obed Starbuck, it was later the birthplace of abolitionist Lucretia Mott. A dozen guest rooms, named for the ships Starbuck commanded, are furnished with period antiques and pretty wall coverings. The basement harbors a restaurant of the same name (delighted murmurings waft up); it generates a wonderful Continental breakfast and afternoon tea. ✉ *13 Fair St., 02554* ☎ *508/228–0040 or 888/872–4052* ⊕ *www. nantucket.net/lodging/shipsinn* ⇨ *10 rooms, 8 with bath* ♿ *Restaurant, refrigerators, cable TV; no kids under 8* ▭ *AE, MC, V* ⊘ *Closed Nov.–Apr.* ⦿*I CP.*

★ $ ▦ **Anchor Inn.** Built in 1806 by Archaelus Hammond, the first captain to harpoon a whale in the Pacific, this inn has been thoughtfully retrofitted to accommodate more peaceful pursuits, such as munching yummy homemade muffins on the cheery breakfast porch or lazing on the brick patio with its impressive view of the First Congregational Church. Innkeepers Charles and Ann Balas have been in residence since 1983, offering beach towels and sightseeing advice, and doing their best to keep tariffs reasonable. ⊠ *66 Centre St.* ☏ *Box 387, 02554* ☎ *508/228–0072* ⊕ *www.anchor-inn.net* ⮡ *11 rooms* ♨ *Cable TV; no kids, no smoking* ☰ *AE, MC, V* ☉ *Closed mid-Dec.–Feb.* ❤ *CP.*

$ ⊞ **Chestnut House.** Innkeepers Jeannette and Jerry Carl are Arts and Crafts fans—hence the Mission-inspired furnishings in the parlor and the William Morris–theme papers that adorn some rooms. A housekeeping cottage with full kitchen makes for a cozy hideaway *à deux* (or *quatre*, if you pull down the living room's Murphy bed). Breakfast vouchers allow you to sample a nearby restaurant. ⊠ *3 Chestnut St., 02554* ☎ *508/228–0049* 🖷 *508/228–9521* ⊕ *www.chestnuthouse.com* ⮡ *1 room, 4 suites, 1 cottage* ♨ *Refrigerators; no TV in some rooms, no smoking* ☰ *AE, MC, V* ❤ *BP.*

$ ⊞ **Easton House.** Third-generation innkeepers Judy and Cyril Ross know that it's the little things that count, like line-dried cotton sheets and homemade granola. The house is a trove of family heirlooms; some of the antique beds, including spool, cannonball, and pineapple posts, have been supersized to queens. The English-style garden, shaded by a spreading catalpa, is a great place to laze. ⊠ *17 N. Water St., 02554* ☎ *508/228–2759* ⊕ *www.eastonhouse.com* ⮡ *10 rooms, 8 with bath; 1 cottage* ♨ *No smoking* ☰ *No credit cards* ☉ *Closed Oct.–late May* ❤ *CP.*

☙ $ ⊞ **The Grey Lady.** Perched above the shops of "Petticoat Row," the Grey Lady has sunny rooms, some with private entrances. Children are more than welcome—pets, too. The parlor is set up for do-it-yourself snackers, with a coffeemaker, microwave, toaster, and ice. Longtime innkeeper Rosalie Maloney also maintains a harbor-view boathouse on Old North Wharf. ⊠ *34 Centre St.* ☏ *Box 1292, 02554* ☎ *508/228–9552 or 800/245–9552* 🖷 *508/228–2115* ⊕ *www.nantucket.net/lodging/greylady* ⮡ *6 suites* ♨ *Some kitchenettes, refrigerators, cable TV, some pets allowed* ☰ *D, MC, V* ☉ *Closed Jan.–Apr.*

$ ⊞ **Woodbox Inn.** Built in 1709, the Woodbox can lay claim to being Nantucket's oldest inn; the architectural details, such as low, hand-hewn beams, dispel any possible doubt. True to the times, the antiques-appointed rooms are somewhat small; the suites have sitting rooms and fireplaces. ⊠ *29 Fair St., 02554* ☎ *508/228–1468* ⊕ *www.woodboxinn.com* ⮡ *3 rooms, 6 suites* ♨ *Restaurant, some refrigerators; no phones in some rooms, no smoking* ☰ *No credit cards* ☉ *Closed Dec.–June.*

★ ¢ ⊞ **Nesbitt Inn.** The last real deal left in town, this homey Victorian has been in the same family since 1914. Dolly and Nobby Noblit are so nice, and the rates so reasonable, one is willing to overlook the shared baths, gently worn furnishings, and the occasional exhausted bed. ⊠ *21 Broad St.* ☏ *Box 1019, 02554* ☎ *508/228–0156* 🖷 *508/228–2446* ⮡ *12 rooms share 3 baths* ♨ *No smoking* ☰ *MC, V* ☉ *Closed Jan.–Apr.* ❤ *CP.*

Nantucket Town Outskirts

See Where to Stay & Eat Outside Nantucket Town map for these properties.

$$$–$$$$ ⊞ **Cliffside Beach Club.** Which way to the beach? You're on it: this snazzily updated 1920s beach club stakes its claim with a flotilla of colorful

umbrellas—somewhat miffing natives, who consider sand rights anathema. Local politics aside, this is one prime chunk of gentle bay beach, and the complex makes the most of its site, with a gorgeous cathedral-ceiling lobby decorated with hanging quilts and rooms of every size and shape enhanced by island-made modern furnishings. Best of all, you can traipse across the sand to the Galley, one of the best restaurants around. ⊠ *46 Jefferson Ave.* ⌀ *Box 449, 02554* ☎ *508/228–0618 or 800/932–9645* ⊕ *www.cliffsidebeach.com* ⟿ *26 rooms, 3 suites, 2 apartments, 1 cottage* ⚲ *Restaurant, in-room data ports, some kitchenettes, refrigerators, cable TV, gym, hot tub, massage, beach, playground* ☰ *AE* ⊙ *Closed mid-Oct.–May* ⦿ *CP.*

★ **$–$$$** ⊞ **Dolphin Guest House.** This 1850s house started out as St. Paul's church: the early Nantucketers, being thrifty, were ahead of their time in terms of creative reuse. Today it's a welcoming inn with traditional decor and hosts Diane and George Metcalfe, who can steer you to unique island pleasures, such as where to catch an optimal sunset or gather beach plums. ⊠ *10 N. Beach St., 02554* ☎ *508/228–4028* ⊕ *www.nantucket.net/lodging/dolphin* ⟿ *12 rooms* ⚲ *No a/c, no smoking* ☰ *AE, MC, V* ⦿ *CP.*

☾ **$–$$** ⊞ **The Beachside at Nantucket.** Nantucket has only one "motel" in the classic rooms-around-a-pool configuration, and it's a honey—not at all out of place amid its tony neighbors. Between the town and Jetties Beach (both are within a bracing 10-minute walk), the complex ascends to two stories; rooms—decor is of the cheery wicker-and-florals school—have little pool-view terraces separated by whitewashed latticework. Families naturally flock here, but business travelers are equally well served. ⊠ *30 N. Beach St., 02554* ☎ *508/228–2241 or 800/322–4433* 🖷 *508/228–8901* ⊕ *www.thebeachside.com* ⟿ *90 rooms, 3 suites* ⚲ *Refrigerators, cable TV, pool, meeting rooms; no smoking* ☰ *AE, D, DC, MC, V* ⊙ *Closed mid-Oct.–late Apr.* ⦿ *CP.*

$–$$ ⊞ **Cliff Lodge.** Debby and John Bennett's 1711 house retains both the architectural detail and the gracious atmosphere of an earlier era. The good-size bedrooms are prettily furnished with pastel hooked rugs on spatter-painted floors, country curtains, and down comforters. In addition to enjoying the attractive common rooms, you're welcome to lounge on the sunporch (set with lovely Shaker rockers) or garden patio, or head up to the roof walk for a terrific harbor view. The breakfast buffets feature homemade muffins, cakes, and crisps; cookies and tea sandwiches turn up as a restorative afternoon snack. ⊠ *9 Cliff Rd., 02554* ☎ *508/228–9480* 🖷 *508/228–6308* ⊕ *www.clifflodgenantucket.com* ⟿ *11 rooms, 1 apartment* ⚲ *No smoking* ☰ *MC, V* ⦿ *CP.*

$–$$ ⊞ **La Ruche Inn.** A bit of a hike (10 minutes) from the center of town, this Greek Revival manse compensates with luxurious, yet understated decor and all sorts of pampering touches, such as silk-blend towels and 600-thread-count sheets. The buffet breakfasts in the garden include fresh–squeezed mimosas, and you're welcome to nosh again at the cocktail hour, on complimentary hors d'oeuvres served with wine. ⊠ *109 Orange St., 02554* ☎ *508/228–4482* 🖷 *508/228–4752* ⊕ *www.larucheinn.com* ⟿ *8 rooms* ⚲ *Refrigerators, in-room VCRs; no smoking* ☰ *AE, D, MC, V* ⊙ *Closed Jan.–Apr.* ⦿ *CP.*

¢–$$ ⌑ **House of the Seven Gables.** Younger than its Salem namesake—this is one of Nantucket's rare Victorians—this inn does have the requisite number of pointy parts, several of which shelter cozy bedrooms decorated in a style appropriate to the period. Guests needn't stir to enjoy a fresh-baked Continental breakfast: it's brought right to the room. ⊠ *32 Cliff Rd., 02554* ☎ *508/228–4706 or 800/905–5005* ⊕ *www. houseofthesevengables.com* ⤳ *10 rooms, 8 with bath* ⬧ *No smoking* ⊟ *AE, MC, V* ☉ *Closed Nov.–Mar.* ⊙ *CP.*

COTTAGES   Housekeeping cottages might better serve families than antiques-filled inns. Those seeking serious self-contained solitude can choose nesting places farther afield in Surfside or Sconset.

$$$$ ⌑ **Mullen Cottages.** There are two cottages (one on Brant Point, one right on the water in Surfside), and they're beauties, fully fitted out with washer/dryer, TV/VCR, outdoor shower—the works. In-season rates run $3,150–$3,850 per week. ⊠ *34 Walsh St., 02554* ☎ *508/228–9545* ⊕ *www.nantucketi.com.*

Real Estate Agents

Coffin Real Estate (⊠ 40 Centre St. ☎ 508/228–1138 or 800/662–8260 ☖ 508/228–8110 ⊕ www.coffinrealestate.com) has been in business since the preboom '60s; it has a branch in Sconset.

Congdon & Coleman Real Estate (⊠ 57 Main St. ☎ 508/325–5000 or 800/325–5232 ☖ 508/325–5025 ⊕ www.congdonandcoleman.com) has been serving buyers and renters since 1931.

Country Village Rentals & Real Estate (⊠ 10 Straight Wharf ☎ 508/228–8840 or 800/599–7368 ☖ 508/228–8804 ⊕ www.cvrandr.com) can set you up in Nantucket (or Stowe, St. Barth's, or the Bahamas).

Denby Real Estate (⊠ 5 N. Water St. ☎ 508/228–2522 ☖ 508/228–6542 ⊕ www.denby.com) has been at work since 1967.

Hamilton Heard, Jr. Real Estate (⊠ 15 N. Beach ☎ 508/228–3838 or 800/325–4264 ☖ 508/325–4859 ⊕ www.heard-real-estate.com) has brokers who live in various areas and can offer the inside scoop.

Killen Real Estate (⊠ 10 Easy St. ☎ 508/228–0976 ⊕ www.killenrealestate. com) has been connecting renters since the '60s.

Lee Real Estate (⊠ 58 Main St. ☎ 508/325–5800 or 800/495–4198 ☖ 508/228–6128 ⊕ www.leerealestate.com) has a varied list, including some historic properties.

Lucille Jordan Real Estate (⊠ 8 Federal St. ☎ 508/228–4449 ⊕ www. jordanre.com) has a broad rental inventory; check the photos lining the storefront windows.

The **Maury People** (⊠ 35–37 Main St. ☎ 508/228–1881 ☖ 508/228–1481 ⊕ www.maurypeople.com), associated with Sotheby's, has over 1,000 private homes in its rental inventory, including historic and beach homes; service is not only knowledgeable but personable.

CloseUp
NAVIGATING THE RENTAL MARKET

I F YOU'RE GOING TO BE STAYING FOR A WEEK OR MORE, *you may want to consider renting a cottage or house—an arrangement that gives you a chance to settle in and get a real taste of island living. Many visitors, especially those with children, find renting more relaxing than staying in a hotel or an inn. With your own kitchen, you'll save money by eating in; plus you can enjoy such homey summer pleasures as barbecues. Though decor can vary from chichi to weatherworn, most cottages come equipped with all you'll need to ensure a comfortable stay. Steer clear of a house without linens; it's a sign of bad things to come. The better houses come fully accoutered: not just with basics such as sheets and towels but with luxury touches like cable or satellite TV, a CD player, gourmet kitchen implements, beach chairs, and bikes.*

Finding a great cottage or house can be tough, however, especially since so many are rented a year or more in advance by returning guests. The time to start your search is a summer ahead, though you can occasionally find a property as late as spring. A good way to shop is to stop in and visit Realtors when you happen to be in town. Be prepared for a bit of sticker shock, though. Prices are generally about twice what you'd have to pay on Cape Cod or even the Vineyard. In summer, very rustic (read shabby) rentals start at about $1,000 a week and can run to many times that ($3,000 and up) for multi-bedroom or waterfront properties. In the off-season, prices drop considerably. Also, discounts up to 10% are standard if you rent for more than a couple of weeks, since it saves the home owners house-cleaning fees (in fact, some owners insist on a two-week minimum). Spring for a whole season, and you could get a real bargain—relatively speaking, of course.

Preferred Properties (⊠ 76 Easton St. ☎ 508/228–2320 or 800/338–7715 🖶 508/228–8464 ⊕ www.preferredpropertiesre.com) is a Christie's affiliate whose offerings range "from cottages in the sand to castles on the cliff."

The Arts

For current listings, see the free tabloid-size weekly, *Yesterday's Island* (⊕ www.yesterdaysisland.com), and the regular island weeklies: the *Inquirer and Mirror* (⊕ www.inkym.com), published since 1821, and the *The Nantucket Independent,* (⊕ www.nantucketindependent.com), introduced in 2003. Posters around town announce coming attractions, and be sure to check the board outside the Hub, a newsstand at the corner of Federal and Main streets.

Dance
Dance Nantucket (⊠ 10 Edgar Ave. ☎ 508/325–6679 ⊕ www.dancenantucket.org) hosts dance parties and leads classes in Latin, swing, and ballroom for all levels.

Giovanna La Paglia (⊠ 10 Surfside Rd. ☎ 508/228–4979) directs a bal-
let studio for children and adults at the Cyrus Peirce Middle School
and welcomes drop-ins; she also gives studio workshops and performances.

Film

With the tag line "Where screenwriters inherit the earth," the **Nantucket
Film Festival** (☎ 508/325–6274 or 212/642–6339 ⊕ www.
nantucketfilmfestival.org), held each June, emphasizes the importance
of strong scripts—a criterion that also informs the juried selection
from hundreds of international submissions. The final playlist—about
two dozen short and feature-length films—always includes a few world
premieres, and many selections have gone on to considerable commercial
success. Tickets go on sale 15 minutes before showtime. A Week Pass,
though pricey ($250), gives you priority in the inevitable lines at the
hosting Dreamland and Starlight theaters. Daily passes ($50) are also
useful, since capacity is often reached before any tickets go on sale. Informal daily coffee-klatch events—such as close-up discussions with
directors, held at a local restaurant, are always interesting. Throughout the festival, you can cast your vote for the best feature and the best
short feature.

The **Dreamland Theatre** (⊠ 17 S. Water St. ☎ 508/228–5356) is housed
in a pleasantly ramshackle old ark of a building, which used to be a Quaker
meetinghouse, then a straw factory, and, finally, an entertainment hall.
It's now a summer cinema (open mid-May–mid-September) running two
shows nightly of first-run mainstream movies and the occasional rainy-
day matinee.

The **Starlight Theatre** (⊠ 1 N. Union St. ☎ 508/228–4435) is a small
screening room appended to an outdoor cafe of the same name. Spiffed
up and rechristened in 2004, it shows mostly foreign, art, and independent films. In summer there are usually two shows nightly, plus spo-
radic matinees.

Fine Arts & Crafts

The **Artists Association of Nantucket** (⊠ Gardner Perry La. ☎ 508/228–
0722 ⊕ www.nantucketarts.org), founded in 1945, leads classes year-
round in various media, often led by some of the island's most note-
worthy artists. The association's **gallery** (⊠ 19 Washington St. ☎ 508/
228–0294) hosts shows and occasional special events.

The **Nantucket Island School of Design and the Arts** (⊠ 23 Wauwinet Rd.
☎ 508/228–9248 ⊕ www.nisda.org), affiliated with the Massachusetts College of Art in Boston, teaches fine-art classes in many media to
artists of all ilk. Look for compelling community lectures and events.

Nantucket Lightship Basket Museum (⊠ 49 Union St. ☎ 508/228–1177)
mounts demos Friday and Saturday in summer.

Shredder's Studio (⊠ 3 Salros Rd. ☎ 508/228–4487) has more than a
dozen art classes for various ages (children and up) in assorted media.

Music

Many concerts are free or reasonably priced at $10–$20. Benefits can ascend into three figures.

The **Boston Pops Esplanade Orchestra** (☎ 508/825–8248) puts on a blow-out concert in mid-August on Jetties Beach to benefit the Nantucket Cottage Hospital.

Jazz on the Veranda (✉ Point Breeze Hotel, 71 Easton St. ☎ 508/228–8674) is a free series held Friday evenings in summer.

The **Nantucket Arts Council** (✉ Box 554, 02554 ☎ 508/228–8588) sponsors a music series (jazz, country, classical) September to June.

The **Nantucket Community Music Center** (✉ 11 Centre St. ☎ 508/228–3352) not only arranges year-round choral and instrumental instruction but sponsors and puts on concerts; choristers are always welcome.

Nantucket Musical Arts Society (☎ 508/228–1287) mounts concerts by internationally acclaimed musicians Tuesday evenings at 8:30 July through August and has done so since 1959. The concerts are mostly classical but have occasionally ventured into jazz.

The **Nantucket Park & Recreation Commission** (✉ Children's Beach bandstand, off Harbor View Way ☎ 508/228–7213) hosts free concerts (and the occasional theater production) from July 4 to Labor Day. Programs begin at 6 PM, range from jazz and classical to pop, and include such local favorites as Ecliff & the Swingdogs. Bring blankets, chairs, and bug repellent.

The **Noonday Concert Series** (✉ Unitarian Universalist Church, 11 Orange St. ☎ 508/228–5466), Thursday at noon in July and August, brings in stellar performers and also showcases outstanding local musicians. Past concerts have included organ, bluegrass, and classical music.

Readings & Talks

The **Coffin School** (✉ 4 Winter St. ☎ 508/228–2505) is the site of lectures sponsored by the resident Egan Institute for Maritime Studies, as well as occasional concerts.

The **Nantucket Atheneum** (✉ 1 India St. ☎ 508/228–1110 ⊕ www.nantucketatheneum.org) hosts a dazzling roster of writers and speakers year-round. Except for a few big-name fund-raisers in summer, all events are free.

The **Nantucket Historical Association** (✉ 15 Broad St. ☎ 508/228–1894 ⊕ www.nha.org) hosts evening talks on a variety of topics touching on local history.

The **Nantucket Island School of Design and the Arts** (✉ 23 Wauwinet Rd. ☎ 508/228–9248 ⊕ www.nantucket.net/art/nisda) hosts a cultural arts lecture series, ranging from artistic to environmental topics, Wednesday nights in July and August.

Theater

The **Point Breeze Players Dinner Theater** (⊠ 71 Easton St. ☎ 508/228–8674), held at Chancellor's restaurant at the Point Breeze Hotel Tuesday evenings July through August, centers on an interactive, Nantucket-based plot.

Theatre Workshop of Nantucket (⊠ Bennett Hall, 62 Centre St. ☎ 508/228–4305 ⊕ www.theatreworkshop.com), a community theater since 1956, stages plays, musicals, and readings year-round. TWN sponsors murder mystery dinner theater at the Jared Coffin House Mondays July through August.

Uptown Players (⊠ Methodist Church, 2 Centre St. ☎ 508/228–9533), a fringe group with professional antecedents, mounts challenging work in an intimate proscenium space.

Kid Stuff

Most of these organizations have supervised evening, short-term, or summer programs for children. For more ideas on what to do with your youngsters or for events you and your children can do together, *see* Sports & the Outdoors.

The **Children's Theatre of Nantucket** (⊠ Nantucket High School, 10 Surfside Rd. ☎ 508/228–8513) takes over the 600-seat auditorium of the Nantucket High School for weekly productions in summer.

Eco Guides Strong Wings (☎ 508/228–1769 ⊕ www.strongwings.org) has courses for children 5–16, including kayaking and mountain-biking.

The **Maria Mitchell Association** (☎ 508/228–9198 office ⊕ www.mmo.org) organizes nature-centered activities for kids of all ages.

Marjory Trott (⊠ 8 Dukes Rd. ☎ 508/228–4209) teaches popular classes in creative movement, dance, and yoga for children as young as 10 months at various venues, including the **Children's Beach bandstand** (⊠ Off Harbor View Way) in-season and the **Atheneum** (⊠ 1 India St.) off-season.

Murray Camp (⊠ 25½ Bartlett Rd. ☎ 508/325–4600) is a venerable day program for ages 5–14, available by the week or season late June–mid August. It has all the usual camp offerings (swimming, sailing, etc.), plus electives such as "Fun French"; it also hosts "Kids' Nights Out" and family evenings.

The **Nantucket Atheneum** (⊠ 1 India St. ☎ 508/228–1110 ⊕ www.nantucketatheneum.org) holds regular storytelling and book-club meetings for various ages.

The **Nantucket Boys & Girls Club** (⊠ 61 Sparks St. ☎ 508/228–0158 ⊕ www.nantucketclub.com), part of the national organization, has a spacious modern facility where recreational and educational after-school, weekend, and vacation-time programs keep 850 kids entertained year-round.

The **Nantucket Community Music Center** (✉ 11 Centre St. ☏ 508/228–3352) offers lessons and concerts.

Nantucket Community Sailing (✉ 4 Winter St. ☏ 508/228–6600 ⊕ www. nantucketcommunitysailing.org) provides affordable access and classes for all ages.

The **Nantucket Historical Association** (✉ 15 Broad St. ☏ 508/228–1894 ⊕ www.nha.org) sponsors special hands-on living-history programs for ages 4–15.

The **Nantucket Ice Community Skating Rink** (✉ 1 Backus Rd. ☏ 508/228–2516 ⊕ www.nantucketice.org) hosts classes, camps, and open skates.

The **Nantucket Park & Recreation Commission** (✉ 2 Bathing Beach Rd. ☏ 508/228–7213) offers free arts-and-crafts and dance programs, puppet shows, plays, films, and family concerts at Children's Beach in season. It also maintains a bring-your-own-equipment skateboarding and blading park near the public tennis courts at Jetties Beach; tennis clinics are available for ages 4–14. The **Teen Center** (✉ First Way ☏ 508/325–5340), open Friday and Saturday nights year-round plus Wednesday and Sunday afternoons, offers activities and just a place to hang out.

Sketching Tours for Kids (☏ 508/527–4057 ⊕ www.sketchingtours.com) are pared-down versions of the "en plein aire" sessions that artist Anne Butler conducts for adults.

The **Toy Boat** (✉ 41 Straight Wharf ☏ 508/228–4552 ⊕ www.thetoyboat. com), a wonderful kids' store, provides a summer schedule of fun and educational activities, all of which are free.

Nightlife

The phrase "Nantucket nightlife" verges on an oxymoron—and, during the off-season, it's virtually a nonentity. If it's glitz and nonstop action you're after, better stick to the mainland. On the other hand, if you like live music, you will never go lacking—at least in season. Although there are only two bars (the Muse and the Chicken Box) that bring in dance bands, they've both got a great scene going, and the lineup ranges widely, from reggae to funk. Also, there are plenty of smaller venues where you can catch a little folk, jazz, or cabaret—DJ'd disco and karaoke, too, if those are to your liking. Each week usually brings a couple of classical concerts as well, and the Boston Pops put in a yearly appearance. Nantucket does have one nighttime draw that big cities lack: stargazing, whether from a quiet meadow or widow's walk or at the historic Loines Observatory.

For listings of events, see the free weekly *Yesterday's Island* (⊕ www. yesterdaysisland.com), the *Inquirer and Mirror* (⊕ www.ack.net), and *The Nantucket Independent* (⊕ www.nantucketindependent.com). Some events may be listed on the Web site www.nantucketfoggysheet.com. Posters around town announce coming attractions. Also be sure to check the board outside the Hub, a newsstand at the corner of Federal and Main streets.

WHERE THE ELITE MEET: "QUIET" BARS

ET'S SAY YOU'RE PAST THE PITCHER-
SHARING PORTION OF YOUR LIFE *and
even the esoteric martini phase.
You're somewhat more mature and
not necessarily on the prowl—just seeking
a relatively refined atmosphere in which to
socialize. Hotel lounges often offer a far
more dignified setting than the typical bar,
along with the possibility of conducting an
audible conversation. Another good
option is to slip into a restaurant to enjoy
a nightcap—and perhaps a dessert—as
they're winding down for the evening.
Nantucket abounds in such hideaways, if
you know where to look. Herewith, a
highly biased survey of favorites (for
specifics, see the Bars and Clubs listings).*

*Year after year, the Boarding House—at
least its sidewalk extension—continues to
delight with its seductive snacks and
central setting: sit here long enough, and
everyone you know on-island will
eventually pass by. The garden patios at*

*Cioppino's and Le Languedoc are a bit
more private and ideal for a romantic
aperitif. The Galley, adjoining the Cliffside
Beach Club, is ultracivilized.*

*Oran Mór offers the premium scotches
that inspired its name, as well as
superlative wines by the glass. Easterly
Sconset has two outstanding attractions:
the wine bar at the Chanticleer (where
connoisseurs can conduct their own
tastings) and the piano bar at the
Summer House, where ocean breezes
and tinkling show tunes are guaranteed
to inspire a sentimental journey.*

Bars & Clubs

American Seasons (⊠ 80 Centre St. ☎ 508/228–7111) has an intimate patio bar serving tapas.

A lively saloon site since the 1930s, the **Atlantic Cafe** (⊠ 15 S. Water St. ☎ 508/228–0570) is a family-friendly joint that still has plenty of appeal for young people.

The **Bamboo Supper Club** (⊠ 3 Chins Way ☎ 508/228 0200) draws a youngish, fairly rambunctious crowd year round with such specialty drinks as the potent Red Bull Purple Haze splashed with Chambord and Absolut Mandarin. There's a pool table upstairs.

Packing a couple of dozen stools, the lounge half of **Blue Fin** (⊠ 15 S. Beach St. ☎ 508/228–2033 ⊕ www.nantucketbluefin.com) is typically wall-to-wall with attractive young sorts scarfing sushi as they sip.

The roar within the bar part of the **Boarding House** (⊠ 12 Federal St. ☎ 508/228–9622) approaches zoo level—it's that popular. Far more civilized are the café tables outside, provided you can snag one.

At the White Elephant's **Brant Point Grill** (⊠ 50 Easton St. ☎ 508/325–1320 or 800/445–6574 ⊕ www.brantpointgrill.com), the setting is country-elegant—Windsor chairs, varnished woodwork with hunter-green trim—and the patrons are patently moneyed, since many are hotel guests. A pianist provides atmosphere (and takes requests).

Cambridge Street (⊠ 12 Cambridge St. ☎ 508/228–7109) is incontrovertibly cool: the patrons themselves, who exhibit an alternative bent, constitute the entertainment.

Cap'n Tobey's Chowder House (⊠ 20 Straight Wharf ☎ 508/228–0836) turns dance bar at night, with occasional karaoke.

The **Chicken Box** (aka the Box; ⊠ 14 Dave St., off Lower Orange St. ☎ 508/228–9717 ⊕ www.chickenbox.com) rocks! Live music—including some big-name bands—plays six nights a week in season, and weekends throughout the year. On the off nights, you can always play pool, foosball, or darts.

Cinco (⊠ 5 Amelia Dr. ☎ 508/325–5151 ⊕ www.cinco5.com) serves tropical drinks to accompany its tapas.

Cioppino's (⊠ 20 Broad St. ☎ 508/228–4622) has a winning wine list; owner Tracy Root used to be the maître d' at Chanticleer. A small bar within the elegant house welcomes all comers, especially aficionados of fine port; late-nighters can find succor in the garden patio.

The **Club Car Lounge** (⊠ 1 Main St. ☎ 508/228–1101) is an actual club car, salvaged from the narrow–gauge railroad that once served Sconset. These days it makes a convivial piano bar, where requests and sing-alongs are encouraged.

Martinis and mellow jazz piano lend atmosphere to **DeMarco** (⊠ 9 India St. ☎ 508/228–1836), as do the heavenly aromas wafting from the kitchen.

Down where the pleasure yachts dock, **Eat Fire Spring Cafe** (⊠ 14 Old South Wharf ☎ 508/228–5756) starts serving drinks as soon as the sun crosses the yardarm; at night live jazz draws a mellow crowd.

At **The Galley** (⊠ 54 Jefferson Ave., at Cliffside Beach ☎ 508/228–9641) you can sip mojitos right on the beach as piano riffs mix with the rhythm of gentle surf.

Longing for an elaborate umbrella drink? The Harbor House Village's **Harbor Wok** (⊠ S. Beach St. ☎ 508/325–1300 or 866/325–9300) mixes esoteric drinks to match its Chinese cuisine.

The under-21 crowd tends to cluster along "The Strip," a series of fast-food joints extending along Broad Street toward Steamboat Wharf. By far the biggest draw, for loiterers of all ages, is the **Juice Bar** (⊠ 12 Broad St. ☎ 508/228–5799), which, despite its name, is famed primarily for its fabulous homemade ice cream.

Kitty Murtaugh's (⊠ 4 West Creek Rd. ☎ 508/228–0781) calls itself a "porter house" and has two pool tables.

Le Languedoc (✉ 24 Broad St. ☎ 508/228–2552) has a small bar area in the cozy subterranean bistro and also serves drinks on the patio.

Refined sorts find their way upstairs to the tiny bar at **Oran Mor** (✉ 2 S. Beach St. ☎ 508/228–8655) to sip fine wines and shots of single-malt Scotch: one such elixir inspired the restaurant's name.

★ You don't have to be fabulous to fit in at **the pearl** (✉ 12 Federal St. ☎ 508/228–9701), but it wouldn't hurt. Patrons tend to be as chic as the white onyx bar itself, whose blue lighting lends a mysterious glow to all assembled.

The always-busy bar at **Ropewalk** (✉ 1 Straight Wharf ☎ 508/228–8886), perched among the yachts at the end of Straight Wharf, is supplemented by a raw bar.

Rose and Crown (✉ 23 S. Water St. ☎ 508/228–2595) is a family-friendly restaurant that morphs into a pub popular with the barely post-collegiate crowd. DJs keep the dance floor moving, as do various frozen drinks and the redoubtable Goombay Smash; occasional karaoke nights are similarly fueled.

A youngish, sporting crowd congregates at **Schooners** (✉ 31 Easy St. ☎ 508/228–5824), a nautically themed eatery near Steamship Wharf.

Expect to find fellow sophisticates bellying up to the dory bar (built to resemble a boat) at **Ships Inn** (✉ 13 Fair St. ☎ 508/228–0040). The restaurant's innovative menu is matched by inventive martinis.

Cineastes and sociable sorts claim the bar stools and patio tables at the **Starlight Café** (✉ 1 N. Union St. ☎ 508/228–4479), which adjoins the Starlight Theatre.

Straight Wharf (✉ 6 Harbor Sq., Straight Wharf ☎ 508/228–4499) is likewise best known as a restaurant, but the café annex draws a lively, attractive clientele.

The bar at the **Summer House Restaurant** (✉ 17 Ocean Ave. ☎ 508/257–9976) is hands down the most romantic spot for a cocktail on-island. A pianist entertains devotees, who cluster around the bar or claim comfortable armchairs.

Open year-round, the **Tap Room** (✉ Jared Coffin House, 29 Broad St. ☎ 508/228–2400 ⊕ www.jaredcoffinhouse.net) is the kind of dark, Tudor-look hideaway that makes a perfect winter haven; in summer, the democratic scene—all ages and strata are made to feel welcome—expands to the garden patio.

The café tables of the **Tavern** (✉ 1 Harbor Sq., Straight Wharf ☎ 508/228–1266) spill out onto a Straight Wharf plaza, at the center of which stands the Gazebo, the island's closest analog to a singles bar. You can stroll around and scan the throng before committing to joining the crush.

The formal interiors of **21 Federal** (✉ 21 Federal St. ☎ 508/228–2121 ⊕ www.21federal.net) make a surprisingly conducive setting for well-heeled camaraderie. The specialty drink is the Bermudian Dark and Stormy.

Shopping

The historic center of town doubles as the commercial district: shops are concentrated primarily in the grid formed by Main, Centre, Broad, and Easy streets, with a few shops trailing off along the periphery. The former boathouses of Straight Wharf and Old South Wharf, retrofitted as shops and galleries, attract well-heeled browsers as well. The necessities of island life—hardware, office supplies, etc.—tend to be clustered mid-island, where new stores offering nonessentials are gradually making inroads as well.

Most of Nantucket's shops are seasonal, opening in time for the Daffodil Festival in late April and closing soon after Christmas Stroll in early December; a hardy few stay open year-round and often offer rather astounding bargains off-season. On summer weekends, many shops stay open late (until 9 or 10). Most galleries hold their openings on Friday evenings.

Antiques

Antiques Depot (⊠ 14 Easy St. ☎ 508/228–1287) has an intriguing mix of furniture, art, and accessories, including decoys.

East End Gallery (⊠ 3 Old North Wharf ☎ 508/228–4515) is a tiny shop featuring chests, paintings, porcelain, and estate jewelry.

European Traditions (⊠ 12 Straight Wharf ☎ 508/325–0038 ⊕ www. europeantraditionsantiques.com) shows antique pine and other furniture within the handsome brick 1846 Thomas Macy warehouse.

G. K. S. Bush (⊠ 13 Old South Rd. ☎ 508/325–0300) carries ultra-high-end American antique furniture, paintings, and decorative arts (winter headquarters are on New York's Upper East Side).

L&E Reid III Antiques (⊠ 39 Washington St. ☎ 508/325–8919) specializes in wine- and food-related antiques.

Leonards Antiques (⊠ 20 Federal St. ☎ 508/228–0620 ⊕ www. leonardsdirect.com) sells fine antique and reproduction furniture with a special emphasis on heirloom-quality beds; ample accessories fill out the look.

Lynda Willauer Antiques (⊠ 2 India St. ☎ 508/228–3631) has amassed a stellar cache of American and English furniture, plus fine collectibles, including Chinese export porcelain and majolica.

Manor House Antiques (⊠ 31½ Centre St. ☎ 508/228–4335) is a multi-dealer collaborative with an emphasis on "smalls" (miscellaneous collectibles).

Nantucket Country (⊠ 38 Centre St. ☎ 508/228–8868) has an especially rich inventory of quilts and flags; another specialty—in addition to maritime and "Nantucketiana"—is antique children's toys.

Nantucket House Antiques (⊠ 2 S. Beach St. ☎ 508/228–4604 ⊕ www. nantuckethouse.com) displays a wealth of well-chosen artifacts, in-spired aggregations; the owners are interior decorators.

Nantucket Stock Exchange (⊠ 25A Old South Rd. ☎ 508/228–9155) has an impressive stash of marine antiques, as well as good general stock, mostly island–derived via consignment. The shop also carries co-owner Cheryl Fudge's refashioned vintage wear.

Nina Hellman Marine Antiques & Americana (⊠ 48 Centre St. ☎ 508/228–4677 ⊕ www.nauticalnantucket.com) carries scrimshaw, whaling arti-facts, ship models, instruments, and other marine antiques, plus folk art and Nantucket memorabilia. Charles Manghis, a contemporary scrimshaw artist, demonstrates and exhibits his craft here.

★ **Rafael Osona Auctions** (⊠ American Legion Hall, 21 Washington St. ☎ 508/228–3942 ⊕ www.rafaelosonaauction.com) holds auctions of fine antiques most Saturday mornings from Memorial Day weekend to early December; the items—furniture, decorative accessories, art, jew-elry, and more—are previewable two days in advance.

Established in 1927, **Sylvia Antiques** (⊠ 6 Ray's Ct. ☎ 508/228–0960 ⊕ www.sylviaantiques.com) retains the richest stash of island-related antiquities.

Tonkin of Nantucket (⊠ 33 Main St. ☎ 508/228–9697 ⊕ www.tonkin-of-nantucket.com) has two floors of fine Continental antiques—in-cluding furniture, china, art, silver, and scientific instruments—as well as sailors' valentines and lightship baskets; larger pieces can be viewed at the mid-island warehouse at 5-7 Teasdale Circle.

Val Maitino Antiques (⊠ 31 N. Liberty St. ☎ 508/228–2747 ⊕ www. valmaitinoantiques.com), founded in 1950, features a broad inventory of American and English furniture and accessories including weather vanes and lightship baskets; antique lighting is a specialty.

Wayne Pratt (⊠ 28 Main St. ☎ 508/228–5200 ⊕ www.waynepratt. com) specializes in American antiques and handcrafted reproduc-tions. Items of special interest include Jose Reyes baskets and mar-itime antiques.

Weeds (⊠ 14 Centre St. ☎ 508/228–5200 ⊕ www.weedsnantucket. com) marries mere age with pure style; it's a delight to peruse.

Art Galleries

The **Artists' Association of Nantucket** (⊠ 19 Washington St. ☎ 508/228–0772 ⊕ www.nantucketarts.org) is the best place to get an overview of the work being done on-island; many members have galleries of their own.

Cavalier Galleries (⊠ 7 Salem St. ☎ 508/325–4405 ⊕ www. cavaliergalleries.com) is fronted by a garden featuring life-size bronzes of children at play; further sculpture can be found inside, along with paintings, prints, and photographs.

The **Gallery at Four India** (✉ 4 India St. ☎ 508/228–8509 ⊕ www. galleryatfourindia.com) is a quiet, spacious refuge, with highly sought-after American and marine paintings dating from the 1850s to 1940s, plus a small sampling of contemporary realism.

Hoorn-Ashby Gallery (✉ 10 Federal St. ☎ 508/228–9314) favors realism, ranging from the whimsical to the highly polished.

At the edge of town, the **Old Spouter Gallery** (✉ 118 Orange St. ☎ 508/ 325–9988) makes a fine showcase for interesting local artists.

Paul La Paglia Gallery (✉ 38 Centre St. ☎ 508/228–8760) offers a range of vintage artworks (mostly with maritime, botanical, or regional themes) and beautiful custom framing.

Robert Wilson Galleries (✉ 34 Main St. ☎ 508/228–2096 ⊕ www. artnet.com/rwilson.html) carries contemporary American marine, impressionist, and other art.

Sailors' Valentine Gallery (✉ 12 Straight Wharf ☎ 508/228–2011 ⊕ www. sailorsvalentinegallery.com) presents an international array of contemporary fine and folk art, plus the namesake keepsakes created by homesick mariners in the 19th century.

Tucked amid a row of shingled former boathouses, the **South Wharf Gallery** (✉ 21 Old South Wharf ☎ 508/228–0406) has been showing top local work since 1978.

Books
Check the Nantucket Room at the back of **Mitchell's Book Corner** (✉ 54 Main St. ☎ 508/228–1080 ⊕ www.mitchellsbookcorner.com) for regional titles. The front is filled with an astute sampling covering a broad range of categories. Author signings are held on summer Saturdays.

Nantucket Bookworks (✉ 25 Broad St. ☎ 508/228–4000 ⊕ www. nantucketbookworks.com) feels like a house gone feral, with books claiming every comfy nook. It carries an extensive inventory, with an emphasis on literary works and Nantucket-specific titles, as well as children's books and gift items.

Candy
Aunt Leah's Fudge (✉ Courtyard, Straight Wharf ☎ 508/228–1017 or 800/824–6330 ⊕ www.auntleahsfudge.com) whips up—and ships—several dozen varieties, including Chocolate Cranberry Nut Supreme.

The Candy Room (✉ at Force 5 Watersports, 6 Union St. ☎ 508/228–0700) is a back-room trove of commercial confections—Candyland incarnate.

The aroma of chocolate confections being cooked up in the back room of **Sweet Inspirations** (✉ 26 Centre St. ☎ 508/228–5814 ⊕ www. nantucketchocolatier.com) will instantly dispel any notions of dieting. Cranberries and chocolate make a surprisingly seductive duo, especially in the form of cranberry cheesecake truffles.

Children's Clothing

Kidding Around (✉ 2 Broad St. ☎ 508/228–7952) carries a festive array of children's clothes and accoutrements, in sizes newborn to 16; some of the goods (including toys and books) relate to Nantucket.

Pinwheels (✉ 7 S. Beach St. ☎ 508/228–1238) stocks the kinds of children's clothes that prompt the "awww" response, plus toys and more.

Clothing

With a branch in Palm Beach, **blu** (✉ 5 S. Water St. ☎ 508/325–6980 ⊕ www.nantucketblu.com) attains laid-back, born-to-it style.

Cashmere Nantucket (✉ 32 Centre St. ☎ 508/228–7611) carries contemporary and traditional original designs for men and women.

Chele's (✉ 1 N. Beach St. ☎ 508/228–6448) carries women's clothes as pretty and ephemeral as summer blooms; sizes range from 0 to XL.

Watch your head as you step down into **Cordillera Imports** (✉ 18 Broad St. ☎ 508/228–6140). Offering casual clothing, sandals, accessories, and crafts from Third World countries, this semi-basement is one of the few shops non-trust-funded teenagers can afford to patronize.

David Chase (✉ 60 Main St. ☎ 508/228–4775) offers neoclassic yet timely women's clothing for displaced urbanites, as well as compatible shoes, including Jimmy Choos.

Eye of the Needle (✉ 14 Federal St. ☎ 508/228–1923) is a microcosm of urban fashion trends, playfully leavened. In summer, a small satellite store is set up at the Summer House in Sconset.

Eye of the Needle Girls (✉ 18 Federal St. ☎ 508/228–4449) offers a similar selection to its stylish parent store, albeit writ small.

Gypsy (✉ 47 Main St. ☎ 508/228–4404) imports cutting-edge European styles; prices are *haute.*

Handblock (✉ 4 S. Water St. ☎ 508/228–4500 ⊕ www.handblock.com) stocks April Cornell clothing (for women and girls) and linens, along with countrified home furnishings.

A cousin of Force 5 Watersports, the **Haul-Over** (✉ 51 Main St. ☎ 508/228–8484 ⊕ www.thehaulover.com) sells clothing and gear for young, active sorts.

Namesake-muse Audrey would have approved of **Hepburn** (✉ 3 Salem St. ☎ 508/228–1548), with its slim-profile, high-fashion dresses; the accessories are especially nice, including an intriguing array of silver.

J. McLaughlin (✉ 1 Salem St. ☎ 508/325–6351) features cheery cotton prints; check out the painted roses climbing the rafters.

Johnston's of Elgin Cashmere (✉ 4 Federal St. ☎ 508/228–5450) stocks classic, contemporary, and couture styles, all quite pricey.

Lady Bird Lingerie (✉ 1 Orange St. ☎ 508/228–6093 ⊕ www.ladybirdlingerie.com) prides itself on fitting all sizes.

CloseUp

NANTUCKET REDS

BERMUDA HAS ITS SHORTS, FIJI ITS SARONGS. *Nantucket's totemic clothing items are made of cotton dyed red so as to fade to a dull salmon shade. The reds were something of a secret code until they were singled out by The Official Preppy Handbook in 1980: "By their pink shirts ye shall know them" might be the watchwords for Nantucketers among the worldwide sailing community. Now reds are as site-specific as Martha's Vineyard's Black Dog line.*

The principal purveyor is Murray's Toggery Shop on Main Street, which has catered to conservative dressers since the early 1900s. (Roland Macy worked here at his father's shop in the early 1800s before setting off to rewrite retailing history.) From baby togs to tote bags, you'll find everything you could want here in the way of reds. But for that weathered look that sets them off so well, you'll have to get out on the water.

She's back! The splashy resort wear so popular in the '60s is experiencing a resurgence at the **Lilly Pulitzer Shop** (⊠ 5 S. Water St. ☎ 508/228–0569 ⊕ www.lillyshop.com).

Marina Clothing (⊠ 5 Old South Wharf ☎ 508/228–6868 ⊕ www.marinaclothing.com) captures an outdoorsy look.

Fodor's Choice ★ **Murray's Toggery Shop** (⊠ 62 Main St. ☎ 508/228–0437 ⊕ www.nantucketreds.com) can claim credit for introducing the signature "Nantucket reds" (⇨ Nantucket Reds box)—now available in a range of styles for men, women, and children. Ranging from staid staples to the borderline outré (e.g., Betsy Johnson), the stock really is suitable for all ages and persuasions.

Murray's Warehouse (⊠ 7 New St. ☎ 508/228–3584 ⊕ www.nantucketreds.com) offers discounts of up to 75% on surplus stock from Murray's Toggery Shop.

Nalu (⊠ 2 Candle St. ☎ 508/325–6110) essays to fill a perceived gap in "hip" clothing: lines includes BCBG and ABS.

Nantucket Rose Garden (⊠ 9B S. Beach St. ☎ 508/325–5877) carries the kinds of frivolities that become necessities: colorful sweaters, decorated slippers, etc.

Something about the Nantucket lifestyle prompts hat hunger. **Peter Beaton** (⊠ 16½ Federal St. ☎ 508/228–8456 ⊕ www.peterbeaton.com) shows an international array of beauties, all customizable with special trim, along with a smattering of clothing.

Pollacks (⊠ 5 S. Water St. ☎ 508/228–9940) outfits both women and men in a rainbow's worth of tailored linens.

Ralph Lauren (⊠ 16 Main St. ☎ 508/228–9541 ⊕ www.polo.com) supplanted The Looms—an island institution—in the spring of '04 and the sky didn't cave in, but locals are still not happy about the incursion of a chain.

Vanessa Noel (✉ 5 Chestnut St., at Centre St. ☎ 508/228–6030 ⊕ www. vanessanoel.com) creates ultraglam shoes—they're expensive, to be sure, but fans gladly toe the line.

★ The inviting windows of **Vis-a-Vis** (✉ 34 Main St. ☎ 508/228–5527 ⊕ www.visavisnantucket.com) display relaxed-luxe women's fashions amid antique home furnishings, some of which, including hooked rugs, quilts, and collectibles, are also for sale.

Wolfhound Imports (✉ 21 Main St. ☎ 508/228–3552) carries Irish clothing for both genders and all ages; the style translates beautifully to Nantucket's windswept moors.

Zero Main (✉ 0 Main St. ☎ 508/228–4401) has striking women's clothes, plus an excellent selection of reasonably priced shoes.

Crafts

Claire Murray (✉ 11 S. Water St. ☎ 508/228–1913 or 800/252–4733 ⊕ www.clairemurray.com) carries the designer's Nantucket-theme and other hand-hooked rugs and rug kits, quilts, and knitting and needlework kits.

The **Dane Gallery** (✉ 28 Centre St. ☎ 508/228–7779 ⊕ www.danegallery. com) showcases splashy glass sculptures and vessels created by internationally renowned designers including shop owner Robert Dane.

Erica Wilson Needle Works (✉ 25 Main St. ☎ 508/228–9881) embodies the enthusiasms of the famous British-born designer, an island resident since 1958. In addition to her own embroidery and needlepoint kits, the store carries winning clothing and accessories for women (look for Heidi Weddendorf's Nantucket knot jewelry), baby gifts, and appealing elements of home decor.

Since 1848, the **Four Winds Craft Guild** (✉ 6 Ray's Ct. ☎ 508/228–9623 ⊕ www.sylviaantiques.com) has showcased local folk arts, including scrimshaw and lightship baskets (old and new), ship models, and duck decoys; the guild also offers a kit for making your own lightship basket. A satellite shop within the historic Pacific Club at 1 Main Street displays outstanding new work.

An outpost of the Boston mother ship, **Lannan Ship Model Gallery** (✉ 12 Oak St. ☎ 508/325–7797) recaptures the graceful sailing vessels of bygone days in miniature; the vessels are painstakingly handcrafted and intricately rigged.

Made on Nantucket (✉ 44 Main St. ☎ 508/228–0110) represents the work of more than 90 local artisans, ranging from quilters to woodworkers. The owner also collects Bakelite and other vintage jewelry.

★ **Nantucket Looms** (✉ 16 Federal St. ☎ 508/228–1908 ⊕ www. nantucketlooms.com) stocks luscious woven-on-the-premises textiles and chunky Susan Lister Locke jewelry, among other adornments for self and home.

Scrimshander Gallery (⊠ 19 Old South Wharf ☎ 508/228–1004) deals in new and antique scrimshaw.

Sheep to Shore (⊠ 14 Sparks Ave. ☎ 508/228–0038) is a knitter's paradise and support center.

The **Spectrum Art Galleries** (⊠ 26 Main St. ☎ 508/228–4606) displays a sampling of top American crafts.

Department Stores
Marine Home Center (⊠ Lower Orange St. ☎ 508/228–0900) carries everything you could possibly need, from major appliances to baby clothes. Prices are unfortunately a bit inflated from mainland norms.

Flowers
In addition to fresh blooms, **Flowers on Chestnut** (⊠ 1 Chestnut St. ☎ 508/228–6007) carries appealing gifts, including books, baby presents, lamps, and picture frames.

Trillium (⊠ 17 Centre St. ☎ 508/228–4450) comes up with truly dramatic designs, using unusual vessels and foliage.

Food & Beverage
LIQUOR STORES   **Fahey & Fromagerie** (⊠ 49A Pleasant St. ☎ 508/325–5644) is a wine specialist as well as purveyor of fantastic house-made and imported foods and cheese. Evenings in season, they sell not only gourmet pizza-to-go but takeout Thai food.

With about 1,500 varieties of wine, **Island Spirits** (⊠ 10 Washington St. ☎ 508/228–4484 ⊕ www.island-spirits.com) has Nantucket's largest selection, much of it elucidated with helpful signage. The store also stocks premium liquors and microbrews.

MARKETS   **Allserve General Store** (⊠ 44 Straight Wharf ☎ 508/228–8170) sells basics for the boat basin—and is the birthplace of Nantucket Nectars.

Annye's Whole Foods (⊠ 95-A Washington St. Ext. ☎ 508/228–4554) has organic staples, including some fresh produce.

Grand Union (⊠ Salem St., Straight Wharf ☎ 508/228–9756) is serviceable, albeit a bit cramped, with good produce.

Stop'n Shop Supermarket (⊠ Pleasant St. ☎ 508/228–2178) is comparable to its mainland peers. In summer, shop at odd hours since parking can be problematic.

Garden Centers
Arrowhead Nursery (⊠ 13 Arrowhead Dr. ☎ 508/228–8131 ⊕ www.arrowheadnursery.com) has an excellent selection of flowering trees, plus handsome outdoor furniture.

Holdgate's Nursery (⊠ 42 Old South Rd. ☎ 508/228–4967 ⊕ www.holdgates-nursery.com) offers the basics, along with an informative perennial show garden.

Moors End Farm (⊠ Polpis Rd. ☎ 508/228–2674) is a great source for perennials.

Surfing Hydrangea Nursery (✉ Somerset Rd. ☎ 508/228–6828) specializes in native and unusual plants.

Gift Shops

Anderson's of Nantucket (✉ 29 Main St. ☎ 508/228–4187) is a mostly white wonderland of laces, crystal, ceramics, mirrors, and more.

Best of the Beach (✉ 19 Centre St. ☎ 508/228–6263 ⊕ www.botbeach. com) celebrates the indoor/outdoor ocean-side lifestyle with fun, tasteful novelties.

Diane Johnston (✉ 35 Centre St. ☎ 508/228–4688) blends select clothing (hand-knit sweaters, needlepoint slippers) with antique quilts, lush rugs (from kilims to contemporary creations), and whatever else strikes the owner's fancy; the mix is magical.

The **English Trunk Show Company** (✉ 8 Washington St. ☎ 508/228–4199) assembles everything for the Anglophile, from tableware and linens to gardening tools; much of the stock is antique.

Expressions of Dan Freedman (✉ 7 Old South Wharf ☎ 508/228–3291) offers a wide assortment of brass clocks and the useful Nantucket Beach Bag Blanket.

FoolsGold (✉ 5 Washington St. ☎ 508/325–6788 ⊕ www.foolsgold.us) is a rare pocket of modernism, offering design elements for the body and home.

L'Ile de France (✉ 18 Federal St. ☎ 508/228–3686 ⊕ www. frenchgeneralstore.com) stocks French essentials such as sailor shirts, aromatic soaps, assorted antiques, and fresh artisanal bread.

Leslie Linsley Nantucket (✉ 0 India St. ☎ 508/325–4900 ⊕ www. leslielinsley.com), the project of a widely published crafts aficionado, carries supplies, tasteful souvenirs, and other decorative touches.

An outreach program of the Nantucket Historical Association, the **Museum Shop** (✉ 11 Broad St., next to Whaling Museum ☎ 508/228–5785 ⊕ www.nha.org) sells island-related books, reproduction furniture and accessories, and toys.

Vanessa @ Seven Seas (✉ 46 Centre St. ☎ 508/228–8010 ⊕ www. vanessanoel.com) gathers everything from handbags and jewelry to antique maps and furniture.

Home Furnishings

Christopher's Home Furnishings (✉ 8 and 31 Washington St. ☎ 508/325–0714) is a bit chichi for these parts, but undeniably fabulous.

At the **Complete Kitchen** (✉ 25 Centre St. ☎ 508/228–2665 ⊕ www. completekitchen.com) you'll find everything you need to furnish a kitchen worthy of a cooking-show studio.

Ensembles (✉ 17 N. Beach St. ☎ 508/325–4500) stocks imported bed linens as well as unusual bed and bath accessories.

Janis Aldridge (✉ 6 Coffin St. ☎ 508/228–6673 ⊕ www.janisaldridge.com) showcases beautiful accents and essentials for the home.

The **J. Butler Collection** (✉ 36 Centre St. ☎ 508/228–8429) assembles handsome furniture and accents in a muted, summery palette.

The **Lion's Paw** (✉ 0 Main St. ☎ 508/228–3837) is full of the sort of furnishings Nantucketers favor, fancy cottage-style.

Nantucket Gourmet (✉ 4 India St. ☎ 508/228–4353) offers the modern kitchen everything from coffeemakers to the Nantucket Peppergun.

Jewelry

Diana Kim England, Goldsmiths (✉ 56 Main St. ☎ 508/228–3766 or 800/343–1468 ⊕ www.dianakimengland.com) creates lightship-basket jewelry, including lockets designed like basket lids. Other lines are more contemporary and feature unusual gems such as tourmaline, chalcedony, and tanzanite.

The **Golden Basket** (✉ 44 Main St. ☎ 508/228–4344 or 800/626–2758 ⊕ www.thegoldenbasket.com) was founded in 1977 by designer Glenaan M. Elliott, who fashioned the first miniature lightship basket. Other popular motifs include starfish and shells.

Jewel of the Isle (✉ 6 Straight Wharf ☎ 508/228–2448 or 800/927–2148 ⊕ www.jeweloftheisle.com) showcases luxury lines (including Rolex) as well as jewelry created on-site.

Jewelers' Gallery (✉ 21 Centre St. ☎ 508/228–0229 or 800/550–0229 ⊕ www.thejewelersgallery.com) shows exquisite estate jewelry (Cartier, Tiffany, et al.) alongside contemporary designs. The display windows are drool-worthy.

Jola Jewelry Designs (✉ 29 Centre St. ☎ 508/325–6999) is a jewel box—the tiny, lovely atelier of Polish-born goldsmith Jolanta Gutnik, who creates "passionate statements" using unusual stones and rare pearls.

Pageo Jewelers (✉ 22 Centre St. ☎ 508/228–6899 ⊕ www.pageo.com) sells high-end, rather showy jewelry from all over the world.

Parham's Gems of the Sea (✉ 9A S. Beach St. ☎ 508/325–5899) purveys pearls in every imaginable size, shape, and hue.

Trianon (✉ 50 Main St. ☎ 508/325–5806) carries contemporary work—including some pieces incorporating Nantucket shells and sand—as well as the mostly nature-motif Seaman Schepps line, established in 1904.

The **Trinity Collection** (✉ 50 Main St. ☎ 508/228–7557) focuses on fine timepieces, both vintage and contemporary.

Music

Musicall (✉ 4 E. Chestnut St. ☎ 508/228–9306) is the sole source of the latest sounds; there's secondhand stock as well, and trade-ins are encouraged.

Pet Supplies

Cold Noses (⌧ The Courtyard, Straight Wharf ☎ 508/228–5477 ⊕ www.
coldnoses.net) has presents for Fido and Fluffy, including canine cookies and catnip treats.

Geronimo's (⌧ 119 Pleasant St. ☎ 508/228–3731 ⊕ www.geronimos.
com) is the mid-island source for pet supplies and pampering accessories.

Sandy Paws (⌧ 18 Centre St. ☎ 508/228–0708) caters to horse, dog,
and cat lovers with literature and gifts.

Pharmacies

There is no 24-hour pharmacy on the island. Call the **Nantucket Cottage
Hospital** (⌧ 57 Prospect St. ☎ 508/228–8100 ⊕ www.nantuckethospital.
org), in case of an emergency.

Congdon's (⌧ 47 Main St. ☎ 508/228–0020) is an 1860 drugstore with
much of its original woodwork intact.

Island Pharmacy (⌧ 122 Pleasant St. ☎ 508/228–6400 ⊕ www.islandrx.
com), the Nantucket Pharmacy's mid-island branch, has easier parking.

Nantucket Pharmacy (⌧ 45 Main St. ☎ 508/228–0180 ⊕ www.
nantucketpharmacy.com) looks lifted from the '50s.

Sporting Goods

For the fly-fishing fanatic **Cross Rip Outfitters** (⌧ 24 Easy St. ☎ 508/228–
4900 ⊕ www.crossrip.com) supplies all the necessary gear, plus related
gifts (clothing, home accessories, literature, and artwork).

Force 5 Watersports (⌧ 6 Union St. ☎ 508/228–0700 ⊕ www.
force5watersports.com) sells kayaks, sail- and surfboards, and related
paraphernalia and clothing.

Indian Summer/Upper Deck (⌧ 6 Broad St. ☎ 508/228–3632 ⊕ www.
surfnantucket.com) stocks boards of all sorts—snow, skate, boogie,
sail, and surf—plus the accessories and attitude that go with. Only the
first category is utterly useless on-island.

With its prime ferry-side location, **Young's Bicycle Shop** (⌧ Steamboat
Wharf ☎ 508/228–1151 ⊕ www.youngsbicycleshop.com) is a sensible
place to rent bikes; with 70 years of experience (note the wall-mounted
antiques) and attentive third-generation ownership, it's also a good
place to buy new wheels.

Thrift Shops

Operating off-season to support community services, the **Seconds Shop**
(⌧ 32 Centre St. ☎ 508/228–6677) has some great stuff, including occasional boutique surplus.

Open in summer, the **Thrift Shop** (☎ 508/228–1125, call for location) is
a whole houseful of used goods, including some real finds; proceeds benefit the Nantucket Cottage Hospital.

Toys

The **Nantucket Kiteman** (⊠ 14 S. Water St. ☎ 508/228–7089 ⊕ www. nantucketkiteman.com) sells, assembles, and repairs kites for flying at local beaches.

Sky's the Limit (⊠ 5 The Courtyard, Straight Wharf ☎ 508/228–4633 ⊕ www.nantucketkite.com) stocks kites, plus other "air toys" and beach games.

Carrying plenty of its namesake items in various sizes and shapes, the **Toy Boat** (⊠ 41 Straight Wharf ☎ 508/228–4552 ⊕ www.thetoyboat. com) also sells other high-quality toys for youngsters, including Nantucket mermaids, and children's books based on local themes (look for Joan Aiken's classic *Nightbirds on Nantucket*).

Sports & the Outdoors

Beaches

A calm area by the harbor, **Children's Beach** (off Harbor View Way) is an easy walk north from the center of town and a perfect spot for small children. The beach has a grassy park with benches, a playground, lifeguards, a café, picnic tables, showers, and restrooms. Tie-dyeing lessons are offered Friday at noon mid-July through August.

A short bike or shuttle-bus ride from town, **Jetties Beach** (Hulbert Ave., 1½ mi northwest of Straight Wharf) is the most popular family beach because of its calm surf, lifeguards, bathhouse, restrooms, and snack bar. It's a good place to try out water toys: kayaks, sailboards, and daysailers are rented in summer. On shore it's a lively scene with playground and volleyball nets on the beach and adjacent tennis courts. There is a boardwalk to the beach and you can watch the ferries pass. Buddhas, dragons, mermaids, and, of course, whales inhabit Jetties Beach during the annual **Sandcastle & Sculpture Day** in August. Creative concoctions, often with maritime themes, emerge from the sand: fish, porpoises, submarines, and crabs are common enough, although they're frequently constructed with a touch of whimsy, as in a giant man-eating clam. Automobiles, spaceships, celestial bodies, flowers, and the famous lightship baskets are carefully and creatively crafted out of sand, shells, seaweed, and even beach litter. You might even see a castle or two! Anyone can stake out a patch of sand. There are prizes in several age groups and categories, so grab a shovel, bucket, turkey baster (a secret weapon for blowing sand), rake, and sunscreen and join the fun. Registration forms are available at the chamber office, 48 Main Street.

Biking

The best way to tour Nantucket is by bicycle. Miles of paved bike paths wind through all types of terrain from one end of the island to the other; it is possible to bike around the entire island in a day. Most paths start within ½ mi of town, and all are well marked. Several lead to beaches. And if you're without your wheels, it's easy enough to rent some. The paths are also perfect for runners and bladers—but not mopeds, which are verboten. Note that Nantucket now requires all riders—including adults—to wear a helmet.

BIKE PATH **Milestone Bike Path,** linking Nantucket Town and Sconset, is probably the least scenic of the paths but is still quite pleasant. It's 6 mi, but when paired with the quite scenic Polpis Path it becomes a 14-mi island loop.

BIKE SHOPS **Island Bike & Sport** (⊠ 25 Old South Rd. ☎ 508/228–4070), though located mid-island, guarantees the best rates and offers free delivery.

Nantucket Bike Shop (⊠ 4 Broad St., Steamboat Wharf ⊠ Straight Wharf ☎ 508/228–1999 or 800/838–5311 for both ⊕ www.nantucketbikeshop. com), open April through October, rents bicycles and mopeds and provides an excellent touring map. Daily rentals cost $12–$22 for a children's or youth bike, $20–$40 for an adult size, and $40–$75 for a moped, though half- and multiple-day rates are available. (Be aware that locals dislike the dangerous, poky mopeds, so expect some dirty looks.) Ask about free delivery and pickup.

Young's Bicycle Shop (⊠ 6 Broad St., Steamboat Wharf ☎ 508/228–1151 ⊕ www.youngsbicycleshop.com), established in 1931, rents bicycles, including tandems and children's equipment ($15–$50 daily), plus cars ($75–$85 daily, in season) and Jeep Wranglers ($179 daily); weekly rates are available. The knowledgeable third-generation Young family and staff will send you off with everything you need—an excellent touring map, a helmet, and a quaint little Portuguese basket for your handlebars.

Bird-Watching

Hundreds of species flock to the island's moors, meadows, and marshes in the course of a year. Birds that are rare in other parts of New England thrive here, because of the lack of predators and the abundance of wide-open, undeveloped space. Northern harriers, rare short-eared owls, and Savannah sparrows nest in the grasslands; oystercatchers, gulls, plovers, and tiny least terns nest on sands and in beach grasses; snowy egrets, great blue herons, and ospreys stalk the marshlands; and ring-necked pheasants, mockingbirds, and Carolina wrens inhabit the tangled bogs and thickets. Almost anywhere outside of town you're sure to see interesting bird life, not just in migratory season but year round.

Set up your spotting scope near the salt marsh at Eel Point any time of year and you're bound to see shorebirds feeding—low tide is the best time. They're particularly abundant during the fall migration. Endangered piping plovers and least terns nest on the ocean side in Spring. Folger's Marsh near the Life Saving Museum on Polpis Road about 3 mi east of town and the Harbor Flats at the end of Washington Street on the eastern edge of town are also good shorebird-watching sites. Inland, a walk through Sanford Farm from Madaket Road to the south shore, traversing upland, forest, heath, and shore habitats, will bring you in range of Savannah sparrows, yellow warblers, osprey, and red-tailed hawks, the island's most common raptor. Be on the lookout for the protected Northern harrier. For woodland species, check out the trails through Windswept Cranberry Bog or the Masquetuck Reservation near Polpis Harbor.

Eco Guides: Strong Wings (⊠ 9 Nobadeer Farm Rd. ☎ 508/228–1769 ⊕ www.strongwings.org) customizes environmentally savvy birding tours based on interest and group size and, depending upon your preferred degree of difficulty, can include a hike, a bike ride, or a casual stroll.

The **Maria Mitchell Association** (MMA; ⊠ 4 Vestal St. ☎ 508/228–0898 ⊕ www.mmo.org) leads marine-ecology field trips and nature and bird walks weekly in the spring and early summer months and three times a week from June through Labor Day.

Boating

During July and August, Nantucket is *the* place to study, close-up, the world's possibly most splendid yachts—and the well-to-do people who own and sail them. Vintage motor yachts and sloops are moored forecastle to stern with multitier, fiberglass cruisers and sleek racing yawls. Don't be surprised if you see yachts with piggyback motor launches, automobiles, and helicopters. Some of the most expensive slips on the East Coast attract vessels bearing flags and registries from around the world. Most of them spend a few days here, many from a tour that originated in the Mediterranean via the Caribbean. Even if you're not usually interested in boats, come visit the Straight, Old South, and Commercial wharves to observe the conditions under which these poor yachters are forced to live.

Fortunately, Nantucket caters to those without a yacht with plenty of boat charters, rentals, and scenic cruises. For chartered fishing tours, *see* Fishing.

BOAT RENTALS **Nantucket Boat Rental** (⊠ Slip 1, Straight Wharf ☎ 508/325–1001 ⊕ www.nantucket.net/boating/boatrentals) rents powerboats. Smaller crafts (13 and 17 feet) are limited to the harbor and 5 passengers; 20- and 22-foot crafts may hold up to 10. Security deposits ($1,500) are required for all boat rentals.

Nantucket Community Sailing (⊠ 4 Winter St. ☎ 508/228–6600 ⊕ www. nantucketcommunitysailing.org) rents Sunfish sailboats, sailboards, and kayaks from Jetties Beach (Memorial Day–Labor Day); it also has youth and adult instructional sailing programs, as well as adaptive watersport clinics for disabled athletes. NCS's Outrigger Canoe Club—a Polynesian tradition—meets on Jetties Monday, Wednesday, and Friday at 5:30 in season.

Nantucket Harbor Sail (⊠ Petrel's Landing, 17 Swain's Wharf ☎ 508/ 228–0424) rents 19-foot sailboats ($80 for two hours, $160 for four hours, $240 per day). Security deposits are not required, although previous boating experience is.

Sea Nantucket (⊠ Washington St., ¼ mi southeast of Commercial Wharf ☎ 508/228–7499) rents kayaks and small sailboats by the hour or half day at the vest-pocket Francis Street Beach.

CRUISES Boats of all kinds leave from Straight Wharf on harbor sails throughout the summer; many are available for charter as well.

Anna W. II (⊠ Slip 11, Straight Wharf ☎ 508/228–1444) is a 1961 Maine lobster boat that's been converted to accommodate tables with booth seating. Kid-friendly trips (ages 4 and up only) include a 10:30 Marine Life Discovery Cruise ($27), on which fisherman and self-taught naturalist Captain Bruce Cowan tours the jetties, trap-hauling for lobsters, fish, crabs and eels; as well as the Ice Cream cruises ($17), which leave at 1:30 and 3:30 and feature complimentary servings of everyone's favorite food. A 5:30 cruise ($20) catches the boats coming into port, and for the Sunset Cruise ($25), couples or families can bring a picnic supper and a bottle of wine.

From early June through mid-September, the Hy-line ferry company offers an **"Around the Sound"** (⊠ Hy-Line, Ocean St. Dock, Hyannis ☎ 508/778–2600 or 800/492–8082 ⊕ www.hy-linecruises.com) cruise: this one-day round-trip ($42) from Hyannis stops at Nantucket and Martha's Vineyard. You'll spend about six hours at sea and have about three hours on each island for sightseeing, shopping, or dining. Or, from Nantucket, you could hop a 2¼-hour ferry for a day or overnight in Martha's Vineyard: there are three round trips ($28) daily. The boats, which hold 300–400 passengers, have a snack bar onboard, with sandwiches, snacks, candy, soda, beer, and wine.

The ***Christina*** (⊠ Slip 1019, Straight Wharf ☎ 508/325–4000) is a classic brass-and-mahogany sailboat. Daily trips cost $25 and depart at 10, 1, and 4. A fantastic sunset trip costs $35.

The ***Endeavor*** (⊠ Slip 1015, Straight Wharf ☎ 508/228–5585 ⊕ www.endeavorsailing.com), a charter replica Friendship sloop, makes four daily 1½-hour trips out to the jetties and into the sound. Departures are at 10, 1, and 4 ($25 per person); the departure times for the sunset cruise vary ($35 per person). Private charters and special theme trips for children—"Pirate Adventure" and "Songs and Stories of the Sea"—are available.

Olde Nantucket Natural History Cruises (☎ 408/277–7444), led by Captain Russ Cleveland aboard a 27-foot cabin cruiser, cover lore from Nantucket's whaling days, in addition to the rare and endangered species present today.

Shearwater Excursions (☎ 508/228–7037 ⊕ www.explorenantucket.com) mount various seaborne ecotours aboard a 50-foot power catamaran. One option is a 2-hour trip to view Muskeget Island's 2,500 resident gray seals; the boat departs at 10 and 3 from Children's Beach or the Town Pier ($50 per adult, $35 for a child under 12). One-hour lobster cruises to nearby Tuckernuck Island are offered on a flexible schedule out of Madaket ($350 for up to 6 people). Sundays are for whale-watching ($100) 15–30 mi southeast of Nantucket; Captain Blair Perkins guarantees a sighting, which means that if no mammals show up, you can go again for free. The Shearwater is also available for private evening charters.

Fishing

Surf fishing is very popular on Nantucket, especially in the late spring when bluefish are running. Blues and bass are the main island catches—bluefishing is best at Great Point—but there are plentiful numbers of other flavorful fish as well. Freshwater fishing is also an option at many area ponds.

FISHING CHARTERS Bob DeCosta, owner of the custom-built **Albacore** (⊠ Slip 1017, Straight Wharf ☎ 508/228–5074 ⊕ www.albacorecharters.com), continues in the tradition his father started in 1968 when he founded what is now the island's oldest family charter business. "No fish, no pay" is DeCosta's appealing motto.

Captain Peter Kaizer likes to say "Fishing's fun, catching's better." A former commercial fisherman, he guarantees you'll bring home something to eat by taking you to the fishies' favorite clandestine hangouts aboard the **Althea K** (☎ 508/228–3471 ⊕ www.altheakcharter.com). Catches can be brought to the Brant Point Inn, where the chef—a friend of Kaizer's—will cook them to order for your waterfront meal. Kaizer also runs whale-watching and charter cruises from an insider's perspective.

Captain Tom's Charters (⊠ Public Landing, Madaket ☎ 508/228–4225 ⊕ www.captaintomscharters.com) win consistent "best of" awards for Tom Mleczko's hands-on expertise. Choose among rips, bars, surf, open water, and flats (the latter for the added challenge of sight fishing with fly rods).

SHELLFISHING A permit is required for **shellfishing**, specifically foraging for littleneck and cherrystone clams, quahogs, scallops, oysters, steamers, and mussels. Permits are $100 per person for nonresidents and last a year. You can pick one up—along with tips on where and how to get the best catch—at the **Marine and Coastal Resources Department** (⊠ 34 Washington St. ☎ 508/228–7261).

TACKLE SHOPS **Bill Fisher Tackle** (⊠ 14 New La. ☎ 508/228–2261) sells and rents equipment and can point you in the direction of the best fishing spots.

Cross Rip Outfitters (⊠ 24 Easy St. ☎ 408/228–4900 ⊕ www.crossrip. com) sells everything you could possibly need, and then some (trinkets for deep-pocketed enthusiasts). They'll also provide guide service or organize a charter.

Fitness Clubs

Nantucket Health Club (⊠ 10 Young's Way ☎ 508/228–4750 ⊕ www. nantuckethealthclub.com) has StairMasters, Lifecycles, treadmills, rowers, Airdyne bikes, New Generation Nautilus, and free weights; aerobics, Spinning and yoga classes; and personal trainers. You can get a short-term pass that covers the machines, fitness classes, or both.

Built in 2002, the **Nantucket Tennis & Swim Club** (⊠ 23 Nobadeer Farm Rd. ☎ 508/825–2020 ⊕ www.nantuckettennis.com) is a three-acre, state-of-the-art complex comprising nine Har-Tru courts (five are lit for night play), plus a fitness center, pool, spa, pro shop, and café.

Hiking & Conservation Areas

Nantucket supports approximately 1,200 species of vegetation: that's a greater variety than is found in any other area of equivalent size in the United States. It has 82 mi of beaches, and though almost 97% of the shoreline is privately owned, it's a point of pride that almost all is open for public use. There are hardwood forests, salt marshes, cranberry bogs, squam swamps, freshwater ponds, and coastal heathlands, and, with Martha's Vineyard and nearby Tuckernuck Island, the island holds more than 90% of the acreage of sandplain grassland *worldwide*. The island is home to a huge number of deer; significant colonies of harbor seals, gray seals, and harbor porpoises; turtles, frogs, rabbits, voles, and other reptiles and small field mammals. A lack of land-bound predators such as skunks and raccoons allows bird populations to thrive, and hundreds of species either live on the island or pass through on their annual migrations. The still-fertile seas are awash with tuna, blues, bass, and shellfish—not to mention, of course, the whales that made Nantucket what it is today. Pretty impressive statistics for a glacial deposit that measures just 14-mi long and 3½-mi wide.

Almost all of the 9,000 acres maintained by the **Nantucket Conservation Foundation** (⊠ 118 Cliff Rd. ☎ 508/228–2884 ⊕ www.nantucketconscrvation.com) are open to the public; though only a few trails are marked, you can feel free to wander knowing that you can't get lost—if you keep going in one direction, you're bound to hit a road or a beach eventually. The foundation, open weekdays 8–5, puts out maps and informative brochures on the three most popular hiking spots, all of which have extensive interpretive trails. Each of the properties—Sanford Farm, Ram Pasture, Squam Swamp, and Tupancy Links—also provide maps and information at their gates. Remember that these conservation areas are set aside to preserve and protect Nantucket's fragile ecosystems—tread carefully—and also be aware that ticks are a serious problem here. Dress accordingly and carry plenty of repellent.

Scuba Diving

The scuba diving around Nantucket is somewhat limited. Visibility is between 5 and 30 feet, and there are no spectacular wrecks to visit; most diving is done off the jetties. The **Sunken Ship** (⊠ 12 Broad St. ☎ 508/228–9226) has complete dive-shop services, including lessons, guided dives, equipment rentals, and charters; it also rents water skis, boogie boards, and fishing poles and sells just about every kind of sporting good and accessory imaginable.

Surfing

The relatively mild breakers at Cisco Beach make picking up the sport easier than it might be in, say, Maui. And **Nantucket Island Surf School** (☎ 508/560–1020 ⊕ www.surfack.com) owner Gary Kohner and his crew can tell you everything you need to know to get up and cruising, from surfing etiquette to ocean safety. Group and private lessons and equipment and wet-suit rental are available.

Swimming

The Olympic-size indoor **Nantucket Community Pool** (⊠ Nantucket High School, 10 Surfside Rd. ☎ 508/228–7262) is open year-round for lap and recreational swimming and lessons. You can buy daily, weekly, and monthly passes.

Tennis

If you need more of a workout than lounging on the beach can afford, sign up early for time at the public court at Jetties, or call ahead to be among the lucky few nonmembers who can get a game in at Siasconset Casino. The Nantucket Tennis and Swim Club is the only place with lighted courts.

The Jetties Beach Tennis Courts (☎ 508/325–5334), six contiguous asphalt courts overseen by the Parks & Recreation department, charge a nominal fee ($20 for singles, $25 for doubles) 8 AM–6 PM in season and are much in demand, so reserve early in the day. Early and latecomers play free, and off-season, you're golden: they leave the nets up year-round.

Nantucket Tennis and Swim Club (⊠ 23 Nobadeer Farm Rd., near the airport ☎ 508/228–3700 ☉ Memorial Day–Columbus Day, daily 7 AM–9:30 PM) has nine fast-dry clay courts, five lighted courts, and a pro shop. Lessons, rentals, clinics, and round-robins are available.

Whale-Watching

Many of the fishing charters will gladly make detours to spot whales.

Shearwater Excursions (☎ 508/228–7037 ⊕ www.explorenantucket. com) makes special trips Sundays in seasons.

Yoga

Marjory Trott (⊠ 8 Dukes Rd. ☎ 508/228–4209) teaches regularly scheduled classes for all age groups.

Nantucket Health Club (⊠ 10 Young's Way ☎ 508/228–4750 ⊕ www. nantuckethealthclub.com) posts its class schedule online.

Sheri Perelman (☎ 508/325–0763 for directions) leads yoga classes and private sessions year-round from a small mid-island studio.

thespace (⊠ 9 Amelia Dr. ☎ 508/825–0900), the island's healing arts center, offers classes year-round.

At **Yoga of Health** (⊠ 15 Seikinnow Pl. ☎ 508/228–7038), Nan Strelnitski, who's also an RN, offers instruction for all levels and specializes in restorative yoga.

Yoga on the Beach (⊠ Children's Beach ☎ 508/257–6921), an hour-long class held at the Bandstand Monday through Saturday at 7 AM in season, is a refreshing option.

The **Yoga Room** (⊠ 49 Fairgrounds Rd. ☎ 508/825–2211 ⊕ www. nantucketyogaroom.com) has classes for all levels; in summer, they run pretty much all day.

SIASCONSET, THE SOUTH SHORE & MADAKET

Siasconset, Polpis & Wauwinet

Siasconset began as a community of cod and halibut fishermen and shore whalers in the 17th century. But even then it was already becoming a summer resort: people from Nantucket Town would come here to escape the smell of whale oil burning in the refineries. In 1884 the Nantucket Railroad was extended to Sconset (as it's known locally), bringing more off-islanders. The writers and artists who came from Boston in the 1890s were soon followed by Broadway actors on holiday during the theaters' summer hiatus. Attracted by the village's beauty, remoteness, sandy ocean beach, and cheap lodgings—converted one-room fishing shacks, and cottages built to look like them—they spread the word, and before long Sconset became a thriving actors' colony.

Today a charming village of pretty streets with tiny rose-covered cottages and driveways of crushed white shells, Sconset is almost entirely a summer community (about 150 families live here through the winter), served by a post office, a general store, and two restaurants, as well as a unique liquor store–cum–informal lending library. Sconset makes a lovely day trip from Nantucket Town—try it on bike or shuttle bus, stopping to take a stroll in the village and continuing on to nearby beaches, bogs, and conservation areas.

Numbers in the text correspond to numbers in the margin and on the Siasconset, Polpis, and Wauwinet map.

A Good Tour

Heading out on foot from Post Office Square, meander south along Ocean Avenue, past the Summer House hotel and explore the side streets: Cottage, Magnolia, and Pochik. They remain much as they were in the 1890s, when a development of tiny rental cottages in the fishing-shack style was built here. The summer rose blossoms climbing over many of the cottages weave fantastic carpets of color. Returning to the square, head up Broadway. Off Broadway Street is the Sconset Pump—your Nantucket Nectars juice cap will tell you it was "dug in 1776." From the pump, walk east on New Street toward the **Siasconser Casino ❶**—it's a social and tennis club—and take a peek at the beautiful entrance of Chanticleer, the ritzy French restaurant across the street. Just east on New Street is the **Sconset Union Chapel ❷** and its pretty garden. Then reclaim your bike or vehicle and head north on Sankaty Road (which turns into Polpis Road) past the striped **Sankaty Head Lighthouse ❸**, best viewed from **Sesachacha Pond ❹**. Continue northwest on Polpis Road past the **Windswept Cranberry Bog ❺**, the smaller of two island bogs. Just a mile or so west of the bog you'll come to the turnoff for **Wauwinet ❻** and **Coatue–Coskata–Great Point**—a terrific exploring area, worthy of a special trip (it's accessible only by foot or, with a special permit, by four-wheel drive). Heading out to Wauwinet, you'll pass **SeaView Farm Art Center ❼**. Returning to Polpis Road, continue 1¼ mi east and turn south

Siasconset, Polpis, & Wauwinet

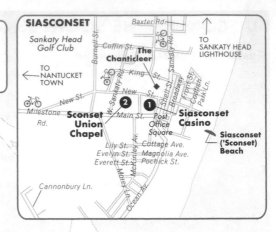

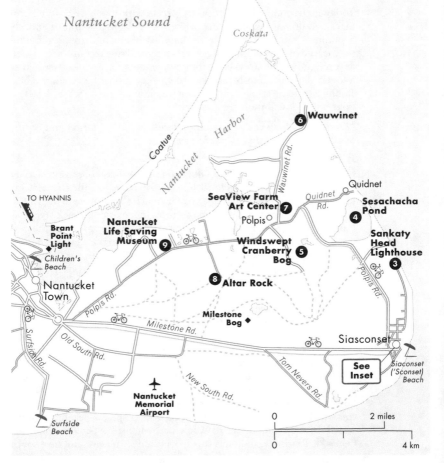

on Altar Rock Road to ascend to **Altar Rock ⓫**, the island's highest point, which affords an incredible view of the surrounding moors, particularly at dawn and dusk. It's about ½ mi from the Polpis Bike Path. Return to Polpis Road, and continue west another ½ mi to the **Nantucket Life Saving Museum ⓭**, where artifacts recovered from the *Andrea Doria* are displayed. After you've visited the museum, take the Polpis Path back toward town.

TIMING Since the last stop on the tour closes at 4, try to get started early, touring Sconset and having lunch there before visiting the sights off Polpis Road. This tour will take most of a day on bike and a half day by car. Note that there are no services in Sconset during the off-season.

Sights to See

★ ⓫ **Altar Rock.** Altar Rock Road, a dirt track about 3 mi west on Polpis Road, leads to the island's highest point, Altar Rock, from which the view is spectacular. The hill overlooks open moor and bog land—technically called lowland heath—which is very rare in the United States. The entire area is laced with paths leading in every direction. Don't forget to keep track of the trails you travel in order to find your way back.

off the beaten path

MILESTONE BOG – The 200-plus acres of cranberry bogs, surrounded by conservation land, is always a beautiful spot to visit, particularly in the fall. The sight of bright red berries and the moors' rich autumn colors is not to be missed. ⊠ *Off Milestone Rd., west of Siasconset.*

⓭ **Nantucket Life Saving Museum.** Items displayed in this re-creation of the 1874 Life Saving Service station that still stands on Surfside Beach (it's a hostel now), include original rescue equipment and boats, artifacts recovered from the *Andrea Doria* wreck, and photos and accounts of daring rescues. There are several rare pieces: for instance, one of four surviving surfboats and an equally well preserved original beach cart. ⊠ *158 Polpis Rd.* ☎ *508/228–1885* ⊕ *www.nantucketlifesaving.org* 💲 *$5* ☽ *Mid-June–mid–Oct., daily, 9:30–4.*

⓬ **Sankaty Head Lighthouse.** The red-and-white-striped beacon overlooking the sea on one side and the Scottish-looking links of the private Sankaty Head Golf Club on the other is one of New England's many endangered lighthouses. On a 90-foot-high bluff that has lost as much as 200 feet of shoreline in the past 75 years, the 1849 lighthouse could be lost, as Great Point Light was in 1984, to further erosion. More Nantucket shoreline disappears every year, especially at Sankaty Head (and on the south shore), where no shoals break the ocean waves as they do on the north shore. Some of that sand is simply moved along shore to the island's other end, but that's no great consolation to Sconset dwellers. The lighthouse is not open to the public, but you can approach it, via a seashell gravel road, for photos. ⊠ *Baxter Rd.*

⓬ **Sconset Union Chapel.** The village's only church holds Roman Catholic mass at 8:45 AM and Protestant services at 10:30 AM on summer Sundays. Even if you're not a churchgoer, it's worth a visit to see the almost 200 kneelers, individually designed by well-known needlepoint artist Erica Wilson, and the beautiful flower garden. ⊠ *18 New St.* ☎ *508/257–6616.*

need a break? **Sconset Market** (⊠ Post Office Sq. ☎ 508/257–9915) is a seasonal shop with fresh-prepared foods and gourmet necessities. For a great picnic in Sconset, stop at **Claudette's** (⊠ Post Office Sq. ☎ 508/257–6622) for a box lunch to go; or dig right in on the shady patio. It's open mid-May through mid-October.

❼ SeaView Farm Art Center. Run by the Nantucket Island School of Design and the Arts and inspired by the island's distinctive environment and history, SeaView nurtures the artist in everyone. Classes for children, teens, adults, and "all generations" range from half-day workshops to summerlong programs; some can be counted toward college credit. Virtually every medium and discipline is addressed. The Center also has a gallery and hosts evening lectures and events. ⊠ *23 Wauwinet Rd.* ☎ *508/228–9248* ⊕ *www.nisda.org.*

❹ Sesachacha Pond. This kettle pond (pronounced *sah*-kah-cha) off Polpis Road is a good spot for bird-watching. It's circled by a walking path that leads to an Audubon wildlife area and is separated from the ocean by a narrow strand on its east side. It provides a good view of Sankaty Head Lighthouse.

❶ Siasconset Casino. Despite its name, this property dating to 1899 has never been used for gambling—the meaning of "casino" was broader back when it was built—but was instead used from the beginning as a theater venue, particularly during the actors'-colony heyday, and as a gathering place. Some theater can still be seen here, but it's primarily a tennis club and cinema. Though the clay-court tennis club is private, nonmembers can play a few hours a week in summer (call first), provided they wear whites and tennis shoes and book on the same day. First-run movies are shown on Tuesday, Thursday, and Saturday in July and August. Opposite the casino is the much-photographed entryway of the Chanticleer restaurant: a trellised arch topped by a sculpted hedge frames a rose garden with a flower-bedecked carousel horse at its center. ⊠ *New St.* ☎ *508/257–6661.*

❻ Wauwinet. Now it's a hamlet of beach houses on the northeastern end of Nantucket. But early European settlers found the neck of sand above it to be the easiest way to get to the ocean for fishing. Instead of rowing around Great Point, fishermen would go to the head of the harbor and haul their dories over the narrow strip of sand and beach grass separating Nantucket Harbor from the ocean. Hence the name for that strip: the haulover.

In 1876 the Wauwinet House inn started luring townspeople to its 75¢ shore dinners. Local historian Jane Lamb, resident of a house called Chaos Corner on Wauwinet Road, relates the story of revelers who, on July 4, 1877, while sailing back to town after dancing until 11 PM, were grounded on shoals and rolled back and forth here until the tide rose with the sun. Happily, Wauwinet dinner cruises didn't die with that night, and you can still sail out to the inn for dinner.

⑤ Windswept Cranberry Bog. Throughout the year, the 205-acre conservation area off Polpis Road is a beautiful tapestry of greens, reds, and golds— and a popular hangout for many bird species. The bog is especially vibrant in mid-October, when the cranberries are harvested. (Although the weekend after Columbus Day has historically been a harvesting holiday, a glut in the market has cancelled the harvesting in recent years. Call the Chamber of Commerce for information.) A map is available from the **Nantucket Conservation Foundation** (⊠ 118 Cliff Rd. ☎ 508/ 228–2884 ⊕ www.nantucketconservation.com).

> off the beaten path

Fodor'sChoice
★

COATUE–COSKATA–GREAT POINT – A trip to an unpopulated spit of sand, comprising three cooperatively managed wildlife refuges, is a great way to spend a day relaxing or pursuing a favorite activity, such as bird-watching or fishing. **Coatue,** the strip of sand enclosing Nantucket Harbor, is open for many kinds of recreation—shellfishing (permit required) for bay scallops, soft-shell clams, quahogs, and mussels; surf casting for bluefish and striped bass (spring through fall); picnicking; or just enjoying the crowdless expanse. **Coskata**'s beaches, dunes, salt marshes, and stands of oak and cedar attract marsh hawks, egrets, oystercatchers, terns, herring gulls, plovers, and many other birds, particularly during spring and fall migration. A successful program has brought ospreys here to nest on posts set up in a field by Coskata Pond. You'll want to bring your field glasses.

Because of dangerous currents and riptides and the lack of lifeguards, swimming is strongly discouraged in the refuges, especially within 200 yards of the 70-foot stone tower of **Great Point Light.** Those currents, at the same time, are fascinating to watch at the Great Point tide rip. Seals and fishermen alike benefit from the unique feeding ground that it creates. The lighthouse is a 1986 re-creation of the light destroyed by a storm in 1984. The new light was built to withstand 20-foot waves and winds of up to 240 mph, and it was fitted with eight solar panels to power it.

You may only enter the area on foot or by four-wheel-drive vehicle, for which a **permit** (⊠ $100–$125 for a year ☎ 508/228–5646 w www.thetrustees.org) is required. Rental vehicles usually come with permits—double-check with your rental agency. Permits are available at the **gatehouse at Wauwinet** (⊠ Wauwinet Rd. ☎ 508/ 228–0006) 9 am–6 pm June to mid-October or off-season from a ranger patrolling the property. If you enter on foot, be aware that Great Point is a 5-mi walk from the entrance on soft, deep sand.

Where to Eat

$$$$ ✕ **The Chanticleer.** Chef Jean-Charles Berruet has been wowing Nantucket's elite with classical French cuisine in a *haute auberge* setting in Sconset since 1970. Don't let the clematis-veiled summerhouse look deceive you: this is very serious stuff. If you're looking for the ultimate in tra-

ditional Gallic finesse (champagne–suffused lobster, perhaps?), supplemented by a select 40,000-bottle wine cellar, you've come to the right place. Lunch can be a bargain—relatively speaking, *bien sur.* ⊠ *9 New St., Siasconset* ☎ *508/257–6231* ⌕ *Reservations essential* ▭ *AE, MC, V* ☾ *Closed Mon. and mid-Oct.–early May.*

★ **$$$$** ✕ **Topper's.** The Wauwinet—an ultraluxuriously restored 19th-century inn on Nantucket's northeastern shore—is where islanders and visitors alike go to experience perfection. Many take advantage of the complimentary launch, the *Wauwinet Lady* out of Straight Wharf, which frames the journey with a scenic harbor tour. Having traipsed past the croquet lawn (with its life-size sculpted chess set), one enters a creamy-white dining room awash with lush linens and glorious flowers. Chris Freeman's cuisine delivers on the fantasy with a classically inspired multiple-choice prix-fixe menu. Preparations seem staider than in the heady early days (the chef has mellowed), but you're assured of an evening blending artistry and finesse. ⊠ *120 Wauwinet Rd., Wauwinet* ☎ *508/228–8768* ⌕ *Reservations essential* ▭ *AE, D, DC, MC, V* ☾ *Closed Nov.–Apr.*

$$–$$$$
Fodor'sChoice
★ ✕ **The Summer House Beachside Bistro.** Where some hoteliers might install a poolside snack bar, the Summer House imported a skilled chef—Paul Restrepo, whose CV includes Cipriani's—to create a real restaurant en plein aire. The terraced potagerie flanking the stairway down to the cluster of white umbrellas attests to the freshness of Restrepo's ingredients (he's a gifted gardener, too, to wrest such bounty from the sand). Some of his dishes, including a light, lyrical clam chowder and fried calamari with a sweet chili mirin glaze, are certifiably addictive. ⊠ *17 Ocean Ave., Siasconset* ☎ *508/257–4542* ▭ *AE, MC, V* ☾ *Closed mid-Oct.–May.*

$$$ ✕ **Sconset Café.** It looks like a modest lunchroom, with chockablock tables virtually within arm's reach of the open kitchen. But this tiny institution, treasured by summering locals since 1983, puts out wonderful breakfasts, great lunches, and outright astounding dinners. The nightly menus shift every two weeks to take advantage of seasonal bounty. If you have trouble getting in (it's not exactly undiscovered, and reservations are accepted for the 6 PM seating only), you can always order out and feast on the beach. (Call in the shoulder season before you head out to confirm that it's open.) ⊠ *Post Office Sq., Siasconset* ☎ *508/257–4008* ▭ *No credit cards* ⌟⌞ *BYOB* ☾ *Closed Columbus Day–mid-May.*

$$–$$$ ✕ **The Summer House Restaurant.** An integral element of the rose-canopied complex that epitomizes Sconset, the dining room is also abloom, with lavish floral displays set against a background of pastel linen and white wicker. The cuisine is energized, rather than rarefied: all sorts of influences agreeably converge. ⊠ *17 Ocean Ave., Siasconset* ☎ *508/257–9976* ⌕ *Reservations essential* ▭ *AE, MC, V* ☾ *Closed mid-Oct.–May.*

Where to Stay

$$$$ ▥ **Bartlett's Beach Cottages.** Located 4 mi southwest of town and a short walk from Cisco Beach, these rustic cottages—running two to four bedrooms—are part of Bartlett's Ocean View Farm, which means that fresh produce and wonderful prepared foods are close at hand. Each has a

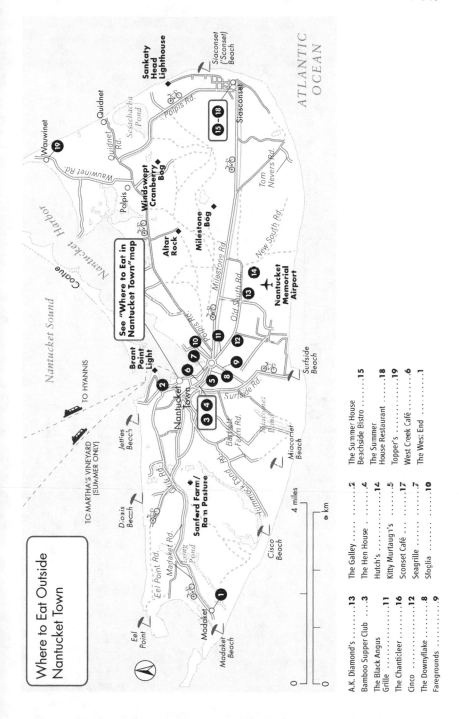

Where to Eat Outside Nantucket Town

See "Where to Eat in Nantucket Town" map

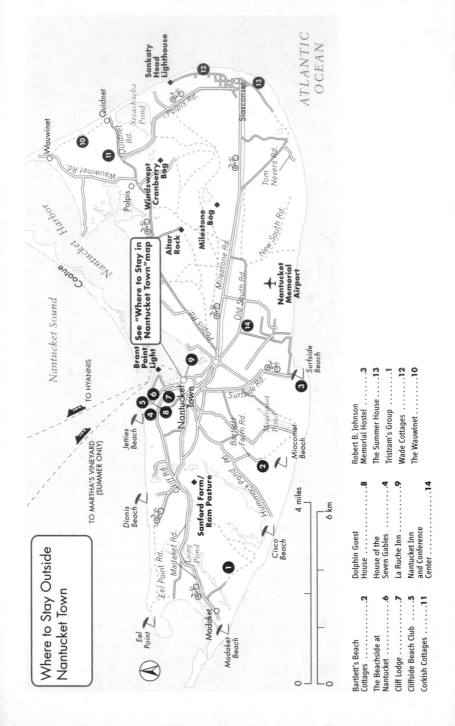

Where to Stay Outside Nantucket Town

See "Where to Stay in Nantucket Town" map

ATLANTIC OCEAN

Nantucket Sound

Coatue

Nantucket Harbor

TO HYANNIS

TO MARTHA'S VINEYARD (SUMMER ONLY)

Eel Point

Dionis Beach

Madaket Beach

Madaket

Jetties Beach

Nantucket Town

Cisco Beach

Surfside Beach

Miacomet Beach

Sanford Farm/ Ram Pasture

Brant Point Light

Altar Rock

Milestone Bog

Windswept Cranberry Bog

Wauwinet

Quidnet

Sesachacha Pond

Sankaty Head Lighthouse

Siasconset

Nantucket Memorial Airport

Eel Point Rd.
Madaket Rd.
Long Pond
Cliff Rd.
Hummock Pond Rd.
Bartlett Farm Rd.
Miacomet Rd.
Surfside Rd.
Old South Rd.
Milestone Rd.
Polpis Rd.
New South Rd.
Tom Nevers Rd.
Wauwinet Rd.
Quidnet Rd.
Polpis

0   4 miles
0   6 km

fireplace, TV, and phone, but you may need to cart in some linens and kitchen supplies. Expect a rate of $1,200–$2,500 per week. ⊠ *Hummock Pond Rd.* ⌂ *Box 899, Nantucket 02554* ☎ *508/228–3906* ⊕ *www.bartlettsfarm.com.*

$$$$ ⊡ **Corkish Cottages.** These family-scale cottages—three bedrooms, plus sundeck—offer plenty of privacy and room to roam. Some are fancier than others, but each is located on its own 10-acre tract. ⊠ *320 Polpis Rd., Nantucket 02554* ☎ *508/228–5686* ⚹ *Some pets allowed* ⊟ *No credit cards* ⊙ *Closed mid-Oct.–Apr.*

$$–$$$$ ⊡ **Wauwinet.** This resplendently updated 1850 resort straddles a
Fodor'sChoice "haulover" poised between ocean and bay—which means beaches on
★ both sides. Head out by complimentary van or launch to partake of utmost pampering (the staff-to-guest ratio exceeds one-on-one). Optional activities include sailing, water-taxiing to a private beach along Coatue, and touring the Great Point nature preserve by Land Rover. Of course, it's tempting just to stay put, what with the cushy country-chic rooms and a splendid restaurant, Topper's. ⊠ *120 Wauwinet Rd., Wauwinet* ⌂ *Box 2580, Nantucket 02584* ☎ *508/228–0145 or 800/426–8718* ⊟ *508/228–7135* ⊕ *www.wauwinet.com* ⇨ *25 rooms, 5 cottages* ⚹ *Restaurant, room service, 2 tennis courts, beach, boating, mountain bikes, croquet, bar, library, concierge, business services; no kids under 12, no smoking* ⊟ *AE, DC, MC, V* ⊙ *Closed Nov.–Apr.* ⑂ *BP.*

$$–$$$ ⊡ **The Summer House.** Perched on a bluff overlooking Sconset Beach, this cluster of rose-covered cottages—cobbled from salvage in the 1840s—epitomizes Nantucket's enduring allure. The rooms, though small, are intensely romantic, with lace coverlets and pale pine armoires; most have marble baths with whirlpool tubs, and one has a fireplace. Contemplative sorts can claim an Adirondack chair on the lawn; others may want to race down to the beach, perhaps enjoying lunch beside the heated pool en route. The dinner restaurant, around which the cottages nestle, has a timeless air: as a pianist plays old standards, you half expect Scott and Zelda to waltz in. Should the Summer House be fully booked (as, alas, it all too often is), inquire about its satellite inns in town, connected by complimentary jitney. ⊠ *17 Ocean Ave., Siasconset 02564* ☎ *508/257–4577* ⊟ *508/257–4590* ⊕ *www.thesummerhouse.com* ⇨ *10 rooms* ⚹ *2 restaurants, pool, bar, piano bar, some in-room hot tubs* ⊟ *AE, MC, V* ⊙ *Closed Nov.–late Apr.* ⑂ *CP.*

$$ ⊡ **Nantucket Inn and Conference Center.** Though rather corporate and bland on the surface, this hotel near the airport, 3 mi from town, has surprisingly nice interiors: some rooms sport cathedral ceilings and decorative fireplaces, and of course all the business-level accoutrements are present and accounted for throughout. Hourly shuttles to town and Surfside Beach solve the isolation problem. It's also a good deal for families because children under 18 stay free with their parents and the room rates cover a full breakfast buffet. ⊠ *27 Macy's La., Surfside 02554* ☎ *508/228–6900 or 800/321–8484* ⊟ *508/228–9861* ⊕ *www. nantucketinn.net* ⇨ *94 rooms, 6 cottages* ⚹ *In-room data ports, refrigerators, cable TV, in-room VCRs, 2 tennis courts, 2 pools (1 indoor), health club, billiards, bar, lounge, meeting rooms* ⊟ *AE, MC, V* ⊙ *Closed mid-Dec.–mid-Apr.* ⑂ *BP.*

🐾 ¢–$$ 🏠 **Wade Cottages.** This Sconset complex of guest rooms, apartments, and cottages couldn't be better situated for beach aficionados. The buildings, in the same family since the 1920s, are arranged around a central lawn with a great ocean view, shared by most of the rooms. Furnishings tend to be of the somewhat worn beach-house school, but you'll be too busy—and happy—to waste a moment critiquing. ⊠ *Shell St.* 🕮 *Box 211, Siasconset 02564* 🕾 *508/257–6308* 🖷 *508/257–4602* ⊕ *www.wadecottages.com* 🖢 *8 rooms, 4 with bath; 6 apartments; 3 cottages* ♿ *Badminton, Ping-Pong, laundry facilities* 🖃 *AE, MC, V* ☺ *Closed mid-Oct.–late May* ⊙◉ *CP.*

Nightlife

BARS The wine bar at the **Chanticleer** (⊠ 9 New St., Sconset 🕾 508/257–6231 ⊕ www.chanticleerinn.com) is a godsend for oenophiles: here, in a warm, aubergelike setting, you can enjoy flights drawn from a 40,000-bottle wine cellar.

The bay-view patio at **Topper's** (⊠ 120 Wauwinet Rd. 🕾 508/228–8768 ⊕ www.toppersrestaurant.com), the Wauwinet's exquisite restaurant, is a lovely setting for cranberry-juice cosmopolitans and "the Wauwinetini": Ketel One vodka splashed with peach liqueur.

FILM The **Siasconset Casino** (⊠ New St., Siasconset 🕾 508/257–6661), a 100-year-old hall, has nothing to do with gambling: at the turn of the 20th century, the term merely meant a place to gather for entertainment. First-run movies are shown, auditorium-style, Tuesday, Thursday, and Sunday evenings at 8:30, June through Labor Day. Old hands know to bring pillows.

Sports & the Outdoors

BEACH **Siasconset Beach** (⊠ end of Milestone Rd., off Codfish Park) has moderate to heavy surf, a lifeguard, and a playground. Restaurants and public restrooms are a short walk away.

BIKING The 8-mi **Polpis Bike Path,** a long trail with gentle hills, begins at the intersection of Milestone and Polpis roads and winds alongside Polpis Road almost all the way into Sconset. It goes right by the Nantucket Life Saving Museum and has great views of the moors, the cranberry bogs, and Sesachacha Pond.

GOLF **Sankaty Head Golf Club** (⊠ Polpis Rd., Siasconset 🕾 508/257–6391), a private 18-hole course, is open to the public Columbus Day through Memorial Day. This challenging Scottish-style links course cuts through the moors and has spectacular views of the lighthouse and ocean from practically every hole.

Siasconset Golf Club (⊠ 360 Milestone Rd. 🕾 508/257–6596) is an easy-walking 9-hole public course surrounded by conservation land. Opened in 1894, it's the world's oldest privately owned public course.

HIKING & CONSERVATION AREAS Probably the most interesting property from a visitor's perspective is **Squam Swamp** (⊠ Wauwinet Rd., ¼ mi past Pocomo Rd.), a 294-acre parcel whose 19 trail markers are coordinated to points on a self-guided brochure. You'll pass through glades of ferns (including fiddlehead, edible in the spring), stands of high-bush blueberries, shadbush, and arrowwood, and portions of hardwood forest. The pamphlet also points out specific markers along the way, such as a partially uprooted tree at the edge of the trail, a boulder that recalls Nantucket's geologic past, and a vernal pool, an ecosystem crucial to the breeding of amphibians and currently threatened throughout the United States. The swamp is on the right as you drive out Wauwinet Road.

TENNIS **Siasconset Casino** (⊠ 10 New St., Siasconset ☏ 508/257–6585) is a private club with 11 outdoor courts. Some nonmember play is available; call ahead for information.

The South Shore

2–4 mi southeast of Nantucket Town.

The immediate presence of the Atlantic Ocean dominates the South Shore. Its beaches—Cisco and Surfside—are known for challenging surf.

Where to Eat

$$$–$$$$ ✕ **The Black Angus Grille.** Done up in hunter green with cranberry-floral accents, this mid-island restaurant addresses the dedicated carnivores in our midst with sizable slabs of steak (naturally), as well as veal, pork, chicken, fish, and lobster. You will not lack for protein; however, preparation and presentation can be a bit plain. Fortunately, there appear to be plenty of die-hard nonfoodies hereabouts, willing to pay a premium for prime ingredients in recognizable configurations. ⊠ 17 Old South Rd. ☏ 508/228–9852 ⊟ AE, D, DC, MC, V ☉ Closed Nov.–Apr. No lunch.

$$–$$$$ ✕ **Cinco.** This eclectic tapas oasis represents popular bartender Michael Sturgis's entry into the restaurant game (he had followings at 21 Federal, then the Brant Point Grill), and he's definitely a player. The lively space, painted rich earth tones, opened to immediate acclaim in the spring of 2004. Tastings range from baby beet salad with mizuna-and-orange mint vinaigrette to lobster gazpacho, seared native fluke with achiote butter, and "large plates" like paella—all begging to be washed down with hibiscus margaritas. ⊠ 5 Amelia Dr. ☏ 508/325–5151 ⊕ www. cinco5.com ⊟ AE, MC, V ☉ No lunch. Closed Jan.–Mar.

☼ $–$$$ ✕ **A. K. Diamond's.** Steaks and seafood rule at this spacious, clubby cousin of Arno's, close to the airport. Natives flock here to take advantage of the early-bird discount (25%) and to bulk up at the salad bar. Expect cravings for the hefty slabs of baby-back ribs to inspire another visit. ⊠ 16 Macy La. ☏ 508/228–3154 ⊟ AE, D, MC, V.

$–$$ ✕ **Hutch's.** Nantucket's airport is almost as cute as the one depicted on the defunct TV show *Wings,* only a bit bigger. The same goes for its restaurant, open for three meals—and not just burgers but all sorts of blue-plate specials—year-round. ⊠ Nantucket Memorial Airport, 30 Macy's La., off Old South Rd., Surfside ☏ 508/228–5550 ⊟ D, MC, V.

$ ✕ **Faregrounds.** Buffalo wings, potato skins, jalapeño poppers—you know the drill. Set mid-island, Faregrounds—along with its adjunct, Pudley's Pub—offers a something-for-everyone menu: munchies, pizza, steaks, seafood, and the de rigueur salad bar. The din can be deafening—the place is that popular—but the prices sure are welcoming, especially at the "All U Can Eat Lunch Buffet," and the vast menu is actually full of tasty finds. ⊠ *27 Fairgrounds Rd.* ☎ *508/228–4095* ▤ *AE, MC, V.*

Where to Stay

¢ ⛺ **Robert B. Johnson Memorial Hostel.** One of the country's most picturesque hostels, this 49-bed Hostelling International facility occupies a former 1873 lifesaving station—known as "The Star of the Sea"—right on Surfside Beach, a 3½-mi ride from town on the bike path. Dorm rooms (no private rooms are available) are divided into men's, women's, and coed; and the common areas include a kitchen. There's no lockout (customary at many urban hostels) in high season, but Cinderella time is 10 PM sharp: show up or you'll be shut out. Reservations are always a good idea, and essential come summer. ⊠ *31 Western Ave., 02554* ☎ *508/228–0433* ⧉ *508/228–5672* ⊕ *www.usahostels.org* ⤳ *49 dorm-style beds* ⚇ *Picnic area, beach, volleyball* ▤ *MC, V* ⊘ *Closed mid-Oct.–late Apr.*

Nightlife

The **Muse** (⊠ 44 Surfside Rd. ☎ 508/228–6873 ⊕ www.museack.com) is *the* place to catch big-name acts year-round. Recent headliners have included Dave Matthews, Hootie and the Blowfish, and George Clinton. DJs spin between sets and on nights when there's no live act. The barnlike Muse accommodates some 370 people, who also have the option of playing pool or Ping-Pong or scarfing pies produced on-site at **Muse Pizza** (☎ 508/228–1471).

Located mid-island, **Pudley's Pub** (⊠ 27 Faregrounds Rd. ☎ 508/228–4095), at the Faregrounds restaurant, is the kind of place where people stop in for a drink after work; it's loud, convivial, and well-priced.

Shopping

★ **Bartlett's Ocean View Farm** (⊠ Bartlett Farm Rd. ☎ 508/228–9403 ⊕ www.bartlettsoceanviewfarm.com) encompasses 100 acres overseen by eighth-generation Bartletts. The plant stock is varied yet well suited to the island ecology. Healthy, tasty prepared foods add incentive to visit. If you're not up for the trek, a produce truck is parked on Main Street through the summer.

The miniconglomerate of **Cisco Brewers, Nantucket Vineyard, and Triple Eight Distillery** (⊠ 5 Bartlett Farm Rd. ☎ 508/325–5929 ⊕ www.ciscobrewers.com) makes boutique beers, wine, and vodka on-site, with visions of "total global beverage domination." Consider it one-stop shopping.

Sports & the Outdoors

BEACHES **Cisco** (⊠ Hummock Pond Rd., South Shore) has heavy surf, lifeguards, but no food or restrooms. It's not easy to get to or from Nantucket Town, though: it's 4 mi from town, and there are no bike trails to it, so you'll have to ride in the road, walk, drive, or take a taxi. Also, the dunes are severely eroded, so getting down onto the beach can be difficult. Still, the waves make it a popular spot for body- and boardsurfers.

Surfside Beach (⊠ Surfside Rd., South Shore) is the island's premier surf beach, with lifeguards, restrooms, a snack bar, and a wide strand of sand. It pulls in college students as well as families and is great for kite flying and surf casting. You can take the Surfside Bike Path or the shuttle here.

BIKING   The easy 3-mi **Surfside Bike Path** leads to Surfside, the island's premier ocean beach. A drinking fountain and rest stop are placed at about the halfway point.

GOLF   **Miacomet Golf Club** (⊠ 12 W. Miacomet Ave. ☎ 508/325–0333 ⊕ www. miacometgolf.com) is a public links-style course owned by the Land Bank and built over natural terrain—mostly coastal heathland. It has 18 very flat holes.

HIKING &   A 5- to 10-minute bike ride from Nantucket Town on the way to
CONSERVATION   Madaket, the **Sanford Farm, Ram Pasture and the Woods** (⊠ Madaket Rd.,
AREAS   between Milford and Cliff Rds.) comprises 300 acres that were saved from developers by the Nantucket Conservation Foundation in 1971. The southern edge of the property borders the ocean and is the best choice for those who have tired of the crowds at the lifeguarded beaches.

The **Tupancy Links** (⊠ 165 Cliff Rd., 1¼ mi west of town) was originally part of the Nantucket Golf Course and runs between the Cliff Road bike path and Nantucket Sound. It's a smaller property that will probably seem more familiar to most hikers, as it passes mainly through grassland populated by plants like false heather, oxeye daisy, and Queen Anne's lace, but it provides wonderful views once you reach the overlook at the water's edge. The cliff is only 42 feet above sea level, but from it you can see great stretches of the island's north shore, from Tuckernuck Island to the church steeples and town clock of Nantucket Town—and even, on a clear day, the Great Point Lighthouse 8 mi to the northeast. The meadow is a popular meet-and-greet place for dogs.

Madaket

6 mi west of Nantucket Town, 14 mi west of Siasconset.

This rural, residential westernmost point of Nantucket doesn't have much to offer by way of a town, but that would be the wrong reason to come. Madaket's beautiful beaches and bird-watching sites, including Eel Point to the north, on the sound side, are wonderful places to relax and explore.

Where to Stay & Eat

¢–$$ ✕ **The West End.** Downstairs, in the bar, a youngish set quaffs Madaket Mysteries (the none-too-secret ingredient is dark rum) and nibbles on café fare. Upstairs, the cathedral-ceiling space with its optimal sunset-over-the-water views used to be a contender on the dining scene, but has gone prole, with a blackboard menu of burgers and fried-seafood baskets. The latter are actually extra-tasty, thanks to Chef Sammy's brown sugar–laced batter. ⊠ *326 Madaket Rd.* ☎ *508/228–5100* 🚭 *AE, D, MC, V* ☾ *Closed Nov.–Apr.*

$$$$ ⌂ **Tristram's Group.** It's a bit condo-y, this complex of 100 fully equipped houses near Madaket beach, but good for families who like to mingle. Facilities and amenities vary. ⊠ *Tristram's Landing, 02554* ☎ *508/ 228–0359 or 800/442–6268* ⊟ *508/228–3771.*

Nightlife

Sunset lovers flock to **The West End** (⊠ 326 Madaket Rd. ☎ 508/ 228–5100) to catch the Cinerama effect from an upstairs aerie. Young and restless Westenders crowd the intimate bar below to quaff Madaket Mysteries.

Sports & the Outdoors

BEACHES **Dionis Beach** (⊠ Eel Point Rd.) is, at its entrance, a narrow strip of sand that turns into a wider, more private strand with high dunes and fewer children. The beach has a rocky bottom and calm, rolling waters; there are lifeguards on duty and restrooms. Take the Madaket Bike Path to Eel Point Road, about 3 mi west of town.

Fodor'sChoice **Eel Point** (⊠ Eel Point Rd. off Cliff Rd., near Madaket) is 6 mi from Nan-
★ tucket Town in one of the ritzier sections of the island. The sand is ¼ mi or so from the end of a dirt road, and it's very soft, so a certain amount of commitment is required to get here. However, once here you'll find one of the most beautiful and interesting beaches. It's not great for swimming (too shallow), but it offers fine beachcombing. There are no services, just lots of birds, wild berry bushes, and solitude.

Known for great sunsets and surf, **Madaket Beach** (⊠ Off Madaket Rd., Madaket) is reached by shuttle bus from Nantucket Town or the Madaket Bike Path (5 mi from Upper Main St.) and has lifeguards, but no rest rooms. The West End, for food, is nearby.

BIKING At 1.2 mi, the **Cliff Road Path,** on the north shore, is one of the easiest bike paths, but it's still quite scenic, with gentle hills. It intersects with the Eel Point and Madaket paths.

The **Eel Point/Dionis Beach Path** starts at the junction of Eel Point Road and Madaket Road and links the Cliff Road and Madaket bike paths to Dionis Beach. It's a little less than a mile long.

The **Madaket Path** starts at the intersection of Quaker and Upper Main Street and follows Madaket Road out to Madaket Beach, on the island's west end and about 5 mi from the edge of Nantucket Town. About one-third of the way, you could turn off onto Cliff Road Path or the Eel Point/ Dionis Beach Path.

NANTUCKET A TO Z

BIKE TRAVEL

The main bike trails are paved, but mountain bikes (or hybrids) are best if you plan to explore the dirt roads; cobblestones on Main Street make for rough riding, too. There are several places to rent bicycles in town. **Obey all bike rules,** including signaling for turns, giving a clear warning when passing, and observing one-way roads. You must **walk your bike**

if you're going the wrong way or you can be fined. Also, biking is not permitted on the sidewalks in town. Note that Massachusetts law requires the use of protective helmets for children under 13 when operating a bike (or riding as a passenger), and that Nantucket, as of 2002, also requires helmets for adults.

Bicycle paths are very clearly marked. Both the Chamber of Commerce and the visitor information bureau have maps and free guides. Bike rental shops have maps, too.

BOAT & FERRY TRAVEL

Both Hy-Line ferries and the Steamship Authority ferries offer traditional and high-speed service from Hyannis year-round. The only way to get a car to Nantucket is on the Steamship Authority.

Freedom Cruise Line runs mid-May through mid-October from Harwich Port on Cape Cod.

FROM HYANNIS Hy-Line ferries makes three daily two-hour round-trips on the basic or traditional-speed vessels, and six daily one-hour trips on its high-speed ferry in the high season (June to mid-September). Call or check the Web site for the reduced schedule during the off-season. Seating ranges from benches on the upper deck to airlinelike seats in side rows of the cabin to café-style tables and chairs in the cabin front. There is a snack bar onboard.

From early May to late October, in addition to basic service, Hy-Line's 800-passenger M.V. *Great Point* has a first-class section ($23 one-way) with a private lounge, restrooms, upholstered seats and carpeting, complimentary Continental breakfast or afternoon cheese and crackers, and a private sundeck.

The Steamship Authority runs car-and-passenger ferries to Nantucket year-round. The trip takes 2¼ hours. If you plan to bring a car in summer or weekends in the fall, you *must* have a reservation. **Book your car-ferry trip as far ahead as possible:** call weekdays from 8 AM to 5 PM. If you have a confirmed car reservation, be at the terminal 45 minutes before sailing time; 30 minutes should be fine during off-season. There are no standby reservations to Nantucket.

Note: Both lines now charge an additional 50¢ embarkation fee each way.

The Steamship Authority's fast ferry, the *Flying Cloud,* makes six daily round-trips from Hyannis mid-June through early September, and takes just an hour; call for the off-season schedule. The regular ferry makes three round-trips in the off-season (late October to mid-May) and six round-trips in high season. Although reservations are not necessary for the fast ferry, they're highly recommended. In the high season, passengers are required to arrive a half hour before sailing time or be subject to loss of reservation.

🚢 Hyannis Ferries **Hy-Line Ferry** ✉ Ocean St. dock, Hyannis, ☎ 508/778-2602 reservations, 508/778-2600 or 888/778-1132 information, 508/228-3949 on Nantucket

⊕ www.hy-linecruises.com ⊠ One-way $14, round-trip $28; bicycles one-way $5 additional, round-trip $10. **Hy-Line High Speed** ⊠ Ocean St. dock, Hyannis ☎ 508/778–0404 or 800/492–8082 ⊕ www.hy-linecruises.com ⊠ One-way $34, round-trip $59; bicycles one-way $5 additional, round-trip $10. **Steamship Authority** ⊠ South St. dock, Hyannis ☎ 508/477–8600 reservations, 508/228–0262 on Nantucket ⊕ www.islandferry.com ⊠ One-way $14; bicycles one-way $6 additional; car one-way May–Oct. $175 [plus passenger rate], Nov.–Apr. one-way $115. **Steamship Authority Fast Ferry** ⊠ South St. dock, Hyannis ☎ 508/477–8600 reservations, 508/2288–0262 in Nantucket ⊠ One-way $27.50; bicycles one-way $6 additional.

FROM HARWICH PORT   Freedom Cruise Line runs passenger ferry service from mid-May to mid-October from Harwich Port. There are three daily round-trips in high season and one round-trip daily late May to mid-June and mid-September to early October. The voyage takes 90 minutes and includes free parking for day-trippers—and an alternative to the Hyannis crowds. Reservations are highly recommended.

🚩 **Harwich Port Ferry** **Freedom Cruise Line** ⊠ Saquatucket Harbor, off Rte. 28 ☎ 508/432–8999 ⊕ www.nantucketislandferry.com ⊠ One-way $30, round-trip $48; bicycles one-way $5 additional, round-trip $10.

FROM MARTHA'S VINEYARD   Hy-Line ferries make three daily 2¼-hour round-trips to Oak Bluffs, on Martha's Vineyard. Service begins in early June and goes through mid-September only.

🚩 **Martha's Vineyard Ferry** **Hy-Line** ☎ 508/778–2600 in Hyannis, 508/228–3949 on Nantucket, 508/693–0112 in Oak Bluffs ⊠ One-way $14, round-trip $28; bicycles one-way $5 additional, round-trip $10.

BY PRIVATE BOAT   Nantucket has first-class marina and mooring amenities for yacht and boat owners.

🚩 **Marina Contacts** **Madaket Marine** ☎ 508/228–1163 ⊕ www.madaketmarine.com. **Nantucket Boat Basin** ☎ 508/325–1333 or 800/626–2628 🖷 508/228–8941 ⊕ www.nantucketboatbasin.com. **Nantucket Moorings** ☎ 508/228–4472 🖷 508/228–7441 ⊕ www.nantucketmoorings.com.

BUS TRAVEL ON NANTUCKET

The Nantucket Regional Transit Authority (NRTA) runs shuttle buses in town and to Madaket, mid-island areas (including the airport, Sconset, Surfside Beach, and Jetties Beach). Service is available May to late September. Each of the routes has its own schedule (you can pick one up at the Chamber of Commerce, Visitor Services, the NRTA office, or at most any bus stop); service generally begins at 7 AM and ends at 11:30 PM. All shuttle buses have bike racks and lifts. Fares are $1 in town or mid-island; $1 to Sconset, Surfside, or Madaket; $12 for a three-day pass, $20 for a seven-day pass, $50 for a one-month pass, and $80 for a seasonal pass. The month-long and seasonal passes are discounted for students, seniors, commuters, and people with disabilities. Pets are allowed on board. Children under 7 ride free.

🚩 **Shuttle Bus Contact** **Nantucket Regional Transit Authority** ⊠ 22 Federal St., Nantucket 02554 ☎ 508/228–7025 for information, 508/325–9571 other business ⊕ www.shuttlenantucket.com.

CAR RENTAL

If you're determined to rent a car during the high season—not a great idea, given the cost and congestion—book early, reserving such amenities as child or infant seats and bike racks. For a midsize car with air-conditioning, you'll spend about $85 a day or $550 a week in July, or $70 a day, $300 a week in the off-season. Four-wheel drive rentals, available at Young's Bicycle, Nantucket Jeep (which has pickup and drop-off service), and Nantucket Windmill are $180 a day, $1,000 a week in the peak season, $150 a day or $800 a week in the off-season; Jeep Wranglers are even more because of their popularity. To drive on the town beaches open to vehicular traffic or Great Point, you'll need an approved four-wheel-drive vehicle and an appropriate pass; check with the rental company.

🛈 **Local Agencies Affordable Rentals** ⊠ 6 South Beach St. ☎ 508/228-3501 or 877/235-3500. **Nantucket Island Rent A Car** ⊠ Nantucket Memorial Airport ☎ 508/228-9989 or 800/508-9972 ⊕ www.nantucketislandrentacar.com. **Nantucket Jeep Rental** ☎ 508/228-1618. **Nantucket Windmill** ⊠ Nantucket Memorial Airport ☎ 508/228-1227 or 800/228-1227 ⊕ www.nantucketautorental.com. **Young's Bicycle Shop** ⊠ 6 Broad St. ☎ 508/228-1151 🖷 508/228-3038 ⊕ www.youngsbicycleshop.com.

REQUIREMENTS & RESTRICTIONS
Most Nantucket rental agencies require you to be 25 or older to rent a car, and rates may be higher if you're under 25. You might have to pay extra (about $10 a day) for additional drivers. There might also be a surcharge for child seats (about $5 a day) if available; be sure to inquire, since they're compulsory for children under five. Non-U.S. residents will need a reservation voucher, a passport, a driver's license, and a travel policy that covers each driver, when picking up a car.

SURCHARGES
It would be extremely expensive, as well as impractical, to rent a car on Nantucket and take it off the island—the price of the car ferry is high, and rental cars are cheaper in Hyannis. If you were to take a car off-island without the agency's permission, you could be subject to some heavy fines. As anywhere, to avoid a hefty refueling fee, fill the tank just before you return the car. Don't try to circumvent additional driver charges by changing drivers out of sight range of the agency. It's illegal for an unauthorized driver to operate a rental car, and if you are in an accident, all insurance (including your own) and waivers become null and void. You will be personally responsible for all damage and injuries.

CAR TRAVEL

Consider not bringing your car to Nantucket. Having one is invariably expensive, and traffic and parking in town are just ghastly in season—foot power, bikes, taxis, or public transportation can take you anywhere you need to go with much less hassle.

OFF-ROAD DRIVING
To drive on the portions of town–owned beach open to vehicles or north of Wauwinet Road to Coskata, Great Point, and Coatue, you'll need a four-wheel-drive vehicle and a permit. You'll be expected to deflate your tires here for easier beach driving.

🛈 Town beach driving permits ($100) are available at the **Police Department** ⊠ 20 S. Water St. ☎ 508/228-1212. Separate permits for Coskata and points beyond ($125 for

nonresidents) are sold by the Trustees of the Reservations (www.thetrustees.org) at the
Wauwinet Gatehouse ✉ end of Wauwinet Rd. ☎ 508/228–5646.

PARKING   During high season, parking in town is difficult unto impossible. A space,
should you find one, is good for only 30 minutes to 2 hours, and the
"summer specials" are always on the prowl, ticketing. There are two
park-and-ride lots within walking distance of town, but they're usually
full by 9 or 10 AM. When in doubt, take the Nantucket Regional Transit Authority shuttles and spare yourself the hassle.

RULES OF THE   Be alert for Nantucket's numerous one-way streets. Be polite at four-
ROAD   and five-way stops; if you're last to arrive, you're last to go. Keep vehicles (and scooters and bikes, for that matter) on roads and paths.
⇨ For details on state laws, *see* Smart Travel Tips *in* the front of this
book.

CHILDREN IN NANTUCKET

There's plenty to do for vacationing families here, from trips to the beach
to child-specific art classes and museum programs. Children's Beach hosts
children's concerts, numerous camps, tie-dyeing workshops, and more.
Murray Camp has two programs: an evening camp for youngsters ages
5–14 (Tuesday to Saturday, 6 PM to 9 PM, from June through September) costs $40 per outing. A full-day program, from 9 AM to 3 PM, of-
fers activities such as swimming lessons, sailing, windsurfing, and
kayaking; kids 5–13 can attend for up to three days at $115 per day or
for a week at $425. It's a great opportunity for parents to get in a lit-
tle alone time while the children have a blast. Remember to **arrange for
cribs, children's beds, and other such amenities** when you book your room
or house rental.

🚹 **Murray Camp of Nantucket** ☎ 508/325–4600.

BABYSITTING   Nantucket Babysitters' Service has year-round professional babysitting
and home-helper services.

🚹 **Babysitting Contact Nantucket Babysitters' Service** ☎ 508/228–4970 🖷 508/228–
6837 ⊕ www.nantucketbabysitters.com.

MONEY MATTERS

ATMS   ATMs are pretty ubiquitous—you'll find them at the airport, ferry terminals, and supermarkets. The following are accessible 24 hours.

🚹 **ATM Locations Fleet Bank** ✉ Pacific National, 15 Sparks Ave.; Pacific Club, Main
and S. Water Sts. **Nantucket Bank** ✉ 2 Orange St.; 104 Pleasant St.; 1 Amelia Dr.

TAXIS

Taxis usually wait outside the airport, on Steamboat Wharf, and at the
foot of Main Street. Rates are flat fees, based on one person with two
bags before 1 AM: $5 within town (1½-mi radius), $8 to the airport, $16
to Sconset, $18 to Wauwinet.

Limo services, except for King's Coach which serves the Cape, are based
on-island, and reservations are necessary.

🚹 **Limousine Service Absolute Limousine** ☎ 508/325–9990 or 877/849–5466 🖷 508/
325–0601 ⊕ www.absolutelimo.com **Cranberry Transportation** ☎ 508/825–9793.

Highland Drivers ☎ 508/228-9556 ⊕ www.highlanddrivers.com. **King's Coach** ☎ 508/771-1000 or 800/272-9892 ⊕ www.kingscoach.com.

🚖 Taxi Service **A-1 Taxi** ☎ 508/228-3330. **All Point Taxi** ☎ 508/228-5779. **Breeze Taxi** ☎ 508/325-2170. **Lisa's Cab** ☎ 508/228-2223. **Roger's Taxi** ☎ 508/228-5779.

TOURS

ADVENTURE TOURS No matter what you want to do around Nantucket, be it kayaking, mountain biking, climbing, birding, hiking, snorkeling, or scuba diving, Eco Guides: Strong Wings can arrange an exceptional private small-group tour. They also run scheduled classes and overnight camping trips for children through high school age. Trips are tailored to your particular interests and experience level, combining sports according to your wishes and showing you parts of Nantucket you can't see in any other way.

🚖 Tour Operator **Eco Guides: Strong Wings** ⊠ 9 Nobadeer Farm Rd. ☎ 508/228-1769 ⊕ www.strongwings.org.

BUS TOURS Barrett's Tours gives 75- to 90-minute narrated bus tours of the island from spring through fall; the Barrett family has lived on Nantucket for generations. Buses meet the ferries; reservations aren't necessary. Nantucket Island Tours are an hour or so long and take place on a 26-passenger bus that goes out to Sconset and back; buses meet the ferries.

🚖 Tour Operators **Barrett's Tours** ⊠ 20 Federal St. ☎ 508/228 0174. **Nantucket Island Tours** ⊠ Straight Wharf ☎ 508/228-0334.

HISTORICAL WALKING TOURS Walking tours generally cover the major sights within the historic district; motor tours in air-conditioned buses typically make a loop through Sconset. The tour operators listed below won't make you feel like a tourist or rip you off like one.

The self-guided Black Heritage Trail tour covers nine sites in and around Nantucket Town that have associations with Nantucket's African-American population, including the African Meeting House, the Whaling Museum, and the Atheneum. The trail guide is free from the Friends of the African Meeting House on Nantucket, which also leads a "Walk the Black Heritage Trail" tour by appointment in season.

Gail's Tours are lively ¾-hour van excursions narrated by sixth generation Nantucketer Gail Nickerson Johnson, who knows all the inside stories and can offer virtually any kind of advice requested. Tours are not canned—they may encompass the moors, the cranberry bogs, or the lighthouses in addition to Nantucket Town, where the bubbly Gail tries to tie history to current events. In season, tours in the 13-passenger cranberry-red van are at 10, 1, and 3; pick-ups at in-town inns can be arranged.

Historic Nantucket Walking Tours are provided by the Nantucket Historical Association at 10:15, 11:15, 1:15, and 2:15 Monday to Saturday and Sunday at 2:15 from late May to early September. The fascinating 90-minute docent-led tours give an overview of the island's history as told through the town's architectural and commercial past and present, encompassing such sites as Petticoat Row, Main Street's residential neighborhood, and the wharfs, churches, and library.

Nantucket Walking Tours, which cover a plethora of special interests, are conducted in the evening. The most popular are the Ghost Tours, which depart from the Post Office at 5 Federal Street at 7:30 Monday through Wednesday and Friday June through mid-October. "Scallywags, Scoundrels, Sinners and Saints" departs Friday at 6. Call for a schedule of tours focusing on nautical Nantucket and the women of Nantucket. Walking Tours with Dirk Gardiner Roggeveen are 1½–to 2–hour lore-packed experiences led by a 12th-generation islander. They're offered every afternoon except Sunday, from May to mid-October and at other times by appointment; children tag along free.

🛈 Tour Operators **Friends of the African Meeting House on Nantucket** ✉ York and Pleasant Sts. ☎ 508/228-9833 ⊕ www.afroammuseum.org/afmnantucket.htm. **Gail's Tours** ☎ 508/257-6557 ⊕ www.nantucket.net/tours/gails. **Historic Nantucket Walking Tours** ✉ Whaling Museum, 15 Broad St. ☎ 508/325-1894 ⊕ www.nha.org. **Nantucket Walking Tours** ☎ 508/228-4572. **Walking Tours with Dirk Gardiner Roggeveen** ☎ 508/221-0075.

NATURE TOURS Great Point Natural History Tours, led by knowledgeable naturalists, are sponsored by the Trustees of Reservations. Group tours are about three hours long, and you see the sights via Jeep. Depending on what's happening that day, you might visit and discuss the swamp-loving tupelo gum tree, the osprey nests maintained by the Nantucket Conservation Foundation, a stranded seal pup, or the skate cases that litter the shore. The Maria Mitchell Association leads marine-ecology field trips and nature and bird walks weekly in the spring and early summer months and three times a week from June through Labor Day.

🛈 Tour Operators **Great Point Natural History Tours** ☎ 508/228-6799 ⊕ www.thetrustees.org. **Maria Mitchell Association** (MMA) ✉ 4 Vestal St. ☎ 508/228-9198 ⊕ www.mmo.org.

VISITOR INFORMATION

You might want to stop by the Visitor Services and Information Bureau, open weekdays 9–5, to get your bearings. You'll find maps, brochures, and island information available year-round.

🛈 Visitor Information Contacts **Chamber of Commerce** ✉ 48 Main St., 2nd floor, 02554 ☎ 508/228-1700 ⊕ www.nantucketchamber.org. **Nantucket Visitor Services and Information Bureau** ✉ 25 Federal St., 02554 ☎ 508/228-0925 ⊕ www.nantucket.net/town/departments/visitor.html.

WEB SITES

For general information and lodging resources, visit ⊕ www.nantucketchamber.org, ⊕ www.nantucket.net, or ⊕ www.massvacation.com. Island ferry information and schedules are available from ⊕ www.hy-linecruises.com (Hy-Line ferry service) and ⊕ www.islandferry.com (Steamship Authority ferry service). For on-island transportation information, visit ⊕ www.shuttlenantucket.com (Nantucket Regional Transit Authority) or ⊕ www.massbike.org (Massachusetts Bicycle

Coalition). For information on accessibility in Massachusetts, see
⊕ www.state.ma.us/dem/access.htm (Directory of Accessible Facilities) or ⊕ www.capecoddisability.org (Cape Cod Disability Access
Directory).

WHEN TO GO
Memorial Day through Labor Day (in some cases through Columbus
Day) is high season. However, shoulder seasons (spring and fall) are terrific times to visit, with fewer crowds and lower prices. Many shops and
restaurants remain open through New Year's, and a hardy few stay open
year-round.

UNDERSTANDING MARTHA'S VINEYARD & NANTUCKET

IN AN INCREASINGLY COMPLEX and artificial world, Martha's Vineyard and Nantucket remain oases of simplicity. Though it's true that the islands, just off the coast of Cape Cod, have become known in recent decades for their pricey real estate and a few high-profile residents, they are nothing like snobbish Palm Beach or the see-and-be-seen Hamptons. Even during the busy summer months, it is possible to get away from it all on these twin jewels of the Atlantic: strolling along the shore gathering shells and beach glass, watching birds dive into the surf and emerge with their struggling supper, tramping through the shady woods, or just being seduced by the setting sun and the rhythm of the waves—all this is somehow life-affirming and satisfyingly real.

Nantucket and the Vineyard share a geologic history. Both were formed during the last ice age by the debris from a retreating glacier. They also share a moderate climate and an astonishing diversity of terrain. In addition to their hardwood forests, salt marshes, cranberry bogs, swamps, freshwater ponds, and coastal heathlands, the islands, together with nearby Tuckernuck Island, hold more than 90% of the acreage of sandplain grassland *worldwide*. Needless to say, this diversity of habitat fosters an equally stunning diversity of flora and fauna. Nantucket and the Vineyard support approximately 1,200 species of vegetation—a greater variety than is found in any other U.S. area of equivalent size. They are home to a huge number of deer; significant colonies of harbor seals, gray seals, and harbor porpoises; and turtles, frogs, rabbits, voles, and other reptiles and small field mammals. More than 350 species of birds either live on the islands or pass through on their annual migrations. Observant beachcombers will find horseshoe crabs, sea stars, sea urchins, sponges, jellyfish, and a plethora of shells, among them spiraling periwinkles, pointy turret shells, conical whelks, and smooth, round moon snails. And the still-fertile shores are awash with oysters, mussels, steamers, quahogs, blue crabs, and scallops—not to mention, of course, the whales that helped to make the islands what they are today.

Much of the land, including 40% of Nantucket's acreage and a quarter of the Vineyard's, is protected from development and laced with well-marked walking and bicycling trails that wind through glades of fern, portions of hardwood forest, and stands of high-bush blueberry, shadbush, and arrowwood. Kayaking is a popular activity; it lets you glide through the eel grass so silently that shorebirds will hardly even notice your presence and rewards you with the brilliant colors and sweet or pungent bouquets of a dazzling variety of aquatic plants invisible from the landward side of the shore, from sweet pepperbush to sheep laurel to the threatened arethusa, a showy magenta orchid named for the woodland nymph of Greek mythology.

In addition to protecting the islands' natural abundance, island trustees also preserve their colorful past with a wealth of small museums that document local history as far back as the days of the Native Americans. Often housed in buildings that are themselves historic, these archives provide a visual history of the lives of the European settlers and their descendants. The past is so important here, in fact, that the entire island of Nantucket has been declared a historic district, with core districts in Nantucket Town and much of Siasconset, an outlying village of rose-covered cottages that once was an actors' colony.

Today, the rigid enforcement of district guidelines has produced a town architecturally frozen in time, with many public buildings and mansions in the Federal style and nearly all of the private homes conspiring to create the island's most enduring symbol, known to historians as the typical Nantucket house. These 2½-story structures with gabled roofs, central chimneys, widow's walks, and the ubiquitous lead-gray shingles reflect the minimalist aesthetic and careful craftsmanship of the Quaker community that dominated the island in the late 18th and early 19th centuries.

Another holdover from that time is the culture and lore of the sea that permeates the island. In the early to mid-19th century, Nantucket was the world's premier whaling port, and its nautical past—and present—is seen in everything from the faux-scrimshaw on the famous (and famously expensive) Nantucket baskets to the charts and maps that line shop walls, as well as the cherished Figawi Race from Hyannis, an annual three-day sailing extravaganza that tends to include as much beer as saltwater.

Martha's Vineyard, too, has several historic areas, including Vineyard Haven, the island's main commercial district; tony Edgartown, with its manicured gardens surrounding old sea captains' homes; and Oak Bluffs, considered America's original African-American summer enclave and bursting with colorful gingerbread cottages. Though it has become known as the celebrity island for its famous summer residents—from Walter Cronkite to Carly Simon—its landscape is still its most dramatic feature, with a 5,146-acre pine forest, rolling farmland enclosed by drystone walls, and striking clay cliffs surging up from the sea.

The "season" used to be strictly from Memorial Day to Labor Day, but the boundaries have blurred. Both islands now have strong fall harvest, Thanksgiving, and Christmas seasons, due in large part to many seasonal events that take advantage of the tourist trade built up over decades of summers. Many shops and galleries now open in April and close as late as December, and a core remain open year-round. Most of the historic sites and museums,

staffed largely by volunteers, are open daily—or nearly so—Memorial Day through Columbus Day and operate on a limited, weekend schedule in the off-season.

But every season on Nantucket and the Vineyard has its own allure. In summer, you have your choice of plunking down on a beach and never moving, filling your schedule with activities, or combining the two in whatever mix suits you. In fall, the crowds are gone, the prices are lower, and the water may be warm enough to swim in as late as October—just around when the yellows and reds of the foliage reach their peak. The moors become a mellow palette of purple and gold and rust, burning bush along the roadsides flames a brilliant red, and the cranberries ripen to a bright burgundy. Even better, fall and winter are oyster and scallop season, and the restaurants that remain open serve a wide selection of dishes made with these freshly harvested delicacies.

Winter is for the most part a quiet time, when many tourist-oriented activities and facilities shut down but accommodation and transportation prices are lower and you can walk the beaches in total solitude. For a romantic getaway or a quiet retreat, country inns provide snug rooms with canopy beds and fireplaces, where you can curl up with a good book or that special someone after a leisurely dinner by candlelight. Both islands go all out to celebrate Christmas, with theatrical performances, concerts, holiday exhibitions, horse-drawn carriage rides, carolers, a festival of lights, shops selling hot chocolate and gingerbread cookies, and, of course, Santa arriving by boat.

As for spring, it gets a bit wet, and Nantucket receives a good dose of fog. Anticipation is in the air—not only because the daffodils come bursting up along the roadsides and the trees begin to bud but also because the seasonal workers descend, the restaurants fine-tune their menus, and the locals begin to gird themselves for yet another bustling summer season.

ORIGINAL VINEYARDERS: THE WAMPANOAGS

FOR SOME 5,000 YEARS before the first Europeans set foot on Martha's Vineyard, the island was inhabited by the Wampanoags, a subgroup of the larger Native American Wampanoag and Algonquin tribes of the northeastern mainland. The Martha's Vineyard Wampanoags called the island Noepe, meaning "Dry Land amid Waters," a prescient name given their traditional endeavors of farming and fishing. The tribe had settled throughout the island but was based in the southwestern peninsula at Aquinnah, from a word meaning "Land Under the Hill," thought to be a reference to the massive Aquinnah Cliffs.

The Wampanoags were, and remain to an extent, a communal group, with an economy based on the distribution of land and goods. Their subgroups were ruled by sachems, or chiefs, organized into a confederacy of the larger Wampanoag tribes under a supreme sachem. They based many of their teachings and legends on the leader Moshup, a giant semideity possessed of great strength and power who resided in the Aquinnah Cliffs and taught his people how to fish and hunt—he was said to wade into the ocean to catch whales, dashing them against the cliffs, which explains the reddish color of their clay today. He ate entire whales and tossed the ocean behemoths ashore for his people, and today the tribal symbol of the Aquinnah Wampanoags shows Moshup on the cliffs hoisting up a great whale. Moshup legends also explain the creation of the island, as well as nearby Nantucket and the Elizabeth Islands.

In the early and mid-17th century, the island's first European colonists found the tribe accepting, if wary. The first years of settlement were marked, by most accounts, by friendly relations as the Wampanoags taught the settlers the ways of the wilderness and the English imported the moder-

nity of Europe, which included guns for hunting, farming implements, and, unfortunately, disease. While many of the Wampanoag tribes on the mainland and Nantucket were eliminated by disease, the Martha's Vineyard tribe managed to avoid complete devastation. There were some skirmishes over land, but none so terrible as King Philip's War of 1675–76, fought in what is now Rhode Island and parts of eastern Massachusetts. A mainland sachem named Metacomet (dubbed King Philip by the English) sought to rally Wampanoag and other Native American forces to battle the accelerated European encroachment of traditional hunting and farming lands. The war was a disaster for the mainland Wampanoags, who lost thousands, including Metacomet himself. He was shot and beheaded, and his skull was placed on a pole and displayed in Plymouth for 25 years. Only 400 mainland Wampanoags remained alive after the war.

The island Wampanoags remained neutral during King Philip's War, but the result was a heightened wariness between the Native Americans and their English neighbors. For hundreds of years thereafter, the English stepped up their Christian proselytizing, turning out hundreds of "Praying Indians," as the converted were called. Evidence can today be seen in Christiantown, an area set aside by a sachem of the Takemmy area known as Josias, who created the township in 1660 for his group of Praying Indians. On the site is an ancient cemetery and the Mayhew Chapel, named after the governor and missionary Thomas Mayhew.

Between Martha's Vineyard and Nantucket, Wampanoags numbered about 700 until an unknown epidemic wiped out nearly all the Nantucket tribe. The last surviving Nantucket Wampanoag died in 1855. Wampanoags from the mainland and Cape Cod emigrated to Martha's

Vineyard, adding to the numbers somewhat, but by the mid-19th century, only about 40 island tribal members were full-blooded Native Americans. Under the federal controls of the Bureau of Indian Affairs, the Wampanoags of Martha's Vineyard and the mainland banded together in 1928 to become the loosely organized Wampanoag Nation. This designation allowed for limited self government within tribal lands and was a precursor to eventual full recognition of the tribe. There are currently five bands of Wampanoags in Massachusetts, but only the Martha's Vineyard Aquinnah group has been granted federal and state recognition as a Native American tribe. Status was approved in 1987 after years of petitioning the U.S. Congress.

Along with the granting of tribal status, the Wampanoags were given back nearly 500 acres of tribal lands in the area formerly called Gay Head. That name was changed back, by a state legislative act, to the original Wampanoag name Aquinnah in 1998. There is no true reservation at Aquinnah, but tribal headquarters are in this most rural section of the island. The Wampanoag tribe is governed by an elected Tribal Council, with traditional positions held by a chief and medicine man, who maintain their status for life.

While the traditions of the Wampanoags have been diluted by time and history, a resurgence of interest in the old ways has been brewing for some time. Wampanoag festivals include the recently revived Legends of Moshup Pageant, where ancient tales are reenacted using traditional dress and performances. The pageant takes place at sunset on the third Saturday in August, at Tribal Headquarters in the Aquinnah tribal lands. Cranberry Day celebrates the traditional harvest with singing and dancing, and a potluck supper. True to their communal origins, the Wampanoags continue to take care of their own: the tribe maintains 31 units of affordable housing for tribal members and elders and operates a shellfish hatchery and water quality testing laboratory. And, throughout Martha's Vineyard, the tangible reminders of the island's aboriginals remain in such place names as Chappaquiddick, Menemsha, Katama, and Takemmy.

WHALING ON MARTHA'S VINEYARD

WHALES HAVE BEEN GOOD TO NEW ENGLAND—so good that, for a time from the early 18th to the mid-19th century, whale hunting and processing just about built the economic infrastructures of New Bedford, Cape Cod, Nantucket, and Martha's Vineyard. During those halcyon years, sea captains' homes were the most lavish in town, and widow's walks on rooftops became all the rage as families waited for their men to return from as long as three years at sea.

During the early 1700s, Martha's Vineyard colonists and the Native American Wampanoags alike profited from the abundance of whales offshore. Whales were so thick in the immediate area that all that was necessary to harvest them was a small boat, a harpoon, and several strong-armed men. The Wampanoags, in particular, used all parts of the whale, including its meat, oil, and bones. So important were whales to Wampanoag culture that the tribe often stipulated rights to offshore whaling and beached whales whenever they sold land to the whites. In fact, the Wampanoags, as indigenous people, to this day retain the right to claim any beached whales.

The settlers, on the other hand, were most interested in whale oil that provided fuel (often for lighthouses); spermaceti, which was used to make candles; ambergris, added to perfumes; and whale bones, which formed the ivory background for jewelry and other items.

By the 1760s, the whale population in the island waters had been depleted to the extent that small boats and crews could no longer sail far enough to capture them. This ushered in the era of large seagoing schooners and ships that sought whales as far away as the Pacific. Edgartown, with its natural and protected deep harbor, as well as Vineyard Haven became important whaling ports, though they never handled the volume of ships that docked in Nantucket and New Bedford.

Edgartown was the whaling capital of the island. Evidence of the town's wealth is seen in the stately sea captains' mansions along North and South Water streets, facing the harbor, and in Main Street's Old Whaling Church, a magnificent Greek Revival structure with immense columns. Edgartown's 1840 Fisher House, open for tours, was the home of Dr. Daniel Fisher, who built factories in town to process the whales and who was at one time the primary supplier of whale oil throughout the region. Herman Melville, one of the whaling industry's greatest chroniclers, shipped into Edgartown on a whaler named the Acushnet. In his seminal 1851 novel, *Moby-Dick; Or The White Whale,* an Aquinnah Wampanoag character named Tashtego is considered to be the most skillful of all harpooners.

American commercial whaling reached its peak in 1846, when 740 vessels and some 70,000 people were engaged in the industry. By the end of the 19th century, the great whaling days were over. Cheaper and easier-to-gather fuel in the form of kerosene was discovered in the process of refining crude oil, and the whale population had been decimated. Attacks by Confederate ships during the American Civil War hindered the great whaling fleets, and the industry dwindled with the onset of the Industrial Revolution. Martha's Vineyard became known more as a vacation retreat than whaling center, and the great captains' manses, once passed along through generations of family, ended up in the hands of investors and outsiders, many destined to become the B&Bs and inns so popular on the island today.

MARTHA'S VINEYARD'S AFRICAN AMERICAN TRADITION

MARTHA'S VINEYARD'S LONG HISTORY of African American presence has added richness to the island's culture and history. The first colonial settlers brought enslaved servants with them as early as the mid-17th century, many of whom remained on the island to work the land and the ocean as freed men. An early mention of land ownership by a person of African descent is found in the 1763 will of a Wampanoag man named Elisha Amos, who left his land to his wife, Rebecca, who was enslaved on a nearby farm. Later, the whaling industry became a major source of employment for African American men, including one William Martin, whose great-grandmother was Rebecca Amos. Martin became a whaler and ultimately a ship's captain in a career that lasted 40 years. During the years before the Civil War, spots on the island were, informally, part of the famed Underground Railroad, which sought to spirit escaped slaves to freedom in Canada and elsewhere. Later, the fishing industry attracted skilled sailors of the Cape Verde islands, a Portuguese possession off the coast of West Africa.

The evolution of the Methodist Camp Ground of Oak Bluffs (then part of Edgartown) in the mid-19th century replaced the ennui of the post–Civil War era and approaching industrial revolution with a new industry—tourism. The first tourists, propelled by the fervor of religion and by the beauty of the seaside spot, first built the town as a place of quiet retreat. It soon grew to its present status as a popular resort town, built, in great part, by the influx of African Americans of the late-19th and early 20th centuries. Attracted to its sense of community and spirit, African Americans settled in large numbers and visited in droves, and succeeding generations have carried on the tradition. Those who made the Vineyard their permanent or vacation home include the late novelist and Harlem Renaissance icon Dorothy West, as well as today's luminaries Spike Lee and Vernon Jordan.

Today's summertime island population is diverse, and the well-established African Americans and other people of color of the year-round population—the police chiefs, the inn owners, the farmers—acknowledge their history through the self-guided African American Heritage Trail. The trail highlights spots and areas on the island important to the history of all islanders and includes the homes of prominent African American islanders, the Shearer Cottage of Oak Bluffs, and spots where African Americans gathered for worship. As of this writing, trail maps were being produced.

THE MAKING OF NANTUCKET

AT THE HEIGHT OF ITS PROSPERITY in the early to mid-19th century, this tiny island was the world's foremost whaling port. Its harbor bustled with the coming and going of whaling ships and coastal merchant vessels putting in for trade or outfitting. Along the wharves a profusion of sail lofts, ropewalks, ship's chandleries, cooperages, and other shops stood cheek by jowl. Barrels of whale oil were offloaded from ships onto wagons, then wheeled along cobblestone streets to refineries and candle factories. On strong sea breezes the smoke and smells of booming industry were carried through the town as inhabitants eagerly took care of business. It's no wonder that Herman Melville's Ishmael, of the novel *Moby-Dick*, felt the way he did about the place:

My mind was made up to sail in no other than a Nantucket craft, because there was a fine, boisterous something about everything connected with that famous old island, which amazingly pleased me.

But the island's boom years didn't last long. Kerosene came to replace whale oil, sought-after sperm whales were overhunted and became scarce, and a sandbar at the mouth of the harbor silted up. Before the prosperity ended, however, enough hard-won profits went into building the grand houses that remind us of the glory days. And wharves once again teem with shops that tend to the needs of incoming ships—ferryboats, mostly, and luxury yachts, whose passengers crave elegant accoutrements in lieu of ropes and barrels.

Thanks in no small part to the island's isolation in the open Atlantic—its original Native American name, Nanticut, means "faraway land"—and to an economy that experienced frequent depressions, Nantucket has managed to retain much of its 17th- to 19th-century character. The town itself hardly seems to have changed since whaling days: streets are still lined with hundreds of historic houses and lit by old-fashioned lamps. This remarkable preservation also owes much to the foresight and diligence of people working to ensure that Nantucket's uniqueness can be enjoyed by generations to come. In 1955 legislation was initiated to designate Nantucket Town an official National Historic District. Now any outwardly visible alterations to a structure, even the installation of air conditioners or a change in the color of paint, must conform to a rigid building code.

The code's success shows in the harmony of the buildings, most covered in weathered gray shingles, sometimes with a clapboard facade painted white or gray. With local wood in short supply, clapboard facades were a sign of wealth. In town, which is more strictly regulated than the outskirts, virtually nothing jars. Islandwide, you'll find no neon, stoplights, billboards, or fast-food franchises. In spring and summer, when the many tidy gardens are in bloom and cascades of roses cover the gray shingles, the scene seems poised for a postcard. Although the current landscape would be all but unrecognizable to denizens of centuries past—when sheep outnumbered human occupants—key historic landmarks are still ensconced in a setting respectful of the past.

The first Europeans came to the island to escape repressive religious authorities on the mainland. Having themselves fled to the New World to escape persecution in England, the Puritans of the Massachusetts Bay Colony proceeded to persecute Quakers and those who were friendly with them. In 1659 Thomas Macy, who had obtained Nantucket through royal grant and a deal with the resident Wampanoag tribe, sold most of the island to nine shareholders for £30 and two beaver-skin hats. These "original pur-chasers" then sold half shares to artisans whose skills the new settlement would need. The names of these early families—Macy, Coffin, Starbuck, Coleman, Swain, Gardner, Folger, and others—appear at every turn in Nantucket, where their many descendants continue to reside.

The first year, Thomas Macy and his fam-ily, along with Edward Starbuck and the 12-year-old Isaac Coleman, spent fall and winter at Madaket, getting by with the as-sistance of local Wampanoags. The fol-lowing year, 1660, Tristram Coffin and others arrived, establishing a commu-nity—later named Sherburne—at Capaum Harbor on the north shore. When storms closed the harbor early in the 18th century, the center of activity was moved to the present Nantucket Town. Relations with the Wampanoags remained cordial; how-ever, the native population—numbering about 3,000 when the settlers arrived—was decimated by plague in 1763. The last full-blooded Wampanoag on the island died in 1855.

Initially the settlers subsisted by farming (crops, they found, did poorly in the sandy soil), raising sheep (free of predators, the island lent itself well to this pursuit), and catching abundant cod. The native Wampanoags also showed them how to spear 50-ton right whales—so-called be-cause they float once killed and can be towed toward land—right from shore. In 1690 the Nantucketers sent for a Cape Cod whaler to teach them to catch whales from small boats just offshore; soon the island's entire south shore was given over to this industry. In 1712 one of the boats hap-pened to be blown farther out to sea and managed to capture a sperm whale, whose spermaceti was much more highly prized than oil. Thus began the whaling era on Nantucket.

In the 18th century, whaling voyages never lasted much longer than a year. By the 19th century the usual whaling grounds had been so depleted that ships had to travel to the Pacific to find their quarry, so trips could last years. Some Nantucket captains actually have South Sea islands named for them—Swain's Reef, Gardner Pinnacles, and so forth. The life of a whaler was very hard, and many never made it home. An account by Owen Chase, first mate of the Nantucket whaling ship *Essex*, of "the mysterious and mortal attack" of a sperm whale, which in 1820 ended in the loss of the ship and most of the crew, fas-cinated a young sailor named Herman Melville and formed the basis of his 1851 novel, *Moby-Dick*. Recently, that story once again captured the public imagina-tion in the form of the best-selling *In the Heart of the Sea: The Tragedy of the Whaleship Essex* by local historian Nathaniel Philbrick.

The fortunes of Nantucket's whaling in-dustry rose and fell with the tides of three wars and the devastating Great Fire of 1846, which destroyed the port and a good part of town. Just as the islanders struggled to recover (many residents de-camped to try to find their fortunes in the California gold rush), the market for whale oil was eclipsed by the introduction of petroleum-based kerosene. By 1861, at the outset of the Civil War (Nantucket had proved its abolitionist mettle early on by outlawing slavery in 1773) the pop-ulation had plummeted from 10,000 to 2,000.

The hard-strapped stragglers were only too happy to take in boarders, which worked out well with the growth of a postwar leisure class. Toward the end of the century the town supported no fewer than 50 guesthouses; a narrow-gauge railroad carried curious tourists out to stroll the quaint town of Siasconset, whose rose-covered fishing shacks at-tracted a colony of summering Broad-way actors. A vestige of those golden days survives as the Siasconset Casino, a magnificent 1899 Shingle-style theater where 'Sconset residents still mount the occasional revue.

Tourism was a steady, if unspectacular, draw (because of its isolation, perhaps, or its Quaker heritage, Nantucket was never as showy as some of its mainland peers) from the late-19th century right up through the 1950s, when the late businessman-benefactor Walter Beinecke Jr. started spiffing up the waterfront for the carriage trade. Since then, tourism has really taken off, becoming the island's bread and butter.

Like the original settlers and the early waves of tourists, most people who visit Nantucket today come to escape—from cities, from stress, and in some ways from the mayhem of the 21st century. Nantucket has a bit of nightlife, including two raucous year-round dance clubs, but that's not what the island is about. It's about small, gray-shingle cottages covered with pink roses in summer, about daffodil-lined roads in spring. It's about moors swept with brisk salt breezes and scented with bayberry and wild roses. Perhaps most of all, it's about rediscovering a quiet place within yourself and within the world, getting back in touch with the elemental and taking it home with you when you go.

FOGGY MOORS, WINDSWEPT SHORES

NANTUCKET'S REPUTATION FOR ENVELOPING FOG—the reason sailors dubbed it "The Grey Lady" centuries back—is perhaps a bit exaggerated. The problem is not so much that the fog is omnipresent but that it can sweep in so quickly, obscuring sight lines and landmarks in a matter of minutes. The upside is that even if one beach is clouded over, you may well find the other side of the island bathed in radiant sunshine.

Island habitués appreciate the weather's fickleness. The moor you're biking through, one moment a patchwork of variegated green, can segue subtly to purplish gray; the moss and lichen clinging to the stunted pines and scrub oak (salt winds inhibit much growth outside the protective confines of town) loom up as if phosphorescent. Another benefit of the moisture-laden, Gulf Stream–borne air is a year-round differential from mainland temperatures of about 10 degrees: Nantucket is warmer in winter (snow doesn't stick around long, and some Mediterranean plants make it through), refreshingly cooler in summer.

As a glance at old maps or close observation of a single beach will attest, the island's very shape is similarly subject to constant change. Pounded by ocean waves, the south shore is steadily if slowly eroding, and the island's western and eastern tips are particularly exposed. In just the past decade, the sea has sheared off an entire 'Sconset beach, along with its low-lying houses; the structures remaining, including picturesque Sankaty Light, teeter at the brink of a high bluff. Countermeasures such as geotubes, installed to stabilize the sand, are generally acknowledged to be mere holding measures. What the ocean wants it will claim, heedless of our puny human powers.

Like the shoreline, the sand under the sea is always in motion. The shifting shoals off Nantucket have grounded hundreds of vessels—most notoriously the ocean liner *Andrea Doria* in 1954. Sophisticated navigation devices seem to be no match for the vagaries of the waves. As recently as 1999, a cruise ship bound from Bermuda made an unscheduled offshore stopover of several days' duration.

Insistent currents can be a hazard for smaller craft. Amateur kayakers can, for instance, easily paddle across Nantucket Harbor to explore the scalloped coves of Coatue, a 4-mi barrier beach. Attempt a similar distance from westerly Smith's Point to the tiny islands of Tuckernuck and Muskeget beyond, however, and you could be in for the struggle of your life.

Nantucket's surf, particularly in the wake of storms, is not to be taken lightly. Whereas the northerly, sound-side beaches, from Children's past Jetties to Dionis, are nearly always placid, with knee-high waves that wouldn't topple a toddler, the ocean-side beaches are known for their "rollers," big round waves that will lift you off your feet (if you see one about to break, dive under it or you could get seriously pounded). The outer beaches, such as Madaket and 'Sconset, present further challenges with strong sidelong currents. And don't forget, the water is cold, peaking in the mid-70s by late summer.

If you're afraid to dip a toe in, much less bodysurf, there's plenty of pleasure to be had walking along the beach, poking about for scallop shells, moon snails, and "mermaid's purses" (the leathery egg sacs of harmless sand sharks). Just a few caveats: in approaching the beach, stick to the middle of a well-established path, and never walk through the dune grass. Not only are these spindly fronds a prime hangout for Lyme disease–carrying ticks (which ought to be disincentive enough), but their vast unseen networks of roots are all that's holding the sand in place. Even minimal damage can take a decade or more to undo.

Plain and hardy as it might seem, Nantucket's ecology is delicate—and already overstressed. The Nature Conservancy estimates that the islands of Nantucket and Martha's Vineyard represent 90% of the world's remaining sand-plain grassland; the rest has fallen prey to industry and development. This particular habitat, besides being extraordinarily beautiful, supports a great variety of wildflowers and plants, some on the brink of extinction and others perhaps as yet unidentified. The scrubby heaths, threatened by a monoculture of invasive pines and scrub oaks, is crucial to the survival of species such as the Northern Harrier and short-eared owl. A consortium of conservation groups are taking steps to preserve the moors.

Nantucket's beaches are an important breeding ground for the endangered piping plover, a tiny speckled shorebird whose eggs, dropped right in the sand, resemble tiny pebbles. Every summer, Smith's Point is cordoned off to give a few dozen survivors the chance to fledge—much to the chagrin of some locals, whose pickups sport bumper stickers proclaiming "Piping Plovers Taste Just Like Chicken." Just as shocking—at least to the eco-concerned citizens, such as *Boston Globe* science writer Sy Montgomery, who confirmed that "a stretch of 'barren' beach can support millions of hidden lives"—are the beach-driving permits you'll see plastered on thousands of SUVs. Permits are cheap and easy to obtain. The same can't be said for the invaluable beauties and benefits of a rare setting left in peace.

F GARDENING WERE A COMPETITIVE sport—and from a quick tour around the island you'd swear it was—Nantucket would be a world contender. The relatively mild climate (for New England) compensates for rather poor, sandy soil and permits a growing season that lasts a good six months. Though not everyone can build a multimillion-dollar house, anyone can garden, and on Nantucket almost everyone does. Lovingly tended, a tiny cottage—such as the rose-festooned former fishing shacks of 'Sconset—can easily outshine a mega-mansion manned by a small army of landscapers. Gardening is a great leveler, capable of creating common ground across the island and islanders.

The season—social as well as horticultural—officially starts with Daffodil Weekend in late April, a beloved tradition of several decades' standing (⇨ Nantucket Garden Club *in* Here and There). Jean McAusland, a former *House & Garden* editor, decided in the 1970s to beautify the island and plant hundreds of hardy daffodil bulbs. Admirers soon followed suit, and now some 3 million blooms line the roadways every spring. The weekend is invariably a sellout among the restaurants and inns, who open early to accommodate the crowds. Meanwhile, in the former ballroom of the old Point Breeze Hotel, the Nantucket Garden Club mounts a show of prize-worthy blossoms. If you think a daffodil is a daffodil, prepare to be amazed by the infinite variations in size, shape, and hue.

Soon the roses follow. The wild Rosa rugosa, or saltspray rose, rumored to have made its way here via China trade ships, prospers everywhere, under the most adverse circumstances, and produces blooms ranging from white to hot pink. The pasture, or Carolina, rose is the only legitimate native, but its ranks have been supplemented by such "volunteers" (garden-speak for cultivars turned runaways) as the

Multiflora. On Rose Sunday in early July—a tradition just as treasured as Daffodil Weekend—the Congregational Church is lavished with rambling roses for a pops concert that is always packed.

You can spot a lot of magazine-worthy spreads just wandering around town. In many instances, the clever use of trellises can convert an entire house into a living 3D display. For a glimpse of some spectacular "secret gardens," sign on for one of the benefit house-and-garden tours (the hot ticket is St. Paul's in mid-July). They offer a chance to check out your neighbors' private backyards—and have a peek at some rarefied Nantucket interiors, themselves the subject of many a glossy coffee-table book.

In recent decades, however, there has been a trend to gut centuries-old interiors, rendering them more modern and leaving the facades intact, or even rebuilding right down to the beams and rafters, all the while paying lip service to the stringent codes of the Historic District Commission. The result is a scattering of costly pseudo-historical nullities, mere architectural simulacra. Stricter regulations are under discussion, and sheer peer pressure may begin to chip away at the insidious newer-and-bigger-is-better mystique.

It's worth visiting some of the properties under the protection of the Nantucket Historical Society to get a sense of the way people used to live—quite nicely, it seems, without gymnasium-size rooms. Instead what islanders have always held in common is an appreciation for and attraction to the outdoors. A love of nature, rather than "house pride," is what keeps them out weeding and watering through the hot dry spells of late summer. It's what sends them biking and hiking all around the island to see what charming tableaux nature has fashioned entirely on its own.

INDEX

NOTES

NOTES

NOTES

NOTES

NOTES

FODOR'S KEY TO THE GUIDES

America's guidebook leader publishes guides for every kind of traveler.
Check out our many series and find your perfect match.

FODOR'S GOLD GUIDES
America's favorite travel-guide series offers the most detailed insider reviews of hotels, restaurants, and attractions in all price ranges, plus great background information, smart tips, and useful maps.

COMPASS AMERICAN GUIDES
Stunning guides from top local writers and photographers, with gorgeous photos, literary excerpts, and colorful anecdotes. A must-have for culture mavens, history buffs, and new residents.

FODOR'S CITYPACKS
Concise city coverage in a guide plus a foldout map. The right choice for urban travelers who want everything under one cover.

FODOR'S EXPLORING GUIDES
Hundreds of color photos bring your destination to life. Lively stories lend insight into the culture, history, and people.

FODOR'S TRAVEL HISTORIC AMERICA
For travelers who want to experience history firsthand, this series gives in-depth coverage of historic sights, plus nearby restaurants and hotels. Themes include the Thirteen Colonies, the Old West, and the Lewis and Clark Trail.

FODOR'S POCKET GUIDES
For travelers who need only the essentials. The best of Fodor's in pocket-size packages for just $9.95.

FODOR'S FLASHMAPS
Every resident's map guide, with dozens of easy-to-follow maps of public transit, restaurants, shopping, museums, and more.

FODOR'S CITYGUIDES
Sourcebooks for living in the city: thousands of in-the-know listings for restaurants, shops, sports, nightlife, and other city resources.

FODOR'S AROUND THE CITY WITH KIDS
Up to 68 great ideas for family days, recommended by resident parents. Perfect for exploring in your own backyard or on the road.

FODOR'S HOW TO GUIDES
Get tips from the pros on planning the perfect trip. Learn how to pack, fly hassle-free, plan a honeymoon or cruise, stay healthy on the road, and travel with your baby.

FODOR'S LANGUAGES FOR TRAVELERS
Practice the local language before you hit the road. Available in phrase books, cassette sets, and CD sets.

KAREN BROWN'S GUIDES
Engaging guides—many with easy-to-follow inn-to-inn itineraries—to the most charming inns and B&Bs in the U.S.A. and Europe.

SEE IT GUIDES
Illustrated guidebooks that include the practical information travelers need, in gorgeous full color. Thousands of photos, hundreds of restaurant and hotel reviews, prices, and ratings for attractions all in one indispensable package. Perfect for travelers who want the best value packed in a fresh, easy-to-use, colorful layout.

OTHER GREAT TITLES FROM FODOR'S
Baseball Vacations, The Complete Guide to the National Parks, Family Vacations, Golf Digest's Places to Play, Great American Drives of the East, Great American Drives of the West, Great American Vacations, Healthy Escapes, National Parks of the West, Skiing USA.

At bookstores everywhere.   www.fodors.com/books